DELILAH'S
EVERYDAY
SOUL

9 8 7 6 5 4 3 2 1
Digit on the right indicates the number of this printing

Library of Congress Control Number: 2006921030
ISBN-13: 978-0-7624-2601-0
ISBN-10: 0-7624-2601-2

Book cover and interior design by Amanda Richmond

Edited by Diana C. von Glahn

Typography: Mrs. Eaves and Gill Sans

Cover photographs © 2006 by John Romeo
Dish pictured on front cover: Red Snapper with Carmelized Yams, page 118
Dishes picured on back cover: Macaroni and Cheese, page 235 and Grape Jam, page 190.

This book may be ordered by mail from the publisher.
Please include $2.50 for postage and handling.
But try your bookstore first!

Running Press Book Publishers
125 South Twenty-Second Street
Philadelphia, Pennsylvania 19103-4399

Visit us on the web!
www.runningpresscooks.com

DELILAH'S SOUL
EVERYDAY

SOUTHERN COOKING WITH STYLE | DELILAH WINDER
WITH JENNIFER LINDNER MCGLINN

RUNNING PRESS
PHILADELPHIA · LONDON

To my mother and daughter.
Your love, constancy, and support nourish me every day.

And to Miss Edna Lewis.
Her recipes, stories, and spirited grace have uniquely captured the charm
and sophisitication of the South and fueled my own passion for Southern food and culture.

CONTENTS

ACKNOWLEDGMENTS

The creation of this book reflects the constantly unfolding adventure that is my passionate food-driven life. My love for eating and cooking largely defines who I am. I need to cook in the same way a painter needs to paint or a writer needs to write. This desire to create and explore is as intensely personal as my inexplicable ability to remember flavors and conjure up delicious aromas from meals past. Despite my singular passion for food, though, the reality is that its successful and most fulfilling expression relies on the participation of others. Just as my appreciation and deep love for all things culinary are intimately connected to people and places, so this book represents a collaboration of ideas, talents, and energies. I came to the table with my favorite essential ingredients, but I was hardly alone in assembling them. Many people assisted me, and together we created a gorgeous and flavorful banquet that many may now enjoy.

First and foremost, I thank Jennifer Lindner McGlinn for her tireless commitment to this project and to me. I've shared so many of my life's stories with her that it is hard to believe we've only known each other for a couple of years. Throughout this process, Jennifer has served as more than just a writer. She has been my greatest advocate and a valuable consultant, time and again going above and beyond the limits of her already lengthy job description to produce the best book possible. Jennifer is a talented writer whose skill is augmented by her sensitivity and empathy. We have spent hundreds of hours talking—in coffee shops, restaurants, offices, and on cell phones while driving in separate states. During every conversation, she hung on my every word while furiously taking notes and posing questions that helped us both to think about the material in fresh ways. With the raw information in hand, she then spent more hours interpreting and shaping my stories and thoughts, ultimately presenting them in a manner that preserved my voice, personality, and style. I now know that Jennifer understood and envisioned the potential of this book before anyone else, myself included. Early on, she saw beyond the recipes and encouraged me to think about my food in a larger context. As much as we talked about ingredients and methods of cooking, we also discussed the people, events, and emotions that have made these recipes so special to me. I am grateful for the respect and thoughtfulness with which Jennifer approached the large themes and small details of my lifelong passion for food and cooking. What a grand adventure this book has been, and I am so pleased to have shared it with her.

Thank you, too, to my many friends and family. Not only have they supported and encouraged me during this project, but they have played integral roles in my life and culinary experiences as well. Without these folks, I would have no stories to tell or memories to share. They have inspired my love for cooking, and constantly remind me that there is no greater pleasure than celebrating around the table with loved ones.

I also thank my chefs at Bluezette, Joe Hunt and Zachary Conover, for all they have done over the past months to assist me with this project. From helping me develop recipes to preparing beautifully designed dishes for photo shoots, they have truly been invaluable.

I am grateful, too, to the talented photographers who have helped bring my food and style to life. Raymond Holman, Jr., John Romeo, and Christopher McGlinn were not only spirited and patient allies in what can be the time-consuming and complex process of picture taking, but they also inspired me with their innovative and creative visions. Thanks for making me look so good, you guys.

Finally, I thank all of the folks at Running Press who worked on this book. I am grateful for their persistence in seeing this multi-faceted project to completion. They created a stunning book of which I am truly proud.

—Delilah Winder

Writing this book has reminded me of creating an enormous, celebratory feast. There were many components to consider, each of which required a particular sort of preparation. Some items came together fairly simply and quickly, while others called for lots of spice and many long hours of simmering. Each ingredient presented to me was unique and called for thoughtful consideration. They were, though, all the same in one respect: these delicious morsels were some of the finest and most inspiring I ever encountered. I felt responsible for preserving their inherent integrity, while, at the same time, I was intent on revealing each one's particularly poignant and enticing qualities.

Of course, creating this elaborate feast required an equally grand collaboration. The ingredients at hand were Delilah Winder's recipes and stories after all, and I thank her first and foremost for sharing them with me. I am grateful to Delilah for her graciousness and the trust she placed in me. Her generous spirit, honesty, and openness inspired passionate, meaningful discussions, and continuously fueled the project with new ideas and perspectives. I thank Delilah, too, for making our work fun. Especially on the days when both of our Starbucks coffee cups appeared more half-empty than half-full. Sometimes we just felt overstuffed with recipe writing, and the stress of looming deadlines reminded us of rushing a perfectly puffed soufflé to the table before it falls. Even on these days, though, we never parted without experiencing at least several bouts of sidesplitting laughter and sharing fashion tips. I left every meeting with Delilah feeling nourished, excited, and energized.

I am also thankful to my family who offered constant support, read bits and pieces of chapters, and contributed valuable feedback. My parents, Albert and Carol Lee Lindner, willingly gave me frank critiques, listened patiently as I read paragraphs to them over the phone, and cheered me on when my daily play with words felt more like a torturous game of hide and seek than an inspired exercise. I am also grateful to my husband, Chris, who encouraged me, reviewed paragraphs late at night, tasted recipes, patiently sidestepped my piles of books and papers, and quietly overlooked baskets of unfinished laundry that I sometimes sacrificed for completed chapters.

Thank you, too, to Antonia Allegra and Don and Joan Fry. This trio of mentors has been a powerful force in my writing life. Together they form a wellspring of support and creative ideas that is not only abundant and ever flowing, but pure and selfless as well. I am grateful for their endless supply of encouragement and, even more importantly, for their friendship.

Finally, I offer much thanks to our editor, Diana von Glahn, who believed in this project, devoted many hours to it, and encouraged Delilah and me to pursue our vision of what we knew this book could be.

—Jennifer Lindner McGlinn

9

FOREWORD

In the agrarian communities of the rural South, food feeds the soul as much as it strengthens the sun-drenched bodies that work the land. It seems that those who remain intimately connected to the fields that provide their daily sustenance are also nourished in meaningful spiritual ways. For these folks, fresh food is part of daily life. Yes, their dishes tend to be simple, but they are delicious, glorious creations, indeed. It is no wonder that for all its modesty and informality, traditional Southern food ranks among this country's most celebrated cuisines.

Today's Southern food is uniquely wonderful because it maintains much of the character it acquired centuries ago. In the early days of the colonies, African and European culinary traditions merged to create a colorful regional style of American cookery. Africans brought a variety of exotic ingredients with them to this developing nation, but they also arrived with a profound sense of spirituality that shaped their everyday activities. Cooking was no exception. It was laborious and time-consuming, but feeding one another was as much an expression of love and gratitude as it was a necessity of daily life. Times have certainly changed, but many of us still adhere to the lessons our ancestors taught us. It is a privilege to nourish our loved ones with delicious, wholesome dishes. When we do so, we grow closer to others, to our own soulful selves, and to our beloved Maker.

If anyone understands the profound nature of cooking, it is my dear Delilah Winder. In *Delilah's Everyday Soul*, she warmly and openly expresses the passion and spirit of her Southern-inspired cuisine. A gorgeous combination of traditional recipes and her own contemporary flair, Delilah's book presents us with a style of cooking that is as much about pleasing others as it is about creatively feeding one's own soul.

I first met Delilah in 2003 when Oprah Winfrey named her macaroni and cheese the best in the country. I took part in Ms. Winfrey's taste testing, and all I can say is I fell in love with Delilah before I even met her. Her cheesy macaroni seduced me from the first bite. In my opinion, her dish sets the standard against which all others should be measured.

Delilah and I became fast friends after the show, and I have been encouraging her to write a book ever since. The one she has fashioned is more beautiful and comprehensive than even I could ever have imagined. I can honestly say that it is one of the most beautiful and insightful Southern cookery books I have ever seen. The recipes call for everyday ingredients, are easy to follow, and are accompanied by gloriously enticing photographs. If this weren't enough, Delilah's stories take us along on culinary adventures that span from her childhood to the present day. She graciously invites us into her world, revealing some of the most intimate and moving events of her life. As a result, we cannot help but be as impassioned about cooking as she is. I'm sure that after turning only a few pages of this book, Delilah will have you running into the kitchen in no time.

From fried chicken, to country pork ribs, to deviled eggs, to lemon chess pie, Delilah shares with us a wide array of traditional Southern dishes. Other recipes, though, reveal the swankier, more cosmopolitan side of her personality and cooking. From skewered coconut shrimp, to crème brûlée with bananas and chocolate mousse, to lobster stuffed with crab and bay scallops, readers who fancy flavorful dishes with flair will find them here as well. I suggest you scoop up your family, choose some of Delilah's recipes, and get cooking together. I'm sure nothing would make her happier than to know that your family is enjoying some of her food around your own table.

My beloved Delilah, I congratulate you on such a beautiful book. It seems like just yesterday that we were sitting at the Sansom Street Oyster House in Philadelphia, slurping those wonderful salty critters, and chatting about the book you would write one day. Well, here it is, and it is as gorgeous and soulful as you are.

—Art Smith, author of *Back to the Table* and *Kitchen Life*

MY LOVE AFFAIR
WITH FOOD

I have been passionate about food all my life; everything about it makes me happy. From shopping for ingredients, to cooking them and drenching my kitchen in gorgeous aromas and flavors, to setting the table, to visiting with friends and family surrounded by numerous platters of delicious dishes, I am happiest when I am in food mode. I admit, this is practically all the time. Cooking inspires my creativity and fulfills my desire to nourish others—body and spirit. Eating, after all, is about more than simply satisfying hunger. It is about joyfully connecting with loved ones, communicating and remembering traditions, and acknowledging and honoring our identities as part of a larger community.

Simply put, for me cooking and eating are soulful endeavors. As a result, this book is as much a collection of recipes as it is a reflective look at the people and events that have inspired me and influenced my culinary style. Food and life experiences are interconnected. I could easily rattle off the recipe for my grandmother's fried chicken, for example, but I can't hardly think of the dish without remembering how she woke up at 6:00 a.m. to prepare it every day. Or how she presented it on her beautifully set dining table. Or how she packed up leftovers in a shoebox for me to take on day trips. All of these memories come rushing back to me when I think "fried chicken." I do believe these memories also make the dish all that much more delicious and satisfying, as well.

I attribute my love of food and cooking to having grown up in a family that celebrated around the table daily. It wasn't always easy. My two younger sisters and I were always heading off in different directions, and my parents worked full time. My father actually worked two jobs—one during the day and another at night. He left in the morning, came home in the early evening, and promptly went to sleep for a few hours, while my mother cooked dinner. We all ate together, and afterward, my sisters and I helped with the dishes, while my father went to his second job—playing drums in a jazz band. He'd return home at 1:00 or 2:00 a.m. and sleep for several hours before rising again to start another day.

Despite this busy and often grueling schedule, my mother prepared fresh, flavorful meals on a daily basis, and my father insisted that our family eat dinner together. There were no excuses. My sisters and I had to be in our seats at the same time every night

12

no matter what was going on. My father didn't care if half of the house fell off. Everybody was to be at dinner. This was our time to reconnect, a.k.a. information hour. As we passed plates of my mother's fried fish, cold-plate salads, and stewed beans, my sisters and I filled my parents in on our latest school events, grades, and boy troubles. Regardless of what teenage crises arose, or what family drama was playing out, we all met at the dinner table to refresh, regroup, and be nourished.

Dinner might have been the main meal of the day for my family, but even as a kid, I was forever itching to cook and bring people around the table more often. Starting in junior high school, I did just that. Nearly every day, I hosted at least three or four girlfriends for lunch. My mother was at work, so I had the run of the kitchen. I would bolt from school and stop off at the corner grocery store where my parents had a running bill. I'd fill several bags worth of groceries, scurry home to meet my friends, and cook up hot lunches of cheeseburgers, fresh-cut French fries, grilled cheese sandwiches with tomato and bacon, root-beer floats, and ice cream sodas. My mother's grocery bill was outrageous, and needless to say, she used to go crazy on me. I didn't mind, though. I just loved cooking for my friends and watching them enjoy my food. I still do.

I am a city girl at heart, and many of my earliest food memories are based in my hometown of Philadelphia. It was there that I first learned to appreciate the quality products sold at the corner deli, and to rely upon the knowledge and friendly helpfulness of the neighborhood butcher. I was also exposed early to the wide selection of ingredients on display at the Reading Terminal Market, as well as to the ethnic foods available in Chinatown and South Philadelphia's Little Italy. My mother taught me how to shop during our frequent trips to the market. She was adamant about forming relationships with local grocers in order to obtain the highest quality products. By watching my mother, I learned to be a smart and informed shopper and to forthrightly ask lots of questions. I have been doing so ever since.

When I was a kid, I led a sort of double life that fueled my passion for food. During the school year, the city nourished my active and burgeoning cosmopolitan spirit, while during the summer months, the quiet streets and open fields of Virginia reawakened my southern soul. My parents grew up in the South and were the only members of their families to move north. Since they continued to work all summer, they developed the perfect plan to keep my sisters and me busy and out of trouble—they shipped us to Virginia.

We spent time at my maternal grandmother's farm in King Queen County and at my paternal grandparents' home in Richmond. We might as well have been in a different country, though, for all I knew. Of course, the pace of everyday life was slower. But more than that, everyone exhibited a refined graciousness and warm hospitality, the likes

13

of which I had never experienced up North. My aunts and grandmothers were true Southern Ladies—strong, direct, yet proper and elegant. My mother knew just what she was doing when she sent my sisters and me to spend time with these women. Over the years, I learned how to keep a proper house, how to set an elegant table, and, of course, how to celebrate life and loved ones through food.

I simply cannot recall those joyful summers without remembering all the wonderful dishes we ate. When I think of King Queen County, I see platters of Smithfield ham, huge bowls of chicken and dumplings, and church tables crowded with cakes and pies. My weeks in Richmond put me in mind of my grandmother's fried chicken and grape jam, eating soft-shell crabs with my cousin Linda, and savoring pineapple sherbet on the porch with my grandfather. The people, places, and food all blend into sparkling memories filled with delicious flavors, intoxicating aromas, and the laughter and loving security of childhood.

Despite my love affair with food, as an adult, I never even dreamed about cooking professionally. Like so many of my peers, I became a successful, well-dressed businesswoman with a chic corner office and generous benefits. My career as a business systems analyst quickly took off, I was respected and admired—and I was unfulfilled. Cooking had remained my greatest passion during these years, and I indulged in it every chance I got. I shopped nearly every day at the Reading Terminal Market,

searching for the freshest ingredients; I took pride in making special school-box lunches for my daughter; and I frequently hosted intimate and lavish gatherings. It was when I found myself busy, week after week, helping my girlfriends entertain that I began to seriously reconsider the course of my work life.

This was the most common scenario: the girls wanted to impress their boyfriends with a home-cooked meal, but were basically hopeless in the kitchen. "Delilah, you cook all the time," they'd say, calling me up at the last minute. "Can you come over and help me with dinner?" The problem was, dinner was often the least of their troubles. Although many of my friends had beautiful kitchens, they lacked basic equipment and know-how. Even the thought of setting a proper table was enough to send them into panic-attack mode. Half the time I had to lend out my own tableware. I was doing everything, from decorating their homes with flowers, to buying and cooking the food, to leaving instructions on how to reheat or finish each dish. I was preparing elaborate tables and cooking fancy dinners to help my friends woo their unsuspecting dates. I felt like Cyrano de Bergerac in an apron.

Don't get me wrong. I really enjoyed helping my friends. But I admit I was disappointed to realize that successful career women often lacked basic cooking and housekeeping skills. Growing up, I was surrounded by women who prided themselves on their domestic abilities. My grandmothers, aunts, godmother, and my own mother considered them essential elements of a woman's success, regardless of her other family, social, or career accomplishments. I began to feel as though women were losing touch with this powerful feminine model, and I wanted to do something about it.

I decided to take action by throwing myself into my greatest passion. In 1984, I exchanged my cushy job and personal secretary for my first daring, and ever so solo, cooking adventure. I opened a stand at the Reading Terminal Market, where I cooked and cleaned and served 24/7. The hours were crazy, the money was scarce, the work was hard—and I loved every minute of it. I called it Delilah's, because it was, in fact, my own little place and a personal expression of my tastes and cooking style. I opened with a simple mission. I wanted to welcome, satisfy, and comfort folks with the fresh southern-inspired food I grew up on.

The stand only sat eight people at a time, so as I cooked and they ate, we chatted and got to know one another. My best customers returned week after week, year after year. I watched babies grow into teenagers, and young adults marry and have their own children. Many of the middle-aged folks who started out with me in the '80s are now seniors, and they still make weekly treks to their favorite seats. These days, I don't even have to be at the restaurant to see these loyal patrons. I bump into them all the time when I'm out and about in town, and we can't help but stop for a while and visit.

I am often in awe of how cooking simple food and serving it in a welcoming fashion has brought so many acquaintances and friends into my life. To think that we nourished our relationships over cups of fresh coffee and plates of cornbread, fried chicken, and eggs makes me pretty proud. For more than twenty years, I have been committed to serving people in a way that not only personally satisfies me, but that makes them happy, too.

As my business has grown in the last two decades, so has my passion for food and cooking. In the past fourteen years, I have opened two more Delilah's restaurants, one at Philadelphia's 30th Street Station and another at the Philadelphia International Airport, as well as a more upscale restaurant, Bluezette, on Market Street. Although I finally said to myself, "Enough with the restaurants already," I was still looking for another project when the idea of a book emerged. *Delilah's Everyday Soul* was born, and like my businesses, it is a reflection of me. Let's face it. Food is my life. The chapters in this book, therefore, represent the many ways in which cooking and eating have shaped my life's journey. From entertaining, to celebrating the seasons, to recalling summers in Virginia, to preparing macaroni-and-cheese for The Oprah Winfrey Show, to creating festive menus—these are the experiences and practices that have shaped me personally and professionally.

Because I was raised in both the South and the North, I decided that *Delilah's Everyday Soul* should

15

reflect this dual identity. On the one hand, as my restaurant customers know, I am a traditional southern cook, while at the same time, I am inspired by contemporary, innovative, and ethnic foods. It seemed only right, therefore, to fill these pages with recipes that represent my own personality with all its varied styles and tastes. I guess, at the end of the day, this is what food is to me—an expression of a lifetime's worth of memories, experiences, and emotions. So far, the paths I've followed have taught me a simple but meaningful lesson. By remaining thoughtful and enthusiastic about how we cook and what we eat, we really can feed our bodies as well as our souls every day.

—Delilah Winder

CELEBRATING WITH SOUL

When Delilah and I first started talking about this book, I felt certain that it was going to be more than simply a collection of her favorite recipes. Delilah's passion for life and food are inseparable. To her, they form one giant, delicious package that deserves to be unwrapped and celebrated every day. Delilah's enthusiasm for cooking and bringing people together around the table is infectious, and her soulful connection to food is truly inspiring. The path this book was to take soon became clear. We determined that our task was not just to create a cookbook, but to also merge Delilah's best-loved dishes with the memories and emotions that continue to make them relevant and special in her daily life. *Delilah's Everyday Soul* is thus as much about the food she creates, as it is about the people and events that continually inspire her to do so.

As we began brainstorming and mapping out chapters, Delilah and I found that most of the recipes were speaking with a discernable Southern accent. This was hardly a surprise. The idea of the book, after all, emerged out of the basic, comforting dishes that Delilah's Southern-style restaurants have made famous. Delilah spent nearly every summer of her childhood in Virginia. As a result, the South not only became a special place for her to visit, but a hallowed region of her spirit as well. Church picnics, family fish fries, glistening jars of homemade grape jelly, and crocks of fermenting peach wine are just some of the events and foods that shaped her personality and influenced her passion for cooking. Delilah and I shared a similar vision of the project from the outset: her Southern experiences and memories would serve as the framework for the book.

It wasn't long, though, before I realized that Delilah's recipes and stories were speaking to me in a variety of accents. Sure, the familiar Southern twang was always there, but sometimes it faded to allow other manners of speech to be heard more clearly. Although her family's roots are in the South, Delilah, in fact, is a city girl of the North. Born and raised in Philadelphia, it's no wonder that she developed a cosmopolitan attitude and swanky style. It was this side of her I was seeing and hearing time and again, and it made me wonder: could we write a book about down-home pickled watermelon rind *and* chichi caviar parties? Delilah and I both answered this question with an enthusiastic "yes!" The project, after all, was to reflect Delilah's food and personality, and the fact is that she merges both worlds in the style of her cooking and the content of her character. A little bit casual country and a little bit glittery rock-and-roll—Donny and Marie Osmond's tune sums up Delilah perfectly.

Delilah and I knew our first responsibility was to the recipes. We were, in fact, charged with writing a cookbook, not a memoir or autobiography. Before long, though, we both realized we were quite hopeless at sticking to straight recipe writing. We tried hard to focus on the food and restrict our conversations to ingredients and cooking methods. Really, we did. Colorful distractions were constant, however. Time and again, we found ourselves utterly defenseless as Delilah's spirited memories of people and events kept crashing our serious and diligent powwows. They just kept showing up like surprise guests on the 1950s TV show, "This is Your Life." What's more, I found myself morphing into host Ralph Edwards, trying to keep all of the invisible characters and scenes organized, while corralling them with pen and paper around the recipes at hand. After months of talking and writing, I felt as though I knew many of Delilah's friends and family. I recognized their voices, became familiar with the way they dressed and carried themselves, and was able to name their favorite foods. All this, and I never actually met a single one of them.

Delilah transported me to a world of previously unfamiliar people and places through her food. She fed me generously, and I ate heartily.

This impassioned and exhilarating process reinforced a truism Delilah and I both already knew well: recipes do not exist on paper alone as though in a vacuum, but, rather, live in our memories, in our kitchens, and on our tables, forever linked to the people who shared them with us. Ironically, although we often eat with others, we experience food in an intimate way. Delilah's stories speak to particular events and scenes that are important to her. This makes them no less relevant to the rest of us, though. In fact, their intensely personal qualities make them even more intriguing. Delilah's recipes and memories might remind some readers of their own similar upbringings. Others who experienced food in an entirely different way might be inspired to revisit their own memories, or even to create new, more meaningful ones.

For Delilah, food and cooking are inextricably woven into the daily pattern of life, and thus the book called for a unique organization. Rather than fit recipes into static categories, such as appetizers, soups, entrees, etc., we chose to shape the chapters in a lively way around basic techniques, events, people, seasons, and celebrations. Chapter one, "Essential Soulful Cooking," introduces Delilah's Southern-style food, and serves as a foundation for the recipes throughout the book. Chapter two, "Cooking for Friends," presents recipes for intimate gatherings and elegant parties. Chapter three, "Bountiful Seasons," discusses the celebration of seasonal ingredients and dishes. Chapter four, "Catherine's Table," pays tribute to Delilah's childhood summers in Richmond, Virginia, and her grandmother, Catherine Howard. Chapter five, "Food from the Country," celebrates more childhood memories from her grandparents' farm in King Queen County, Virginia. Chapter six, "Ah, Ha! Macaroni and Cheese," features the story and the dish that launched Delilah into the national spotlight. Chapter seven, "Graceful Celebrations," is made up of a collection of menus, each designed with a special occasion in mind.

If you don't know Delilah already, chances are you will after reading through the recipes to come. Maybe you've never picked grapes fresh off of your grandmother's backyard trellis, roasted a Smithfield ham big enough to feed the neighborhood, feasted on a bowl of steaming hot red beans and rice, or hosted lavish caviar parties with your closest friends. Perhaps you have. It's no matter, though, if your food experiences are quite different from Delilah's. Her stories and recipes will quickly seep into your reality like cool butter on a hot biscuit. Whether you are already a whiz with a chef's knife, or are just learning how to turn on the stove, Delilah's passion for cooking and eating are sure to seduce you into the kitchen before you even know you're hungry. I hope these soulful dishes inspire you to celebrate food and make your own memories at the table every day.

—Jennifer Lindner McGlinn

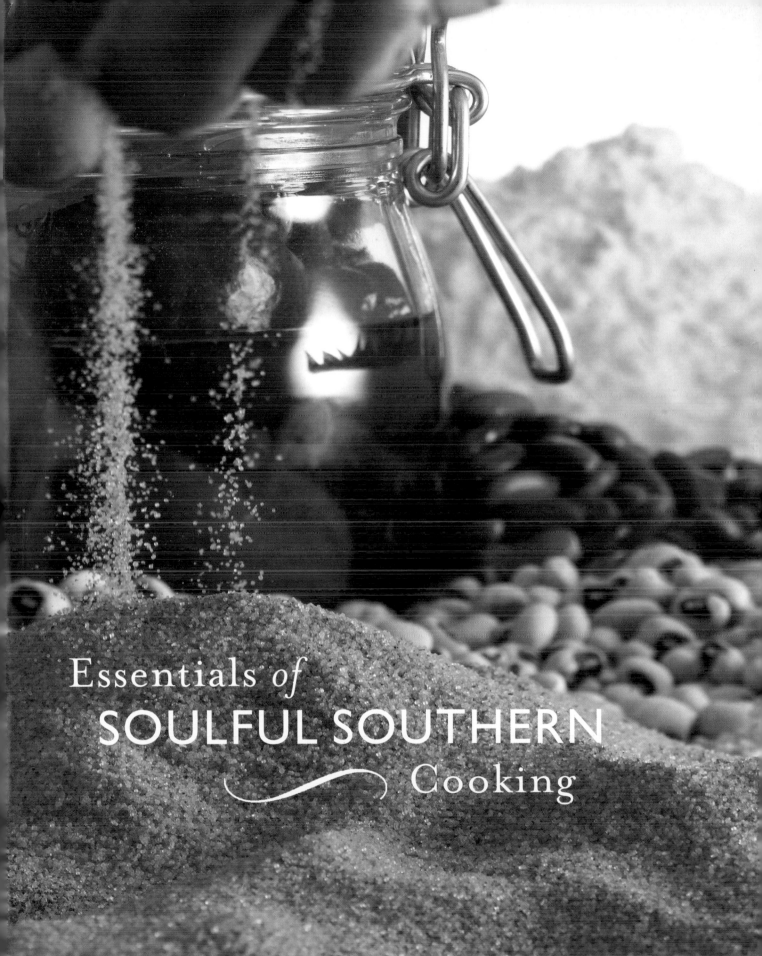

Essentials of
SOULFUL SOUTHERN
Cooking

ESSENTIALS *of* SOULFUL SOUTHERN COOKING

Before we get on with the recipes, I thought I'd begin by discussing what I consider to be the essentials of my cooking. It's not that my food is complicated, but it does have its own unique personality—one based on Southern traditions and inspired by my own style and tastes. Ingredients, of course, are the foundation of every cuisine, and I will talk about some basics to keep on hand in your pantry. Most of these are a combination of traditionally Southern items and those we use a lot in my own household. They are all easy to find, and as long as you have them on hand, you can prepare every recipe in this book without too much fuss.

Now, I just have to address the question—the elephant in the middle of the room—that many of you might be asking: "Isn't Southern food really unhealthy and fattening?" Here's the thing: Southern cooks are known for relying primarily on pork fat, cooking their vegetables way down, and using ample amounts of sugar and salt. I am hardly advocating a diet of overindulgence, or one laden with fat, sugar, and salt at every meal. I do believe, though, that when such ingredients are used in moderation, our stomachs and our souls are satisfied and happy. You'll see that most of my essential ingredients are filled with flavor, not fat and calories, and certainly not chemicals or preservatives. I never use canned or frozen foods. That's another thing about Southern cuisine. It has gotten a bad rap for its bacon fat and such, but few folks hail it for its reliance on fresh, seasonal produce and wholesome sources of protein. If it's not in season and I can't get it fresh, I don't eat it. All of my Southern relatives ate like this, too, and most lived into their nineties. Add a little exercise and relaxed living into the mix, and maybe we'd all live a little longer—and be happier.

I just couldn't talk about basic ingredients without also mentioning essential cookware, kitchen equipment, and knives. I realize most of you probably already have a lot of this stuff in your cupboards. Again, I am simply recommending those items that will assist you in preparing my recipes. You will see that the lists are actually pretty short. You hardly need a vast array of fancy gadgets, or professional chefs'-quality pots and pans to make my food.

I also just have to say a few words about tableware. I am crazy about china, flatware, glassware, linens—anything and everything that goes into setting a table. I realize that many folks are choosing to forgo a lot of these items, especially if they entertain infrequently. I encourage you, though, to at least pay attention to basic multipurpose tableware. I really consider it essential, not only to Southern cooking and entertaining, but also to soulful, fulfilling eating in general.

Finally, I have included a handful of basic recipes that appear frequently throughout the book and which I find useful to have on hand. Despite its name, there is no chicken in Chicken Flour, but southerners use this seasoned flour to dredge all sorts of poultry and vegetables before frying. Fish Flour is similar but, as the name suggests, we use it mostly for dredging fish. These seasoned flours not only add flavor to fried foods, but give them gorgeous, crispy crusts as well. The stock recipes are basics I turn to often. Homemade stocks are always best and making them is no big thing, but I realize you might want to dedicate your time to other activities. If this is the case, make life easier and use prepared stocks. As with everything else, though, just be sure to buy the best quality stocks you can, and look for those with fairly low amounts of sodium.

I hope these essentials prove helpful to you. Once your pantry and kitchen are well stocked, you will be ready to jump right into the recipes and experience the tasty, satisfying goodness of my Southern-inspired cuisine.

23

OILS AND FATS

CANOLA AND VEGETABLE OILS: Canola oil is my favorite, and it is the one I turn to the most in my kitchen. It is lower in saturated fat than any other oil, contains more monounsaturated fat than any oil (except olive oil), and is rich in Omega-3 fatty acids. I like vegetable oil, too, though, for its equally mild flavor. I use both oils almost interchangeably for frying, sautéing, and making salad dressings.

PEANUT OIL: I love using peanut oil. It has a distinctively "peanutty" flavor, and its high smoking temperature makes it ideal for frying. This oil is typically used in West African cuisine, and I turn to it when I am making dishes inspired by that region. Be aware, though, that many people have peanut allergies and cannot consume food prepared with this oil.

PALM OIL: I must admit I am very fond of palm oil, despite its 79 percent saturated fat content! It has a strong, distinctive flavor popular in West African and Brazilian dishes. I highly recommend you try this oil, but if you choose not to or have trouble finding it, you can certainly substitute peanut oil.

LARD: Like all good Southern cooks, my mother and grandmother cooked with lard (pork fat) more than any other fat. I use it more sparingly now than in the past because it is so rich, but, really, you can't cook true Southern dishes without it. Lard makes fried chicken flavorful and dark golden brown; biscuits incomparably light and flaky; and pie crusts seductively tender. Emeril is totally right: "Pork fat rules."

BACON FAT: Virtually nothing goes to waste in Southern kitchens, and that includes the fat rendered from cooked bacon. Like lard, bacon fat makes crispy, dark golden brown fried chicken and adds great flavor to sautéed vegetables. All good Southern cooks know that cooking with pork fat is the key to flavorful, perfectly seasoned Southern food.

BUTTER: Although the Southern obsession with pork fat is intense, we never say 'no' to butter. In keeping with what my mother and grandmother taught me, I use lightly salted butter when cooking a variety of vegetables, fish, and poultry, as well as for spreading on bread and biscuits and when making pie dough. Like many bakers, I generally use unsalted butter in cakes, but, other than that, I do prefer salted butter.

HERBS and SPICES

SEASONED SALT: There are many varieties of seasoned salt available on the market, each of which contains different combinations of salt flavored with other ingredients, such as onion salt, garlic salt, and celery salt. My favorite brand is Lawry's, as I think it has just enough paprika for flavor, but not so much that it turns food red. I like seasoned salt so much that I actually often use it in place of table or kosher salt.

KOSHER SALT: Rather than using kosher salt to season dishes during cooking, I like to use it in brines for meat and poultry. Kosher salt mixed with lemon juice and water is a great brine for chicken; this flavorful liquid flavors the meat and helps draw impurities out of the bird. I also like to use kosher salt for cleaning counters and cutting boards. A paste of salt, lemon juice, and water is an affordable, natural, and gently abrasive cleanser.

TABLE SALT: This salt plays an important role in the southern kitchen, but is actually used more for flavoring food at the table than for seasoning dishes during cooking. I grew up using table salt in this manner and continue to do so today.

BLACK PEPPER: I realize it seems counter-cultural, but I only suggest using prepared ground black pepper in my recipes. Traditional Southern cooks don't bother with freshly ground black pepper. Use it if you wish, but it certainly isn't necessary. I recommend buying just regular (medium-ground) black pepper. The finer it is, the stronger the flavor.

LEMON PEPPER: This slightly tangy pepper is a flavorful alternative to the regular black variety. Its lemony zing is particularly good for seasoning fish and chicken.

GARLIC: Fresh garlic is a staple in the Southern kitchen, but I also use a lot of granulated garlic. This form of dehydrated garlic is similar to garlic powder, but the bits are bigger, and I think it has more flavor. You can certainly use either equally well, but I prefer granulated.

CAYENNE PEPPER AND DRIED RED PEPPER FLAKES: Rich Southern dishes can handle a good bit of kick, especially dishes featuring beans, meats, and hearty greens, like collards. I wouldn't recommend using these hot spices with delicate vegetables like green beans, though, as the heat will overpower them.

OLD BAY SEASONING: I use Old Bay mostly for cooking crabs and shellfish, although you can use it on meat and poultry as well. This blend of celery salt and spices, including mustard, red pepper, black pepper, bay leaves, cloves, allspice, ginger, mace, cardamom, cinnamon, and paprika is, in my opinion, the quintessential seafood seasoning.

CAJUN SEASONING: This blend of spices, onion and garlic powders, salt, paprika, and sometimes sugar is also sold as "blackening seasoning," as it is often used for blackened dishes. I use it as a rub on chicken and seafood, as well as a seasoning agent during cooking.

PAPRIKA: I use a lot of paprika in my cooking to both add color and flavor. Paprika can be mild, sweet, or hot. Use whatever type you like best, but my favorite is mild Hungarian paprika.

DRIED SHRIMP: You're probably thinking, "What is this doing here? Isn't this an Asian ingredient?" And you'd be right, but Southern cooks like it, too, and use these flavorful critters for seasoning and adding texture to a variety of dishes. They are particularly handy to serve to folks who don't eat meat or poultry. In addition to, or in place of, smoked turkey, I add dried shrimp to stews and long-cooking dishes like simmered red or black beans. Dried shrimp are really salty, so if you add them to an existing recipe, cut back on the amount of salt you normally use. They are available in Asian markets and, these days, in some supermarkets as well.

POULTRY SEASONING: This blend of sage, thyme, marjoram, rosemary, nutmeg, and black pepper is, of course, just the thing for roasted chicken and turkey. I like rubbing it throughout the cavity of the bird.

RUBBED SAGE: What is bread stuffing and roasted turkey or chicken without sage? Dried sage is available whole, ground, and rubbed (crumbled). I prefer the latter for its texture and flavor.

FRESH HERBS: Like most Southern cooks, I happily use a wide variety of dried herbs in my dishes, but I like to use fresh herbs whenever I can. My favorites are thyme, rosemary, oregano, and basil.

VANILLA, CINNAMON, AND NUTMEG: Whether I'm baking cakes and pies or serving cooked yams or apples, vanilla is my favorite flavoring, and ground cinnamon and nutmeg are my favorite spices. They naturally bring out the sweetness of whatever dish I'm making and add depth and complexity without getting too fancy. As far as nutmeg goes, these days everyone seems adamant about only using the freshly grated variety. I'm really of two minds about this. Some recipes, especially baked goods and custards, truly benefit from the vibrant spiciness of freshly grated nutmeg. In other dishes, such as French toast or pancakes, I personally find it unnecessary to take the extra trouble, and simply reach for my little container of prepared ground nutmeg.

FLOUR AND MEAL

ALL-PURPOSE FLOUR: You might think it's ridiculous to mention flour here, but it is truly an essential ingredient in my cooking and, of course, in traditional Southern cooking as well. It is the only type of flour I use in baking (I don't fuss with pastry or cake flour), and it is essential for dredging and frying. I like to use sifted flour when baking, but it's unnecessary when dredging fish and chicken.

YELLOW CORNMEAL: Like flour, cornmeal is essential to my cooking. It is the main ingredient in such staples as cornbread and corn cakes, as well as in the Fish Flour I use in a variety of dishes. Cornmeal is available in fine, medium, and coarse grinds. I like a basic medium-ground cornmeal, such as that sold under the Indian Head label.

CONDIMENTS

YELLOW MUSTARD: When I say yellow mustard, I mean plain ol' hot dog mustard. Whole-grain, brown, and Dijon types are delicious, and I like them in fancier preparations, but they are rarely used in Southern cooking. French's is my favorite brand, but choose whatever variety you like best.

HOT SAUCE: I can't think what my food would be without hot sauce. My restaurants literally go through gallons of the stuff weekly. Hot sauce (not to be confused with pepper sauce like Tabasco Brand or Asian-style hot chili sauce) is available in many varieties, each of which has a different degree of heat and a unique flavor. They are all prepared with vinegar, but I like hot sauces with a punch based more on the flavor of vinegar and spices rather than on heat. Crystal Hot Sauce, Goya, and Pete's are among my favorite brands. I like hot sauce drizzled on such rich dishes as fried chicken, French fries, hamburgers, and fish sandwiches, but I also use it as an ingredient in marinades for chicken, meat, and fish cooked on the bone.

MAYONNAISE: I admit that we should eat mayonnaise in moderation for health reasons, so for goodness' sake, use the richest variety you can find. Don't even bother with the light or fat-free stuff. And, no, you don't have to prepare your own. Who has time for that? I like prepared mayonnaise best anyway, and my brand of choice is Hellmann's.

SWEET PICKLE RELISH: This relish is a welcome addition to a variety of foods, including hamburgers, deviled eggs, and potato salad. Buy it already prepared, or finely chop sweet gherkin pickles instead.

WORCESTERSHIRE SAUCE: This flavorful sauce—made of vinegar, molasses, anchovies, onions, salt, and garlic—is certainly popular not only in the Southern kitchen, but in every kitchen in America as well. Even the most neglected refrigerator usually contains a bottle of Worcestershire. It is essential to keep on hand for use as a condiment and to add flavor to many meat marinades.

BEANS

I love beans of all kinds, and they are staples in the Southern kitchen. Some of my favorites include black-eyed peas, navy beans, and red beans. All varieties are incredibly economical; a one-pound bag of dried beans costs pennies per serving and cooks up enough to serve about four people. Yes, I did specify dried beans. I don't use canned beans and I suggest you don't either. They are filled with added salt and preservatives and are hardly worth any time you might save by opening a can. There is no good reason to use canned anything, and the "I-need-to-save-time" excuse is really a poor one. In reality, it will take you all of 15 minutes to put together a pot of beans. I don't bother with soaking them first, so all you need to do is cover the beans with water, bring them to a boil, and then reduce the heat and let them simmer. Sometimes I do this overnight so the beans are ready for me the next day. At other times, it doesn't matter to me that they take some time to cook. Let's face it, there are times when you don't need to be quick.

If you're stuck in the house on a snowy or a rainy afternoon, you can hardly be in a rush. In fact, the aroma of the beans cooking will happily drive you crazy all day. Or maybe you're cleaning all day. Put a pot of beans on the back burner and let them cook while you attend to other things. Serve up hot bowls of beans with pieces of warm cornbread on the side and you have a warm and delicious meal.

COOKWARE

Buying cookware can be daunting. There are so many choices these days that we can easily become overwhelmed. Many of us think we need to outfit our kitchens with lots of pans in all different sizes and shapes, but this is not so. Purchasing cookware should be an extended process, not a short-term, hurried endeavor. In addition, we ought to regard the pieces themselves as smart investments that will help make our cooking more enjoyable.

Here are my cookware rules: buy the best you can afford; don't lend them out; and add on as you go, piece by piece. Follow this advice and I suspect you'll have your cookware for the rest of your life.

I recommend starting with these pieces:

- 1-quart saucepan
- 6-inch sauté pan
- 12-inch sauté pan

- Medium roasting pan
- Cast-iron skillet

EQUIPMENT

Just as with cookware, you really need a minimal amount of kitchen equipment to cook well. Buy the essentials and then add on as you go. I recommend starting with these tools:

- One pair tongs

- Two rubber spatulas—one large and one small

- Set of three stainless steel or glass

    bowls—small, medium, and large

- At least one wooden spoon

- Meat thermometer

- Medium or small whisk

- Medium or small strainer

- Medium or small colander

- Hand mixer

- Peeler

- Slotted spoon

- Rolling pin

- Baking sheet

KNIVES

Knives certainly fall under a special category of equipment. The good ones (and you really only want the good ones) tend to be expensive, but you only need a few to start, and the cost is worth it in the end. My advice again is to buy the best you can afford, buy one at a time, and don't lend them out. Look for knives that fit comfortably in your hand. It is also important to keep them sharp; you cut yourself more frequently with dull knives than with sharp ones. If you take care of your knives and store them properly, they should stay sharp for a good while. When they do get dull, though, most kitchenware stores can sharpen them for you. Here are the knives I find most useful:

- Paring knife
- 6-inch chef's knife

- 10-inch chef's knife
- Serrated bread knife

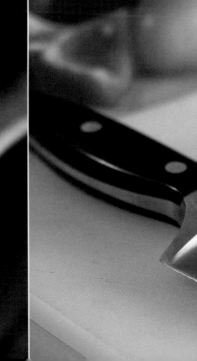

TABLEWARE

I love collecting and using tableware—flatware, china, glasses, linens, etc. My grandmother always set a proper table for every meal, and I have come to do the same. Dining is about more than just food, it's about taking time to sit and enjoy the presentation as well. Even when I am eating alone, I set a place for myself at the table with linen napkins, glasses, china, and silver. I encourage you to do the same. It just makes you feel good.

When you buy nice things, store them within reach so you can *use* them. There is no sense in having pretty tableware if you keep it locked away for "special occasions." Who is more special than you? Taking the time to regularly set the table will also make you more comfortable with the whole process. If you have children, they will benefit from this practice, too. Eating at a proper table will soon become routine, and there will be no need to panic about which fork to use, or which bread plate belongs to whom when next you are at a restaurant or formal dinner.

If you are just starting out, I suggest you purchase tableware for four to eight settings. The more you have, the better, as glasses and plates are bound to break over time. Buy good stainless steel flatware, glassware, and china that match your style and décor. And do not, for any reason, loan pieces to friends. These are not the pieces that you send out of the house with guests when they take leftovers home. You *know* you rarely get those things back, and you risk breaking your set.

I adore linen napkins and tablecloths and readily admit my obsession often gets the best of me. Still, I keep collecting all the same. If you are just beginning to set up house, I encourage you to buy a selection of neutral, but colorful, linens. I'm not a big placemat girl; I prefer tablecloths, but I will occasionally use a linen napkin in place of a mat. And for heaven's sake, don't worry about making everything match. Experiment with mixing and matching colors and patterns and don't be afraid to try new combinations. You will only learn what you like best by trying different combinations.

ESSENTIAL RECIPES

Chicken Flour

Makes 2 cups

2 cups all-purpose flour

½ teaspoon black pepper

1½ teaspoons seasoned salt

1 teaspoon granulated garlic

Combine all of the ingredients in a medium bowl and store at room temperature in an airtight container.

Fish Flour

Makes 2¾ cups

2 cups all-purpose flour

¾ cup yellow cornmeal

1½ teaspoons seasoned salt

¼ teaspoon black pepper

1½ teaspoons Cajun seasoning

Combine all of the ingredients in a medium bowl and store at room temperature in an airtight container.

Beef Stock

Makes 2 quarts

7 pounds beef bones, cut into
   2-inch pieces
1 (6-ounce) can tomato paste
2 cups chopped onions
1 cup chopped celery
1 cup chopped carrots
2 cups red wine
20 whole black peppercorns
5 cloves garlic, peeled
5 dried bay leaves
4 springs fresh thyme
4 springs fresh flat-leaf parsley
1½ gallons water

Preheat the oven to 400°F.

Arrange the bones in a large roasting pan and roast until well browned, about 1 hour. Remove from the oven and brush the bones with tomato paste. Scatter the vegetables over the bones and roast until the vegetables are caramelized and softened, about 30 minutes.

Place the roasting pan over medium heat and add the wine to deglaze, stirring with a wooden spoon to release any browned bits from the bottom of the pan. Pour the bones, vegetables, and liquid into a large stockpot, add the remaining ingredients, and bring to a boil over medium-high heat. Reduce the heat to low and simmer for about 4 hours, occasionally skimming any foam and fat that rise to the surface.

Strain the stock into a large container and cool in an ice bath. Store, covered, in an airtight container in the refrigerator for up to 2 weeks.

35

Smoked Turkey Stock

Makes 1 quart

3 smoked turkey wings, roughly cut into
   about 2¹/₂-inch pieces
1 onion, peeled and roughly chopped
¹/₂ cup granulated garlic
¹/₂ cup onion powder
1 teaspoon dried red pepper flakes
¹/₄ teaspoon black pepper
1 tablespoon plus 1 teaspoon seasoned salt
2 cups hot sauce

Place the turkey wings in a large stockpot and add enough cold water to cover by 2 inches. Bring to a boil over medium-high heat, reduce the heat to medium, and simmer for about 20 minutes, skimming any foam that rises to the surface.

Add the remaining ingredients and continue to simmer for 1 hour.

Strain the stock into a large container and cool in an ice bath. Store, covered, in an airtight container in the refrigerator for up to 2 weeks (see *Chef's Note*).

> CHEF'S NOTE: You can either strain this stock or store it unstrained. The turkey meat and bones and bits of onion are delicious additions to the soups or stews you might like to prepare with this stock. If you choose to leave it unstrained, the stock will keep fresh for less time—about 1 week.

Chicken Stock

Makes about 1¹/₂ quarts

5 pounds chicken wings, rinsed
2 medium onions, peeled and quartered
2 small carrots, peeled and halved widthwise
2 ribs celery, halved widthwise
1 dried bay leaf
1 teaspoon whole black peppercorns
8 sprigs fresh flat-leaf parsley
2 sprigs fresh thyme, or 1 teaspoon dried

Place the chicken wings in a large stockpot and add enough cold water to cover by 2 inches. Bring to a boil over medium-high heat, reduce the heat to medium low, and simmer for about 20 minutes, skimming any foam that rises to the surface.

Add the remaining ingredients and continue to simmer for 2¹/₂ hours.

Strain the stock into a large container and cool in an ice bath, skimming off any fat that rises to the surface. Store, covered, in an airtight container in the refrigerator for up to 2 weeks.

Shrimp Stock

Makes about 1½ quarts

1 dried bay leaf

¼ teaspoon dried thyme

¼ teaspoon coarsely ground black pepper

4 sprigs fresh flat-leaf parsley

2½ pounds shrimp shells, rinsed

7 cups cold water

1 teaspoon tomato paste

1 cup chopped onion

½ cup chopped carrots

½ cup chopped celery

1 tablespoon chopped garlic

Place the bay leaf, thyme, black pepper, and parsley sprigs on a piece of cheesecloth (about 6 inches square). Wrap in a bundle using kitchen twine to create a sachet and set aside momentarily.

Combine the remaining ingredients in a 1-gallon stockpot, add the sachet, and bring to a boil over high heat. Reduce the heat to medium low and simmer for about 45 minutes, skimming any foam that rises to the surface.

Strain the stock into a large container and cool in an ice bath. Store, covered, in an airtight container in the refrigerator for up to 1 week.

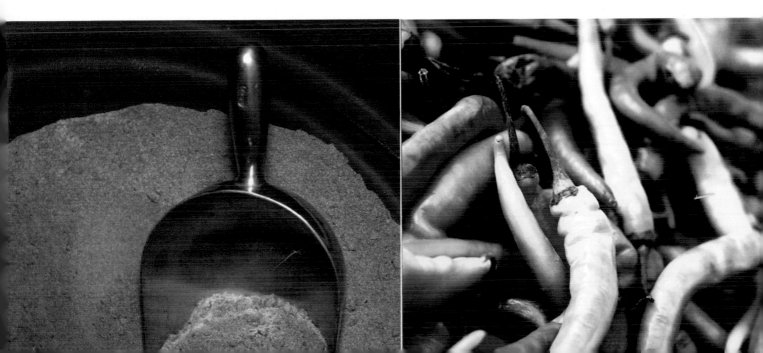

Cooking *for* FRIENDS

COOKING for FRIENDS

I have always loved to entertain. When I was growing up, my parents had frequent parties, and my mother belonged to an active social club. I guess I learned early on to appreciate great friends, and my passion for cooking and their enthusiasm for eating naturally drew us all together time and again.

I actually started entertaining as a teenager, often much to my parents' dismay. During high school, I would run to the store during lunch break, charge a huge bag of groceries to my parents' account, and then scurry home to make quick, delicious meals like burgers and fresh-cut French fries for my girlfriends. Even then I had a reputation for preparing abundant quantities of flavorful dishes. For me, cooking became a way of connecting with people, and I took great pleasure in watching them enjoy my food.

Many years later, this joy often experienced in my youth inspired me to plunge full-time into the restaurant world. Of course, cooking professionally day in and day out for large numbers of folks is not always a party. Even though I enjoy feeding people and watching them relish my food, the hours are long and the work is demanding. You would think, then, that when I leave my restaurants I would want to

remain as far as possible from a kitchen. But actually, it is when I am away from the restaurants that I really start to cook!

I readily admit that I am obsessed with food, cooking, and entertaining. I love to shop for ingredients, I look forward to developing menus, and I relish organizing all of the elements that make up a successful party. While some people plan weeks ahead for dinner parties and gatherings, I tend to invite people over at the last minute, and for no other reason than that I just want to cook for them. Many times it has happened that I stop by a farm stand on a Saturday afternoon and start going crazy over the fresh fruits and vegetables. When I realize I've filled numerous grocery bags, I just start calling friends, telling them, "I've bought a lot of stuff and I want to cook!" Needless to say, it's easy for me to get people to come over. The usual response is, "Yeah, girl, we'll be there!" And then it starts. Most people worry about enough folks showing up. I, on the other hand, try—usually unsuccessfully—to keep the numbers down!

Sometimes I don't even *have* to invite people to my parties. They invite themselves or just show up. Believe it or not, virtual strangers even occasionally appear at my door. This happened, in fact, just recently. A friend and I were sitting at the bar in a restaurant, enjoying drinks and a bite to eat, when I started talking about a party I would be hosting in a few days. I was going on and on about all the folks I was inviting and the many traditional Southern dishes I was making, including collard greens, ham, and biscuits. Suddenly, the woman standing behind me nudged me and asked, "Excuse me, did you say you're making collard greens? I've never made 'em, but I adore them." I thought, 'Do I know this woman?' It soon became clear, though, that not only was she a stranger, but she also had no idea I was a restaurateur. She was just excited to hear me talking about the food. So we got to chatting, and in no time I invited her to come to the party. "Oh, my Lord," she said. "Are you serious? Would you really mind if I came? I just love collard greens! Are you making black-eyed peas?" We talked a while longer that night, and I gave her my address, just in case. At that point, I was thinking, 'The woman doesn't know me from Adam. She probably won't show up, but who knows?' Well, she *did* show up, and with two other friends, no less. I spotted her during the evening with various people having a great time, meeting, greeting, and eating. At one point, we bumped into each other and she said, "I'm having so much fun!" Who knew talking about collards could lead to such joy? Oh, and, yes, we've become friends and have been out to dinner together since then.

I love everything there is about entertaining. I realize many folks think it is just too much work,

bringing all of the components together, but I think that's what makes it fun. I adore planning, shopping, cooking, etc., but, more than anything, I enjoy bringing people together. I especially like to have parties at which people can meet new friends and make connections that they otherwise might not have made.

Because I want my party guests to have the best experience possible, I take the time to decide on the tone or theme of the evening, and then take great pains to choose my tableware accordingly. You might ask, "Delilah, why is this all so important? Who cares how the table is set as long as you're together? Can't you use paper plates and be just as happy?" In my opinion, the answer is "no." Of course, being together is the *most* important thing. But, come on! Why keep your good tableware in the cupboards? What are you waiting for, anyway? Don't you feel better eating off of nice plates, drinking out of proper glasses, and using linen napkins? Well, I do, and when my friends come to my house, they know they will be treated right.

I admit, I'm fussy about getting everything together before a party and making sure the presentations are *just so*. But everyone who has been to my parties knows that once things get started, I just chill out with the crowd. I don't get crazy about people spilling stuff or breaking things. This happens when you entertain and you *cannot* get upset about it. I'm telling you, my house is in *perfect order* every day, but when I have a party, I willingly let the guests do as they please. The night my collard greens friend came over for the first

time, she actually brushed up against a table as she was leaving and a number of glasses crashed to the floor. Oh, she was a wreck. She was truly sick about it and kept apologizing. Honestly, it hardly fazed me. I told her not to worry and gave her my standard answer for such occasions: "There are plenty more glasses where they came from!" Even if there *were* no more in the pantry, I'd just go and get more. Things break. You just can't fret about that stuff. Believe me, entertaining is not that deep!

This chapter approaches entertaining on two levels: Informal Gatherings and Swanky Parties. The recipes that follow are divided into these two categories, but don't let that stop you from experimenting and serving the dishes you like best at whatever kind of affair you host. Again, there are very few rules. Entertaining is not nearly as complicated as we tend to make it. Pick a day. Invite some friends over. Cook a few things you like to eat and pour some tasty drinks. And have fun! No one will have a good time if you're a worried mess.

Now, go! Your friends are waiting.

43

The inspiration for most of my informal parties is, well, pretty informal. The planning usually begins before I even know it, like when I'm shopping at local markets on the weekends. I'll be taking my time, looking at all the fresh ingredients and choosing some beautiful produce, and then realize that I have way too much for just myself. So, I start making some calls and then, before you know it, I'm having a party. Other times, my parties are somewhat more planned, such as, say, on Super Bowl Sunday, or on a summer weekend when I organize a barbecue shindig, or when I invite friends over for brunch.

Knowing me and my high-styling ways, you might be wondering what exactly makes these gatherings informal. You *know* I don't do paper plates and plastic flatware—ever! So it's not necessarily the tableware that makes a party informal. I can make creamy grits fancy, and gorgeous stuffed whole bluefish "down home," so it's not even the food that always determines the tone. I suppose a variety of elements are at work here. Probably the most important is that I present dishes that require little tending to. Pulled Pork can sit in a huge pot on the stove while folks dig in at their own pace. I pile Spicy Shrimp on a large serving platter so my friends can pick and nibble. I serve Fried Oyster and Caesar Salad as soon as the oysters are ready, so it's a "dig-in-right-now-hungry-people" kind of meal. It's not meant to sit out and look pretty. I serve all sorts of dishes at my informal parties: those that I can prepare and serve immediately, as well as those that (like my friends) can sit around all afternoon.

I suppose what makes a party truly informal is the leisurely pace and relaxed feel you set as the host. Whether you are presenting a sit-down meal or snacking in the family room, as long as you create a calm, comfortable atmosphere, it doesn't really matter what color plates you use or what style food you serve. Every party is supposed to be a celebration. Informal gatherings, though, are meant to be particularly easy-going, stress-free, and just pure fun for the host as well as for the guests.

44

Banana Pancakes

Regardless of what time of day I serve these pancakes, they are always a hit. What could be more comforting and satisfying than fluffy pancakes and sweet caramelized bananas, served dripping with golden maple syrup and topped with more bananas, butter, and pecans? One thing you might want to consider: once your guests sit down, they may never leave your house.

Makes about six 5-inch pancakes

1 1/2 cups all-purpose flour

3 tablespoons sugar

1 tablespoon baking powder

1/4 teaspoon salt

1/8 teaspoon ground nutmeg

5 tablespoons unsalted butter

2 large eggs, at room temperature

1 1/4 cups buttermilk, at room temperature

1/2 teaspoon vanilla extract

3 to 4 medium bananas, peeled and cut into about 1/4-inch-thick slices (about 2 cups)

6 tablespoons vegetable oil, for cooking

Maple syrup, for serving

Butter, for serving

Chopped pecans, for serving

Whisk together the flour, sugar, baking powder, salt, and nutmeg in a large bowl. Melt 3 tablespoons of butter in a small saucepan over medium heat. Set aside to cool to room temperature. Whisk the eggs in a medium bowl just to loosen. Add the buttermilk, vanilla, and cooled melted butter, whisking until combined. Pour the egg mixture into the flour mixture, stirring until the batter is smooth and thick.

Melt the remaining 2 tablespoons of butter in a large sauté pan, add the banana slices, and sauté on both sides until caramelized and golden brown. Stir half of the banana slices into the batter, reserving the remaining banana slices for topping the pancakes.

Heat 2 tablespoons of oil in a large sauté pan or skillet over medium-high heat. When the oil is hot (the surface will appear to shimmer when it is ready), ladle 2 pancakes, about 5 inches each, into the pan. Cook until bubbles appear on the tops of the pancakes and flip to brown on the other sides. Remove from the pan, setting aside to keep warm, and carefully wipe out the pan. Repeat the process two more times with the remaining oil to make 6 pancakes.

To serve, arrange the pancakes on individual plates or on a serving platter and top with the reserved caramelized bananas, syrup, butter, and pecans.

45

Blueberry Buckwheat Pancakes

These pancakes combine sweet, tangy blueberries and the unique, slightly nutty flavor of buckwheat, so beloved in the South. I strongly suggest you serve these pancakes with my blueberry syrup—especially if you are a serious blueberry lover—but they are just as yummy drizzled with maple syrup.

Makes about six 5-inch pancakes

PANCAKES

1½ cups buckwheat flour

1 tablespoon baking powder

¼ teaspoon salt

2 large eggs, at room temperature

1¼ cups buttermilk, at room temperature

½ teaspoon vanilla extract

3 tablespoons unsalted butter, melted
  and cooled to room temperature

3 tablespoons honey

4 cups blueberries, crushed

6 tablespoons vegetable oil, for cooking

Blueberry Syrup (recipe follows), for
  serving

BLUEBERRY SYRUP

2 cups fresh blueberries

½ cup maple syrup

2 tablespoons butter

Whisk together the buckwheat flour, baking powder, and salt in a large bowl.

Whisk the eggs in a medium bowl just to loosen. Add the buttermilk, vanilla, butter, and honey, whisking until combined. Pour the egg mixture into the flour mixture, stirring until the batter is smooth and thick, and fold in the blueberries.

Heat 2 tablespoons of oil in a large sauté pan or skillet over medium-high heat. When the oil is hot (the surface will appear to shimmer when it is ready), ladle 2 pancakes, about 5 inches each, into the pan. Cook until bubbles appear on the tops of the pancakes and flip to brown on the other sides. Remove from the pan, setting aside to keep warm, and carefully wipe out the pan. Repeat the process two more times with the remaining oil to make 6 pancakes.

Serve the pancakes topped with Blueberry Syrup on individual plates or on a serving platter.

Combine all of the ingredients in a medium saucepan and bring to a boil over medium-high heat.

Reduce the heat to low and simmer until the syrup is thickened and glossy. Serve warm or at room temperature.

Ackee and Salt Cod

I came to adore this dish during my trips to Jamaica. To this day, whenever I visit, I order Ackee and Salt Cod nearly every morning for breakfast. It is almost always served with Callaloo and Fritters on the side, the recipes for which I have also included on the next page in case you want to experience this mouth-watering combination.

Ackee is a tropical fruit that, when cooked, resembles scrambled eggs. It is sold fresh and canned in Jamaican markets; you will probably have the most luck finding the canned variety. In its fresh form, ackee is truly strange and exotic to behold. When ripe, the red fruit opens to reveal three large black seeds surrounded by silky white flesh. If you are unfamiliar with this product, there is yet another reason to purchase the canned variety: portions of underripe ackee are actually toxic.

Salt cod is a traditional component of many cuisines, including those of the Caribbean islands. Dried and preserved in salt, the cod requires soaking or cooking in water to reduce its saltiness and rehydrate the flesh. This dish is the perfect combination of contrasting textures and flavors. The ackee is mild and creamy, the salt cod is salty and flaky, and the hot pepper is fiery and crisp (use it sparingly). If you have been to Jamaica, this recipe will transport you back there. If you have never been, prepare to experience a memorable culinary excursion.

Serves 6 to 8

1 pound salt cod

¼ cup vegetable oil

1 large onion, peeled and sliced

1 tomato, cored and chopped

1 green bell pepper, cored, seeded, and chopped

¼ Scotch bonnet chili pepper, cored, seeded, and thinly sliced

Salt & black pepper

2 (20-ounce) cans ackee, drained

2 scallions, trimmed and thinly sliced

Bring a large saucepan of water to a boil. Add the cod, reduce the heat to low, and simmer for 30 minutes. Taste a piece of the cod, and if you think it is still too salty, continue to simmer for up to another 30 minutes. Drain the cod and cool completely. Flake into 2-inch pieces and set aside.

Heat the oil in a large sauté pan over medium heat, add the onion and sauté until softened and translucent. Add the tomato, green pepper, chili pepper, and cod, season with salt and pepper, and sauté until the vegetables are softened, about 5 minutes. Stir in the ackee, simmering until heated, and toss in the scallions. Serve on a large serving platter.

Fritters

To me, these fritters are wonderful little bundles of flavor that are an alternative to bread at breakfast or brunch. I like them best served with Ackee and Salt Cod, but they are also enjoyable eaten with scrambled eggs and slab bacon. Although they are served without condiments in the Caribbean, I highly recommend serving these fritters hot with butter and marmalade. If you do, I guarantee you will become instantly addicted.

Makes about 20 to 24

4 cups canola oil, for frying

1 1/2 cups all-purpose flour

1 teaspoon baking powder

1/8 teaspoon salt

1 cup milk

Butter, for serving

Marmalade (such as pineapple or mango), for serving

Heat the oil in a medium saucepan over medium-high heat.

Whisk together all of the ingredients in a medium bowl until smooth. Check if the oil is hot enough by sprinkling a bit of flour into it. If the flour sizzles right away, the oil is ready. Carefully drop about 5 or 6 walnut-size balls of the batter into the hot oil and fry until golden brown. Remove to a paper-towel-lined baking sheet to drain while frying the remaining fritters. Serve the fritters hot with butter and marmalade.

Callaloo

Callaloo greens are the large green leaves of the taro root. They are popular in the Caribbean and prepared very much like turnip or collard greens. Combined, as they are in this recipe, with red onion, tomatoes, chili peppers, and herbs, they make a delicious side dish, especially when paired with vibrantly spiced jerk dishes or my favorite, Ackee and Salt Cod.

Serves 6 to 8

2 teaspoons canola oil

1 small red onion, peeled and thinly sliced

3 cups cooked callaloo (fresh or canned),
    drained of excess liquid

1 cup finely chopped plum tomatoes

1/2 teaspoon finely chopped Scotch bonnet chili pepper

1 teaspoon chopped fresh thyme

Salt & black pepper

Heat the oil in a large sauté pan over medium heat. Add the onion and sauté until translucent and softened. Add the callaloo, tomatoes, chili pepper, and thyme and sauté, stirring occasionally, until the callaloo is wilted. Season with salt and pepper and serve on a serving platter.

49

Poached Eggs with Spinach and Crabmeat

I love poached eggs, and what better way to eat them than with crispy corn cakes, tender crab, fresh spinach, and velvety hollandaise sauce? This dish offers a tempting array of flavors and textures. It takes a bit of organization, but it is worth it in the end. I love crab in this dish, but you can certainly substitute other ingredients to create the combination of flavors you like best. In place of the crab, try sliced avocado and smoked salmon. Rather than garnishing with scallions, try dill and finely chopped bell peppers. The possibilities are endless—and delicious.

Serves 4

CORN CAKES

3 cups fresh corn kernels

½ onion, peeled and finely chopped

I cup milk

3 eggs

1½ cups all-purpose flour

¾ cup yellow cornmeal

I teaspoon salt

½ teaspoon black pepper

I tablespoon butter, melted

3 scallions, trimmed and finely chopped

½ cup canola oil, for frying

HOLLANDAISE SAUCE

4 egg yolks

I tablespoon lemon juice

¼ pound (I stick) butter, melted

⅛ teaspoon cayenne pepper, or to taste

About ½ teaspoon hot chili sauce, or to taste

Salt

Preheat the oven to 250°F.

To make the corn cakes, combine the corn kernels, onion, milk, and eggs in a large bowl and whisk until smooth. Whisk in the flour, cornmeal, salt, and pepper, until smooth. Stir in the butter and scallions and set aside at room temperature to rest for about 15 minutes.

To finish the corn cakes, heat the oil in a large sauté pan or skillet over medium-high heat. When the oil is hot (the surface will appear to shimmer), ladle 2 corn cakes, about 3 inches each, into the pan. Cook until bubbles appear on the tops of the corn cakes, then flip to brown on the other sides. Remove from the pan and drain on a paper-towel-lined baking sheet. Place in the oven to keep warm while repeating the process three more times to make 8 corn cakes. Keep all of the corn cakes warm in the oven while preparing the rest of the dish.

To make the hollandaise, combine the egg yolks and lemon juice in a medium stainless steel bowl and whisk vigorously until thickened and doubled in volume. Fill a medium saucepan with about I inch of water and bring to a boil over high heat. Reduce the heat to low and maintain at a bare simmer. Set the bowl of whisked egg yolks in the saucepan (the bowl should not touch the water) and begin whisking rapidly. While whisking, gradually incorporate the

SPINACH

½ teaspoon canola oil

2 cups fresh spinach, stemmed

⅛ teaspoon salt

CRAB

½ cup jumbo lump crabmeat

EGGS

½ teaspoon white vinegar

3 cups water

8 eggs

Thinly sliced scallions, for garnish

Hot sauce, for serving

butter, drizzling it in until the hollandaise sauce is thickened and smooth. (Make sure the water remains at a bare simmer; if the water is too hot, the hollandaise will scramble.) Remove from the heat, whisk in the cayenne pepper and chili sauce, and season with salt. Cover tightly with plastic wrap and set in a warm area while preparing the rest of the dish.

To make the spinach, heat the oil in a large sauté pan over medium heat. Add the spinach and sauté, tossing occasionally, until wilted. Season with salt, transfer the spinach to an ovenproof dish, and set in the oven to keep warm, reserving the sauté pan.

To make the crab, wipe out the reserved sauté pan and heat over medium heat. Add the crab and toss gently until heated, being careful to keep the lumps in whole pieces. Remove from the heat and set in the oven to keep warm while preparing the eggs.

To make the eggs, bring the vinegar and water to a boil in a large sauté pan over high heat. Reduce the heat to low and maintain at a bare simmer. Carefully drop in four of the eggs and simmer until poached, about 3 minutes. Remove from the water using a slotted spoon and set aside to drain on a paper-towel-lined baking sheet. Repeat the process with the remaining eggs.

To serve, set 2 corn cakes on each serving plate, top with spinach, crab, and a poached egg. Spoon hollandaise overtop, garnish with scallions, and serve with hot sauce.

Spicy Shrimp

This is one of my most popular party dishes. I make platters of spicy shrimp, and my guests just hover around them nibbling for hours. This is also an easy recipe to reduce or multiply, depending on the number of guests you are hosting. The shrimp are delicious hot, right out of the pan, as well as at room temperature.

Serves 4 to 6

2 pounds jumbo shrimp, shells on

1 tablespoon crushed garlic

2 teaspoons cayenne pepper

1 teaspoon dried oregano

1 teaspoon dried thyme

½ teaspoon paprika

1 teaspoon seasoned salt

¼ cup canola oil

4 tablespoons butter

Combine the shrimp, garlic, cayenne pepper, oregano, thyme, paprika, and seasoned salt in a large bowl, tossing to coat the shrimp completely.

Heat the oil and butter in a large sauté pan or skillet over medium-high heat. Add the shrimp and sauté, tossing frequently until just pink, being careful to prevent them from burning. Serve the shrimp on a large serving platter.

53

Late Night Burger

I could say that this recipe is great for serving at relaxing weekend lunches, on Friday nights before going to the movies, or even for a quick weekday supper. While these are all true, the real story, as the title implies, is that this is the burger I make in the early morning hours after returning home from a night of partying and drinking. I'm telling you, this burger will absorb all of the alcohol you consume and will downright put you out! I guarantee you will sleep through the night after finishing off one of these sumptuous burgers at 3 a.m.

For those who would prefer it, you can certainly substitute ground turkey for the sirloin, or use any mushrooms and cheese you like. This happens to be my favorite way to prepare these burgers, and I am not shy to admit that I have enjoyed many a one.

Serves 2

BURGERS

2 pounds ground sirloin

1 tablespoon Worcestershire sauce

2 tablespoons granulated garlic

1 tablespoon seasoned salt

1 teaspoon black pepper

½ cup canola oil

MUSHROOMS AND ONIONS

2 cups sliced shiitake mushrooms

2 Vidalia onions, peeled and thinly sliced

Salt & black pepper

1 tablespoon chopped fresh flat-leaf parsley

ASSEMBLY

2 hamburger buns

About 2 to 3 ounces sliced cheddar cheese

1 head iceberg lettuce, cored and leaves
   separated

2 ripe tomatoes, cored and sliced, for serving

Combine the sirloin, Worcestershire sauce, garlic, seasoned salt, and pepper in a medium bowl, mixing gently to prevent overworking the meat, and shape into 2 burgers.

Heat the oil in a medium sauté pan or skillet over medium-high heat. Place the burgers in the pan and brown on both sides until cooked to desired doneness.

Meanwhile, carefully pour some of the sirloin drippings into a medium sauté pan and heat over medium heat. Add the mushrooms and onions, season with salt and pepper, and sauté until softened and lightly browned. Stir in the parsley, tossing to combine, and remove from the heat, keeping warm.

To assemble, place each bun on a plate and set the burgers on top. Divide the cheese between them and spoon the sautéed mushrooms and onions overtop. Serve the burgers with lettuce and tomatoes on the side.

Mustard Catfish with Rémoulade

It used to be that the fish you ate said a lot about where you grew up. During my summers in Richmond, Virginia, we feasted on lots of porgies, croakers, and spots, but we enjoyed catfish only every so often. One of my close friends, though, grew up in Mississippi and ate so much catfish that he thought it was the only kind of fish there was!

These days, catfish are mostly farm raised, making them widely available. Their mild flavor and firm texture make them well suited to traditional frying and blackening, as well as to vibrant marinades and robust sauces like those in this recipe. I like catfish simply served hot and crispy with sauce like the one below, but you can easily vary this recipe to suit your mood and taste. Serve the sautéed fillets on hoagie or steak rolls with lettuce and tomato, or enjoy them with grits for a hearty breakfast.

Serves 4

CATFISH

2 cups Dijon mustard

½ cup yellow mustard

1 tablespoon soy sauce

¼ cup white wine

4 catfish fillets (about 5 to 8 ounces each)

RÉMOULADE

1 cup mayonnaise

1 teaspoon Dijon mustard

1½ tablespoons capers

2 tablespoons chopped fresh flat-leaf parsley

2 tablespoons chopped fresh tarragon

2 teaspoons paprika

1 teaspoon cayenne pepper

Juice of ½ lemon

1 clove garlic, peeled and finely chopped

2 anchovy fillets, very finely chopped

⅛ teaspoon Worcestershire sauce

1 cup ketchup

Salt & black pepper

TO FINISH

3 cups canola oil

2 cups Fish Flour (see page 34)

At least 1 hour before frying the catfish, combine the mustards, soy sauce, and wine in a shallow dish. Add the catfish fillets, turning to coat, cover with plastic wrap, and set in the refrigerator to marinate for about 1 hour.

Meanwhile, stir together all of the rémoulade ingredients in a medium bowl and set aside in the refrigerator.

When you're ready to finish the catfish, heat the oil in a large sauté pan or skillet. (There should be about 1 inch of oil in the pan.) Place the fish flour in a large shallow pan. Place the marinated catfish in the flour, dredging to coat the fillets liberally.

Check if the oil is hot enough by sprinkling a bit of flour into it. If the flour sizzles right away, the oil is ready. Place the catfish fillets in the pan and sauté on both sides until golden brown. Remove from the pan and drain on paper towels. To serve, place each fillet on a serving plate and spoon the rémoulade overtop.

55

Barbecue Pulled Pork Sandwich with Cole Slaw

This recipe was inspired by the traditional pork sandwiches I remember eating regularly in Virginia. When I was growing up, it seemed that nearly every corner store and small restaurant served these sandwiches. Each of us would order three or four at a time and spend the next half hour or so relishing every juicy bite.

These days, I love serving this dish at informal get-togethers with family and friends. It is always a hit, and I guarantee that once everyone starts nibbling on yours, they will not be able to put down their forks! I have served this dish for lunch and dinner with or without the buns. It is great with crunchy chips, or take it to the next level and serve it with freshly cut French fries. If you're trying to be "good," a side salad works well, too.

This recipe takes a while to prepare, so plan ahead. In fact, my recent acquisition of a lime-green Dutch oven inspired me to actually increase the cooking time. Excited to use my new toy, I decided to cook the pork and the barbecue sauce together for yet another hour after already having roasted it in the oven for nearly five hours. I was thrilled with the results and I think you will be, too. It might even inspire you to splurge on your own colorful Dutch oven.

Serves 6

PORK

1 boneless pork shoulder (about 8 to 10 pounds), skin on

1 tablespoon vegetable or canola oil

1/2 cup chopped fresh flat-leaf parsley

1 tablespoon granulated garlic

1 small clove garlic, peeled and chopped

2 tablespoons seasoned salt

2 teaspoons black pepper

At least 8 hours before roasting the pork, rub the pork shoulder all over with oil, parsley, granulated and fresh garlic, seasoned salt, and pepper. Set it in a large dish, cover with plastic wrap, and set in the refrigerator to marinate for at least 8 and up to 24 hours. (The longer the pork marinates, the better.)

When you are ready to proceed with the dish, preheat the oven to 350°F.

Place the pork in a medium roasting pan and roast it skin side up for about 3 hours. After 3 hours, raise the oven temperature to 400°F. and roast until the meat is very tender and begins to fall off the bone, about 1½ hours more.

COLE SLAW

½ medium head red cabbage,
    cored and finely sliced

½ medium head green cabbage,
    cored and finely sliced

1 Spanish onion, peeled and finely chopped

2 carrots, peeled and grated

2 cups mayonnaise

½ cup sour cream

¼ cup apple cider vinegar

¼ cup sugar

Salt & black pepper

FINISH THE PORK

3 cups Barbecue Sauce (recipe follows)

6 hamburger buns, for serving

BARBECUE SAUCE

1 tablespoon canola oil

1 medium onion, peeled and chopped

1 clove garlic, peeled and finely chopped

1 cup ketchup

1 cup cider vinegar

½ cup water

6 tablespoons brown sugar

5 tablespoons chili powder

3 tablespoons tomato paste

3 tablespoons Worcestershire sauce

1 tablespoon yellow mustard

1 tablespoon black pepper

2 tablespoons corn syrup

1 tablespoon dried red pepper flakes

Meanwhile, to make the cole slaw, combine the cabbages, onion, and carrots in a large bowl. Add the mayonnaise, sour cream, vinegar, and sugar, tossing to coat, and season with salt and pepper.

To finish the pork, remove it from the oven, cut away the skin, and set the pork in a medium (about 4-quart) Dutch oven. Pour the barbecue sauce overtop and bring to a vigorous simmer over medium heat. Reduce the heat to low and simmer gently for 1 hour.

Remove the pork from the heat and, while it is still in the Dutch oven, shred it into pieces. (The pork will be very tender at this point.) To serve, place the buns on individual plates or a serving platter, divide the pork among them, and top with cole slaw.

Heat the oil in a medium saucepan over medium heat. Add the onion and garlic and sauté until softened and translucent.

Stir in the remaining ingredients, reduce the heat to low, and simmer, stirring occasionally, until the sauce thickens to the consistency of steak sauce, about 1½ hours. Remove from the heat and use immediately, or cool and store in the refrigerator in an airtight container for up to 2 weeks.

Bibb Salad with Buttermilk Dressing

This unique salad is a colorful combination of complementary textures and flavors. Tender lettuce and string beans come together with sweet roasted beets, crunchy cornbread croutons, salty bacon, and rich buttermilk dressing, which gets an extra bit of flavorful tang with the addition of blue cheese. It is as pretty as it is delicious, and I'm sure your guests will enjoy it as much as mine do. You can serve the salad in a large serving bowl, but I personally prefer to plate it individually.

As for the dressing, there is actually enough here for twice the amount of salad. I suggest making the whole recipe and either serving extra on the side, or refrigerating the rest for your next salad. I just bet, though, it won't sit around for long.

Serves 6

BUTTERMILK DRESSING

1 1/2 cups mayonnaise

3/4 cup buttermilk

2 teaspoons chopped garlic

2 teaspoons chopped onion

1/2 cup cider vinegar

2 teaspoons chopped fresh flat-leaf parsley

1/2 teaspoon salt

1/2 teaspoon white pepper

1/2 cup Maytag blue cheese

ASSEMBLY

2 heads Bibb lettuce, cored and
  leaves separated

About 1/4 pound string beans

1/4 cup Cornbread Croutons (see page 60)

1/4 cup chopped browned bacon

1/2 cup roasted beets (see *Chef's Note*),
  for serving

1/2 cup Maytag blue cheese, for serving

Combine all of the dressing ingredients in a large bowl, mixing until smooth. (The cheese might still be somewhat lumpy, but that's fine.)

Combine the lettuce, string beans, croutons, and bacon in a large bowl. Pour about half of the dressing overtop and toss gently to coat. To serve, place the salad on individual plates, divide the beets among them, and sprinkle with blue cheese. Serve the extra dressing on the side, if desired.

CHEF'S NOTE: Roasted beets are delicious as a side dish or incorporated into salads. Roasting brings out their sweet flavor, and their deep red color enhances every presentation. To prepare a few or a bunch of roasted beets, cut off the stems and any fibrous roots and slice them in half lengthwise, keeping the skins on. Toss with some vegetable oil, arrange on a baking sheet, and roast in a 325°F. oven until just tender, about 20 minutes. When the beets are cool enough to handle, remove the skins and cut into about 1/2-inch cubes.

58

Fried Oyster and Caesar Salad

Oh, how I love oysters! They are my favorite food in the world. I will eat them in just about any form: fresh, in fritters, and, of course, fried as they are in this salad. I always look forward to making this dish for friends, but, honestly, I could eat this whole thing myself.

Like so many of my recipes, each component here is integral to the dish as a whole. The cool and crisp romaine lettuce, the juicy tomatoes, the crunchy, hot, succulent oysters, and the golden croutons all marry beautifully with the pungent dressing. All of the ingredients come together to offer an explosion of flavors and textures.

I serve this salad for lunch or dinner. The one thing about fried oysters that you should keep in mind, though, is that they must be served hot right out of the pan. You need to assemble and serve this salad immediately. This is not a dish that sits around on a buffet table. This is a hearty salad for people who are willing to dig right in when the cooks says, "Come and get it!"

Serves 4 to 6

OYSTERS

2 cups shucked oysters

1 cup buttermilk

CAESAR DRESSING

2 egg yolks

2 tablespoons Dijon mustard

6 to 8 anchovy fillets, very finely chopped

2 tablespoons chopped garlic

¼ cup cider vinegar

3 teaspoons fresh lemon juice

⅛ teaspoon Worcestershire sauce

½ cup olive oil

1½ cups canola oil

2 tablespoon warm water, as needed

1 cup freshly grated Parmesan cheese

TO FINISH THE OYSTERS

About 1½ cups canola oil

2 cups Fish Flour (see page 34)

1 teaspoon cayenne pepper

ASSEMBLY

2 heads romaine lettuce, cored and chopped

4 plum tomatoes, cored and finely chopped

1 cup Cornbread Croutons (see *Chef's Note*)

Freshly grated Parmesan cheese, for serving

At least 1 hour before serving the salad, strain the oysters, place them in a medium bowl, and pour in the buttermilk, tossing to coat. Cover with plastic wrap and set in the refrigerator to marinate for 1 hour.

Meanwhile, whisk together the egg yolks, mustard, anchovies, garlic, vinegar, lemon juice, and Worcestershire sauce in a medium bowl. Add the oils in a slow, steady stream, whisking constantly until the dressing is emulsified. If the dressing appears too thick during the process, stop adding the oil, whisk in some water, and then continue whisking in the oil. Stir in the cheese and set aside while finishing the oysters.

Heat the oil in a medium sauté pan. (There should be about ¼ inch of oil in the pan.) To check if it is hot enough, sprinkle a bit of fish flour into the oil. If the flour sizzles right away, the oil is ready.

Combine the fish flour and cayenne pepper in a large shallow pan. Drain the oysters, patting dry with paper towels, and dredge in the flour. Carefully drop about half of the oysters in the oil and fry until golden brown. Remove the oysters using a slotted spoon (metal, not plastic!) and set on a paper-towel-lined baking sheet to drain while you fry the remaining oysters.

To assemble the salad, toss the lettuce, tomatoes, croutons, and dressing together in a large serving bowl and arrange the fried oysters on top. Serve sprinkled with additional Parmesan cheese.

CHEF'S NOTE: Cornbread croutons are a delicious alternative to plain bread croutons. They also make great use of leftover cornbread, which goes stale and becomes firm fairly quickly. Use one- or two-day-old cornbread if possible, as its dry texture makes it easier to cut into cubes.

Cut the cornbread into about ½-inch cubes, spread them out on an ungreased or parchment-lined baking sheet, and bake at 250°F. for about 50 minutes or until dry and light golden brown. Use immediately or store for a day or so in an airtight container.

60

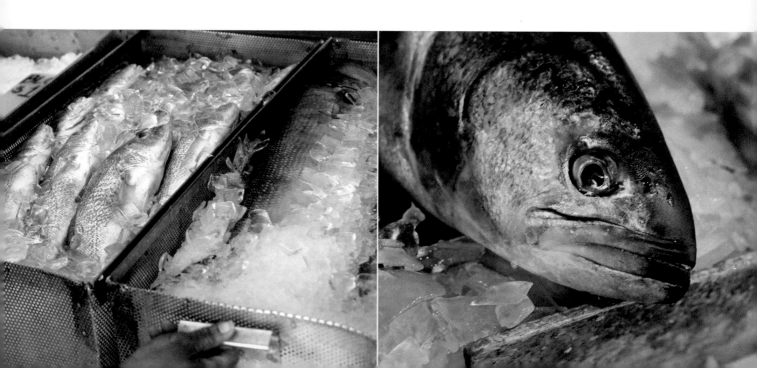

Stuffed Bluefish

I love fish, and I have found that this recipe is a flavorful and easy alternative to serving fillets. I especially like to serve this dish to friends who prefer to stay away from meat. Whole bluefish is great for stuffing, as it is firm and holds together during roasting. The richness of the fish pairs nicely with the fresh pungent cornbread stuffing, which soaks up all the fish's natural juices as it cooks.

Serves 6

2 tablespoons canola oil

½ red onion, peeled and finely chopped

1 teaspoon finely chopped garlic

2 yellow bell peppers, cored, seeded, and
  finely chopped

2 red bell peppers, cored, seeded, and
  finely chopped

2 teaspoons chopped fresh dill

2 teaspoons chopped fresh flat-leaf parsley

1 teaspoon cayenne pepper

1 teaspoon lemon pepper

Salt & black pepper

2 cups crumbled day-old cornbread
  (see page 130)

¼ cup water

1 whole bluefish (about 2 to 3 pounds),
  cleaned and scaled

Heat the oil in a large sauté pan over medium heat. Add the onion and garlic and sauté until softened and translucent. Stir in the peppers and sauté until softened. Toss in the dill, parsley, cayenne pepper, and lemon pepper and season with salt and pepper. Remove from the heat and set aside to cool to room temperature.

Meanwhile, preheat the oven to 350°F.

Combine the cooled pepper mixture with the cornbread in a medium bowl, tossing gently.

Coat a medium baking dish with vegetable spray, or line a baking sheet with parchment paper. Place the bluefish in the dish or on the baking sheet and top with the cornbread mixture. Roast for 30 minutes, raise the oven temperature to 400°F., and roast for another 10 minutes.

Serve the fish on a serving platter.

61

Sweet Potato Cheesecake

I do like cheesecake, but I admit that this dessert is just another excuse to eat sweet potatoes. Every self-respecting Southerner is crazy for sweet potatoes, so I oblige my family and friends by making this rich dessert every so often.

This recipe is based on traditional, dense New-York-style cheesecake prepared with a graham cracker crust. I have enhanced the crust with pecans (another Southern favorite), which add richness and complement the sweet, slightly spicy, and creamy filling. Top the cheesecake with sweetened sour cream and you just don't need anything else on your dessert plate. In fact, you will probably be so satisfied that you won't even think about eating until the next day.

Makes one 10-inch cheesecake

CRUST
1 1/2 cups finely ground graham crackers
1/2 cup finely ground pecans
1 teaspoon ground cinnamon
1/2 cup light brown sugar, packed
1/4 pound (1 stick) unsalted butter, melted

FILLING
3 (8 ounce) packages cream cheese,
  at room temperature
1 1/4 cups sugar
4 eggs
1 cup sweet potato purée (about 1 medium
  sweet potato, cooked, peeled, and puréed)
1 teaspoon ground cinnamon
1/2 teaspoon ground ginger
1/4 teaspoon ground cardamom
1 teaspoon vanilla extract

SOUR CREAM TOPPING
2 cups sour cream
1 cup sugar

Preheat the oven to 325°F.

To make the crust, combine all of the ingredients in a medium bowl, mixing until crumbly. Press into the bottom of a 10-inch springform pan and set aside while preparing the filling.

To make the filling, combine the cream cheese and sugar in a large bowl and beat on high speed using a hand mixer until smooth. (You can also do this on a stand mixer using the paddle attachment.) Add the eggs one at a time, mixing until incorporated and stopping occasionally to scrape the sides of the bowl. Add the sweet potato purée, spices, and vanilla and beat until just incorporated. Pour the filling into the prepared pan and bake until the center is almost completely set. (The center will still jiggle slightly.) Place the cheesecake on a wire rack to cool completely.

To make the sour cream topping, stir together the sour cream and sugar in a small bowl.

To serve, carefully remove the cooled cheesecake from the pan, place on a cake plate, and spread the sour cream topping over the top.

Unlike my easy-going, informal gatherings, my swanky parties are well-planned, often extremely detailed productions! This is not to say that they are always complicated or stressful to organize. I simply mean that there are usually more elements involved and that these parties, therefore, often require more organization and preparation.

I am a big fan of swanky hors d'oeuvre parties, at which the food can be simple or complex, depending on your taste. I do, of course, adore hosting gorgeous sit-down dinners. For the purposes of this chapter, however, I have focused on dishes you can present on platters as passed treats, or set on a buffet table for people to visit as they wish. If a sit-down meal is more your style, you can use most of these recipes for that purpose. Just keep in mind that the serving size of each recipe will, in most cases, be reduced by half.

Whenever I entertain, I am mindful that my party is a reflection of my tastes, my style, and my skill as a hostess. Sadly, many women today know very little about entertaining, let alone cooking. If they are unaccustomed to making dinner for the family, hosting an elegant party might seem really intimidating. I was actually inspired to open restaurants and share my food with others because I was surprised at how few of my acquaintances and friends knew how to cook and entertain. In my opinion, it doesn't matter how career-minded you are; it is important to know the basics of keeping house and being a good hostess. After all, every woman, at some point will have to entertain, and when she does, the event will reflect her level of comfort with the whole ordeal.

Both novice and experienced party-givers can benefit from fresh ideas, so I would like to offer some general suggestions. When hosting a swanky party, consider all of the details associated with the food presentation. Choose a theme for your affair— a particular event, a color scheme, or a seasonal celebration. Use your best tableware. Arrange a variety of barware. Set the stage with flowers, decorations, and music. This all takes time, but your guests will really appreciate your effort.

I realize this kind of entertaining can be a lot of work, but I personally like the hustle and bustle of getting ready. All this activity gives me an adrenaline rush! For me, hosting swanky parties is pure theater. Once I set the stage with my table settings and food, I am ready to put on a great show. This might sound a little backwards, but I often greet my guests and get them started with drinks and nibbles *before* I even get myself ready. While they're visiting and carrying on, I escape to dress and do my make-up and then make my own entrance. "Oh, the diva is here!" my friends often announce as I walk into the room, and then the production kicks into high gear.

The recipes I have chosen for this chapter are just a selection of some of my favorites. They are always hits at my parties, and I hope they will be at yours, too. Just be sure to serve them with great drinks, style, and lots of celebration and laughter.

Collard Green Rolls

These crispy rolls are my version of spring rolls. In true Southern fashion, I like using hearty collard greens and dipping the finished rolls in hot sauce. Once your greens are ready, this recipe comes together quickly. You can even prepare the rolls in advance and leave them, covered, in the refrigerator for several hours or overnight until you are ready to fry them. They also freeze well. Once you decide to finish the rolls, though, be prepared to serve them right away. They are best piping hot and really crispy. Let's face it—no one likes a soggy roll.

While I prefer to use collard greens in this dish, you can easily vary the recipe by using callaloo instead. You might also want to add extra flavor by incorporating small pieces of ham, smoked turkey, or finely chopped onion. Serve the hot rolls on a gorgeous white platter and enjoy them with glasses of sparkling wine or Champagne for an easy, swanky affair.

Makes 8 rolls

4 cups canola oil

2 cups cooked Collard Greens
   (see page 208), drained well

8 spring roll wrappers (about 1 package)

Hot sauce, for serving

Heat the oil in a medium saucepan over medium-high heat. (The oil will appear to shimmer on the surface when it is ready.) Place the greens in a clean kitchen towel and press firmly to extract any excess liquid. (It is imperative that the greens are as dry as possible.)

Begin shaping the rolls. Place a spring roll wrapper on a work surface so that it appears like a diamond rather than a square. Spread a horizontal "log" of greens (about ½-inch-wide) in the center of the wrapper, making sure there is about ⅓ inch between the end of the greens and the point of the wrapper at each end. Wet all four edges of the wrapper with water and fold the points of the wrapper at the sides over the ends of the greens. Lift the point closest to you and fold it over the greens. Roll the wrapper the rest of the way to form a compact cylinder. Repeat the process with the remaining wrappers and greens.

Carefully place about 3 or 4 rolls at a time into the hot oil, turning occasionally until golden brown. Remove the rolls with a slotted spoon and drain on paper towels while frying the remaining rolls. Serve the rolls piled on a serving platter with hot sauce on the side.

67

Asparagus Wrapped in Turkey Bacon

This dish is always popular on a buffet table. Tender, bright green asparagus is delicious on its own, but when wrapped with salty turkey bacon, it becomes something truly special. I like serving this dish hot or at room temperature. You can also easily multiply the recipe to feed whatever size crowd you are entertaining.

Serves 6

Butter, as needed

2 bunches asparagus (about 1½ pounds), trimmed to even lengths and blanched for 4 minutes in boiling salted water

Salt & black pepper

About 4 strips turkey bacon, or as needed

Preheat the oven to 400°F. Butter a large, shallow baking or casserole dish.

Season the asparagus with salt and pepper. Slice each strip of bacon into 3 thin strips, one strip for each stalk. (You might need more strips of bacon depending on the number of stalks you have.) Set 1 strip of turkey bacon on a work surface so that it is perpendicular to the edge of the work surface. Set an asparagus stalk on the end of the bacon strip closest to, and parallel with, the edge of the work surface. Roll to enclose the center portion of the asparagus with bacon. (The tip and about ½ inch of the stem should remain visible.) Place in the prepared baking dish and repeat the process with the remaining asparagus stalks and bacon.

Bake until the bacon is crisp and golden brown, about 10 minutes. Serve hot or at room temperature on serving platter.

Skewered Coconut Shrimp

Here's another of my favorite shrimp dishes. It is always a hit at my parties, and when I serve it at restaurant functions, the platters are always picked clean. Coconut and shrimp love each other. Even unsweetened coconut is naturally sweet and complements the fresh sweetness of the shrimp. When the coconut is combined with coarse Japanese panko breadcrumbs, it creates a coating that enrobes the shrimp in a golden shell that is virtually unequalled in its gorgeous crispness.

I decided to have some extra fun here and use thin strips of sugarcane for skewering the shrimp. This makes for an especially impressive presentation, but you can certainly use wooden skewers if you like.

Serves 4

½ cup all-purpose flour

1 teaspoon salt

½ teaspoon black pepper

2 eggs

¼ cup water

1 cup unsweetened flaked coconut

2 cups panko breadcrumbs

8 jumbo shrimp, peeled and deveined

1 (14-ounce) can sugarcane, drained and cut lengthwise into ⅛-inch-wide strips, or one 12-inch piece fresh sugarcane, peeled, cut widthwise into 4-inch cylinders, and sliced lengthwise into ⅛-inch-wide strips

2 cups canola oil

Hot honey mustard, for dipping

Combine the flour, salt, and pepper in a shallow pan. Combine the eggs and water in a second shallow pan, whisking just until the eggs are loosened. Stir together the coconut and breadcrumbs in a third shallow pan.

Begin coating the shrimp, first dredging in flour, then in the eggs, and finally in the coconut mixture. Skewer 1 shrimp onto each sugarcane strip (you will probably have more strips than shrimp), arrange the skewers on a parchment-lined baking sheet, and set in the refrigerator until the coating is firm, about 1 hour.

Heat the oil in a large sauté pan over medium-high heat. (Check to see if the oil is hot enough by carefully placing the end of a sugarcane strip in the oil. If the oil gently bubbles around the edges of the strip, it is ready.) Carefully lower about 3 shrimp skewers at a time into the oil and fry until the shrimp are golden brown. Set on paper towels to drain and keep warm while frying the remaining skewers.

To serve, arrange the skewers on a large platter and set the mustard on the side for dipping.

69

Jerk Shrimp with Grits

I have so many favorite foods it's downright ridiculous, and shrimp is right up there, close to the top of the list. I will eat shrimp almost any way it's put in front of me. But shrimp and grits together? The combination is beyond wonderful. This jerk season-ing is a good all-purpose recipe. Make it and keep it on hand for any jerk preparation. Once it's made, the shrimp part of the dish comes together quickly. I toss the peeled and deveined shrimp in the seasoning and then quickly sauté them in a hot pan. This recipe for grits is also very basic. Grits, water, salt, and about 15 minutes are all you need.

At my swanky gatherings, I make a fuss over presenting the shrimp and grits. After all, a little theater once in a while is fun. You certainly don't have to go to the trouble of filling individual petite cups as I do, however. The dish is equally pleasing served in individual bowls or arranged on a serving platter. I really like thinking outside of the box, though, and I encourage you to do the same, especially when serving new recipes at your own parties.

Serves 4 to 6

JERK SEASONING

1 tablespoon kosher salt

1 1/2 teaspoons ground allspice

1 teaspoon brown sugar

1 teaspoon granulated garlic

1 teaspoon onion powder

1/2 teaspoon finely chopped Scotch
    bonnet chili pepper

1/2 teaspoon cayenne pepper

1/2 teaspoon dried oregano

1/2 teaspoon ground nutmeg

1/2 teaspoon black pepper

1/2 teaspoon ground ginger

1/4 teaspoon ground cinnamon

1/4 teaspoon dried thyme

To make the jerk seasoning, combine all of the ingredients in a small bowl and set aside momentarily.

To make the grits, bring the water and salt to a boil in a medium saucepan over high heat. Add the grits, pouring in a steady stream and stirring constantly. Reduce the heat to medium-low, cover, and simmer for about 12 minutes. Remove from the heat, stir, and set aside, covered, to keep warm while preparing the shrimp.

GRITS

1 cup water

⅛ teaspoon salt

¼ cup grits

SHRIMP

1 pound jumbo shrimp,
   peeled and deveined

2 tablespoons canola oil

Thinly sliced scallions, for garnish

To make the shrimp, toss together the shrimp, oil, and jerk seasoning in a large bowl. Heat a large sauté pan over medium-high heat, add the shrimp, and sauté, tossing frequently, until they just turn pink.

To serve, spoon some grits into 8 to 12 espresso cups, hang a shrimp over the edge of each cup, and garnish with scallions.

Herb-Roasted Lamb Chops

My friends are truly unbelievable. Rather than wait for an invitation, they will request that I make them dinner. On top of that, they will ask, "Will you make lamb chops?" Fortunately for them, I adore lamb just about as much as I enjoy entertaining. This recipe comes together quickly and relies on traditional ingredients like rosemary and garlic, as well as on my personal favorites, seasoned salt and cayenne pepper. The racks also cook quickly because I use baby lamb from New Zealand, which is very tender and therefore should be roasted only to medium doneness at the most. You will see that this recipe calls for "frenched" racks. This simply means that the meat has been cut away from the ends of the bones, leaving them exposed. You can buy the racks already frenched, or your butcher can prepare them for you.

For those of you who live in or near Philadelphia, I highly suggest you visit my favorite butcher, Harry Ochs, at Reading Terminal Market in Philadelphia. He knows everything there is to know about meat and has coached me over the years to make some of my best roasts, chops, and steaks. Harry taught me how to roast the perfect rack of lamb, and I owe this recipe largely to him.

Serves 4 to 6

½ cup olive oil

¼ cup canola oil

2 teaspoons seasoned salt

1 teaspoon black pepper

2 sprigs fresh rosemary, stemmed
  and roughly chopped

6 cloves garlic, peeled and crushed

1 tablespoon balsamic vinegar

1 teaspoon cayenne pepper

2 racks of baby lamb, frenched

Fresh rosemary springs, for garnish

At least 8 hours before roasting the lamb, combine the oils, seasoned salt, pepper, rosemary, garlic, vinegar, and cayenne pepper in a large zip-top plastic bag. Add the lamb, shaking and rubbing the bag around the racks to coat with the seasonings. Press all of the air out of the bag, seal, and set in the refrigerator to marinate for at least 8 hours or overnight.

The next day or when you are ready to proceed with the dish, preheat the oven to 375°F.

Arrange the lamb on a baking sheet and roast for about 35 minutes, or until cooked *nearly* to desired doneness. Remove from the oven, cover loosely with foil, and set aside to rest and come up to temperature (I like it medium-well—160°F.), about 10 minutes.

To serve, slice the racks into individual chops and arrange on a serving platter garnished with rosemary.

Smithfield Ham with Currant Biscuits and Cherry Marmalade

These biscuits, filled with salty Smithfield ham and sweet cherry marmalade, are one of my most popular party dishes. I especially like to serve them at Christmas and New Year's celebrations because I am most likely to have leftover Smithfield ham from large family gatherings.

Although marmalade and biscuits are wonderful with holiday ham, I happily make them year-round. They come together easily and are great for breakfast, brunch, or snacks. The key here, though, is that I make the marmalade and biscuits to go with the ham, not the other way around. Preparing Smithfield ham is a production and there is always extra. So, in addition to nibbling at it and making sandwiches, I have found other creative ways to celebrate it. Pile these biscuits prettily on a platter, set them on a buffet table, and your guests won't know they're eating leftovers. They will just be glad they came to your party.

Makes 10 biscuits

CHERRY MARMALADE

3 pounds fresh sweet cherries
  (such as Bing), stemmed and pitted

1 1/4 cups sugar

2 tablespoons cider vinegar

1 tablespoon lemon juice

1/2 teaspoon ground cloves

1/2 teaspoon ground cinnamon

1/4 teaspoon cayenne pepper

BISCUITS

1/2 cup currants

1/2 cup water

3 cups sifted all-purpose flour

2 teaspoons salt

2 tablespoons baking powder

1/4 pound (1 stick) unsalted butter,
  chilled and cubed

1 cup buttermilk

To make the marmalade, combine all of the ingredients in a large saucepan and bring to a boil over medium-high heat. Reduce the heat to low and simmer gently, stirring frequently, until the marmalade is thickened and translucent, about 25 minutes. Remove the marmalade from the heat and spoon into a jar. Cool and set aside while preparing the biscuits. (If you'll be using the marmalade for another purpose, seal the jar while the marmalade is still hot and store in the refrigerator for up to 1 month.)

To make the biscuits, preheat the oven to 325°F. Combine the currants and water in a small bowl and set aside to soak for about 10 minutes.

Combine the flour, salt, and baking powder in a large bowl. Using a pastry cutter or your fingertips, work the butter into the flour until the mixture resembles coarse meal. (It's alright if some pea-size pieces of butter remain visible.) Add the buttermilk and mix lightly to form a soft dough. (The dough should be gooey, but not wet.) Drain the currants, and knead them gently into the dough.

Turn the dough out onto a lightly floured work surface,

ASSEMBLY

About ¾ pound Smithfield ham, cut into about 2-inch pieces (see page 216)

sprinkle with additional flour, and roll to about ½ inch thick. Cut into 10 biscuits using a round cutter about 2 inches in diameter. Arrange the biscuits about 1 inch apart on a parchment-lined baking sheet and bake until risen and golden brown, about 15 minutes. Set on wire racks to cool.

To assemble, split open the biscuits and place the ham slices on the bottom half of each biscuit. Spoon some mar- malade over the ham and cover with the tops of the biscuits. To serve, arrange the biscuits on a large serving platter.

Crème Brûlée with Bananas and Chocolate Mousse

Heaven knows that crème brûlée is just about as far from my Virginia culinary roots as you can get, but oh, how I have come to love it! It is a dessert characterized by contradictions. Perhaps this is why it is so seductive. On the one hand, crème brûlée epitomizes simplicity. It relies on only a handful of ingredients and requires just a few steps. On the other hand, the dish's very simplicity makes it challenging. The ingredients must be spectacularly fresh, and once combined, they depend on the cook's skillful and exacting cooking techniques.

It is this dessert's dual nature that makes it so tempting and thrilling, and yet so often disappointing. I can be in a restaurant and turn down one dessert after another until I see crème brûlée on the menu. When it arrives in front of me, I am able to tell almost instantly whether or not the experience will live up to my expectations. The sugar topping should be crisp and caramelized to a rich amber color, not soggy and a wishy-washy pale gold. The custard must be just set and silky with visible specks of real vanilla bean. I know I'm in real trouble if the serving is large. Good crème brûlée is so rich that a small portion satisfies even the biggest craving. I'll tell you one thing: If the crème brûlée I order in a restaurant is substandard, I am one upset sister; I just ate 400 calories for nothing!

Having said all this about my favorite classic dessert, I now present a recipe for an extravagant version of it, complete with caramelized bananas and chocolate mousse. Maybe my Southern roots have inspired me to marry all of these luscious ingredients in one dish, or maybe it's that, especially when entertaining good friends, more really does seem better. Whatever the reason, I encourage you to try this crème brûlée at your next special party. You will all roll away from the table grinning from sweet intoxication.

Serves 6

CRÈME BRÛLÉE

9 egg yolks

¾ cup superfine sugar

1 vanilla bean

1 quart heavy cream

1 teaspoon vanilla extract

Preheat the oven to 325°F.

To make the crème brûlée, combine the egg yolks and sugar in a large bowl and whisk vigorously until thickened and pale yellow in color. (You can also do this with a hand mixer or on a stand mixer using the whip attachment.)

Using a sharp paring knife, split the vanilla bean down the middle, scrape out the seeds, and place the bean and seeds in a medium saucepan. Add the cream and vanilla extract to the pan and bring to a boil over medium heat. Immediately remove from the heat and incorporate into the egg yolk and sugar mixture, pouring in a slow, steady stream and whisking the custard constantly. (Add the cream gradually to prevent the egg yolks from scrambling.)

CHOCOLATE MOUSSE

½ cup sugar

1½ tablespoons water

1 teaspoon banana liquor

3 large egg yolks

½ pound bittersweet chocolate, chopped

2 tablespoons unsalted butter

1¼ cup heavy cream

ASSEMBLY

About ½ cup sugar

About 3 ripe bananas, peeled and sliced
 into ⅛- to ¼-inch rounds

Banana slices, for garnish

Cookies, for serving

Arrange six 6-ounce ramekins in a shallow roasting pan. Divide the custard among them (each ramekin should be about half full) and fill the roasting pan with enough water to come halfway up the sides of the ramekins. Bake until the edges are just set and the centers still jiggle somewhat, about 40 minutes. Remove from the oven and set aside to cool in the pan of water. Remove the crème brûlées and set in the refrigerator to chill for about 2 hours.

Meanwhile, make the chocolate mousse. Combine the sugar, water, and banana liquor in a small saucepan, bring to a boil, and boil until the sugar is dissolved, about 1 minute.

Place the egg yolks in a medium bowl and beat with a hand mixer on high speed until thickened and light yellow in color, about 2 minutes. (You can also do this on a stand mixer using the whip attachment.) Reduce the mixing speed to medium and *gradually* drizzle the hot sugar syrup into the egg yolks. When all of the syrup is incorporated, raise the mixing speed to high and continue whipping for about 3 more minutes. Set aside to cool to room temperature. (If you're using a stand mixer, reduce the mixing speed to low and continue mixing until cooled.)

Combine the chocolate and butter in a medium stainless steel or glass bowl. Bring a medium saucepan filled with about 1 inch of water to a boil over high heat, reduce the heat to low, and maintain at a bare simmer. Set the bowl of chocolate in the saucepan (the bowl should not touch the water) and stir occasionally until melted and smooth. Remove from the heat and cool to room temperature.

Whip the cream in a medium bowl to soft peaks using a hand mixer or whisk.

Fold the cooled melted chocolate into the cooled whipped egg yolk mixture until nearly completely incorporated. Fold about one-third of the whipped cream into the chocolate and egg mixture until nearly completely incorporated, and then fold in the remaining cream, mixing until no streaks of egg or cream are visible. Put the mousse in the refrigerator until set, about 2 hours.

To finish the crème brûlée, prepare a hot broiler. Sprinkle each cooled crème brûlée with about 1 tablespoon of sugar, shaking the ramekin to completely coat the top of the custard. Arrange the crème brûlées on a baking sheet and set under the broiler just until the sugar is bubbly and caramelized. (Watch closely as the sugar burns quickly.) Remove from the broiler and set aside for about 3 minutes to cool to room temperature.

Arrange banana slices on top of each crème brûlée, covering the caramel almost completely. Divide the chocolate mousse among them, smoothing the tops or creating decorative peaks. Sprinkle the mousse with the remaining sugar (you might not need all of the sugar), arrange again on the baking sheet, and set under the broiler once more, just until the tops are caramelized.

To serve, place each crème brûlée on a serving plate, garnish with banana slices, and serve with cookies.

Duke's Delicious Dessert Royale

*Sometimes opportunities show up on your doorstep in the most wonderful and unexpected ways. In my experience, you just have to be ready to greet them warmly and invite 'em right in. That's what happened with this dessert. Developing it was one of my first big challenges as a restaurateur. I opened **Delilah's** in October of 1984, and almost exactly two years later, I put myself on Philadelphia's culinary map with this cake.*

*It all started when Elkman Advertising Agency asked several local caterers, including me, to submit food-related themes for the upcoming premiere of Duke Ellington's opera, **Queenie Pie**. This was to be no small affair. The opera was opening at the renowned Annenberg Theater, and the party was to be held in the lobby before the performance. Competition has always been just the thing to get my juices flowing, and I wanted this gig. So I immediately started doing research on Duke. I went to the Free Library of Philadelphia and read everything I could find. I talked at length with my father, who happens to be a jazz musician, and learned a lot about Duke's music and the jazz culture of Harlem. The thing that struck me most was that the man loved his sweets. He was known for piling different desserts on top of one another and eating them all at once. That man knew how to live.*

All of this gave me the idea to design a cake that was a "controlled" mish-mash of delicious desserts and confections: cake, preserves, pudding, applesauce, and chocolate frosting. Needless to say, I won the competition, and the advertising agency decided to theme the party as a dessert reception. Both the party and I were a hit. I attended the event, slicing and serving the many huge cakes I had prepared. There was so much cake, I can't even tell you. What a sight! I was also featured in newspapers with pictures showing me assembling the layers.

As you can imagine, this recipe is very special to me and conjures up wonderful memories of the whole experience. The cake takes some time to prepare, so I only serve it on special occasions. It is well worth the effort, though, and I hope you make it for the dessert-lover or Duke-enthusiast in your own life.

81

Makes one 9-inch cake

CHOCOLATE CAKE

1¾ cups all-purpose flour

1 cup cocoa powder (not Dutch process)

1½ teaspoons baking powder

1¾ teaspoons baking soda

1¼ teaspoons salt

1 cup milk, at room temperature

2½ teaspoons vanilla extract

Preheat the oven to 350°F. Butter and flour two 9 x 2-inch cake pans and line the bottoms with parchment paper.

To make the cake, sift together the flour, cocoa, baking powder, baking soda, and salt into a medium bowl.

Combine the milk and vanilla in a small bowl.

Place the butter in a large bowl and, using a hand mixer, beat on medium speed until smooth. Add the sugar and continue beating until light. Incorporate the eggs, one at a time, beating until the mixture is light and fluffy. (You can also do this on a stand mixer using the paddle attachment.)

1/4 pound (1 stick) unsalted butter,
   at room temperature

2 cups sugar

2 eggs, at room temperature

1/2 cup boiling water

1/2 cup prepared strong coffee

CHOCOLATE FROSTING

1/2 pound unsweetened chocolate,
   chopped

1/2 pound (2 sticks) unsalted butter

2 (16-ounce) boxes confectioners' sugar,
   sifted

1 cup milk

1 tablespoon plus 1 teaspoon
   vanilla extract

ASSEMBLY

About 3/4 cup apricot preserves

About 3/4 cup vanilla pudding

About 3/4 cup applesauce

Vanilla ice cream, for serving

Reduce the mixing speed to low. Alternately add the flour mixture and milk mixture in thirds, beginning and ending with the flour and stopping once or twice to scrape the sides of the bowl. Raise the mixing speed to medium high and beat for about 1 1/2 minutes until the batter is smooth. Reduce the mixing speed to medium low and gradually pour in the water and coffee. Stop to scrape the sides of the bowl again and continue beating until smooth. (The batter will appear thin.)

Divide the batter evenly between the prepared pans and bake until a skewer inserted in the centers comes out clean, about 25 minutes. (If a few crumbs stick to the skewer, it's okay. Do not over bake, or the cake will be dry.) Set the cakes on wire racks to cool in the pans for about 10 minutes. Turn out of the pans to cool completely.

Meanwhile, to make the frosting, combine the chocolate and butter in a medium saucepan and heat over medium-low heat, stirring frequently until melted and smooth. Remove from the heat and cool to room temperature.

Whisk together the sugar, milk, and vanilla in a large bowl and stir in the melted chocolate. Set the bowl in a larger bowl of ice water. Using a hand mixer, beat on high speed until the frosting has lightened in color and is fluffy, about 2 minutes.

To assemble the cake, slice each cake in half horizontally to create 4 thin layers. Place the bottom layer on a cake plate or serving platter and spread with apricot preserves. Set the second layer on top and spread with vanilla pudding. Place the third layer over the pudding and spread with applesauce. Set the final layer of cake over the applesauce and coat the entire cake with frosting.

Serve slices of the cake with scoops of vanilla ice cream.

Cherry Turnovers

I love to serve big, gorgeous cherry pies, but sometimes, especially at parties, it's fun to arrange platters of delicate, miniature turnovers like these. These crescent-shaped pastries are not only pretty, but absolutely luscious as well. I fry them until they are glistening and golden and then give them a snowy dusting of confectioners' sugar. You can certainly serve them at room temperature, but I like them best still warm; with each bite, the sugar leaves a powdery trail around my lips, and the ruby-red filling drips down my chin. Pure seduction.

Makes about 24 turnovers

PASTRY DOUGH

1¾ cups all-purpose flour

1 tablespoon sugar

½ teaspoon salt

¼ pound (1 stick) unsalted butter, chilled
   and cut into small cubes

2 tablespoons vegetable shortening, chilled

About 3 tablespoons ice water

FILLING

2 cups pitted fresh or frozen tart cherries

¾ cup sugar

1 tablespoon cornstarch

⅛ teaspoon almond extract (optional)

ASSEMBLY

6 cups canola oil, for frying

1½ tablespoons unsalted butter, chilled
   and cut into small cubes

Confectioners' sugar, for serving

To make the pastry, combine the flour, sugar, and salt in a large bowl. Incorporate the butter and shortening using a pastry cutter or your fingertips until the mixture resembles coarse meal. Add 2 tablespoons of the ice water and work gently into the mixture until the dough just comes together, adding more water as needed. Shape the dough into a disk, wrap tightly in plastic wrap, and set aside to rest and chill in the refrigerator for at least 30 minutes.

To make the filling, place the cherries in a medium saucepan and cover. Bring to a simmer over medium heat, cooking until the cherries release some of their juice, about 4 minutes. (This will take longer with frozen cherries.) Remove from the heat.

Combine the sugar and cornstarch in a small bowl and sprinkle into the hot cherries, stirring to incorporate. Add the almond extract and bring to a boil over medium-high heat, stirring frequently. Continue to boil for about 1 minute until thickened and glossy, remove from the heat, and pour into a medium bowl. Set in the refrigerator until completely cooled, about 30 minutes.

To assemble the turnovers, heat the oil in a large saucepan over medium-high heat.

Place the chilled pastry on a lightly floured work surface and roll to about ⅛ inch thick. Cut the dough into 3-inch

84

rounds using a biscuit or cookie cutter and arrange on a parchment-lined baking sheet. Place about ½ teaspoon of filling into the center of each round and dot with 1 or 2 cubes of butter. Moisten the edges of the pastry with water, fold into crescents (half moons), and crimp the edges with a fork.

Check to see that the oil is hot enough by sprinkling a bit of flour into the oil. If the flour sizzles right away, the oil is ready. Carefully place about 4 turnovers at a time into the hot oil and fry until golden brown, about 4 to 6 minutes. Remove to a paper-towel-lined baking sheet to drain and cover loosely with a dish towel to keep warm while frying the remaining turnovers.

To serve, sprinkle the turnovers with confectioners' sugar and arrange on a serving platter.

A SWANKY CAVIAR PARTY

Of all my swanky parties, my caviar and drinks parties are my swankiest and sassiest. These glitzy Friday or Saturday night affairs are just for the girls, and we sure do them right. We always dress up and sometimes assign a theme for the evening. "Breakfast at Tiffany's" recently became one of our most successful themes, each of us channeling our most fabulous inner (and outer) Audrey Hepburn. We were our swankiest retro selves that night!

Although the themes, music, and fashions we choose for any given party can vary widely, the girls and I strictly enforce the central event: feasting on caviar with all of the traditional accompaniments. When it comes to the caviar, I keep it fairly simple, but I do insist on presenting it beautifully. Sometimes I set the caviar in a martini-style glass that sits in a bowl of ice to keep it cold. Other times I like to use my silver caviar server, complete with a glass bowl insert for the caviar, vodka shot glasses that fit around it, and, of course, mother-of-pearl caviar spoons. You might think these spoons are too fussy and expensive. I'm telling you, though, if you're going to spend good money on caviar, stay away from metal spoons. They will bruise those gorgeous black eggs!

My two favorite types of caviar are osetra and, believe it or not, American sturgeon caviar from Kentucky. The difference in price is enormous. Ose-

tra sells for about $150 per ounce, depending on where you buy it, while the American varieties vary between $20 and $40 per ounce. If you're just starting out on your caviar excursion, begin with the less expensive varieties and work your way up if you choose to do so. You might find that you don't need to indulge in the really costly caviar, though. Just because it's more expensive doesn't necessarily guarantee that you will like it better.

As for accompaniments, I stick to the traditional assortment of chopped hard-cooked egg yolks and egg whites (served separately), chopped red onion, whole capers, crème fraîche, and, of course, buckwheat blinis, which I purchase already prepared. I'm too busy setting out glasses and deciding what to wear to bother with the blinis! I also usually serve other little nibbles that complement caviar. My girls and I like beautiful platters of smoked fish, composed of salmon, trout, bluefish, scallops, mussels, trout pâté, and crackers. We'll go back and forth between the caviar and smoked fish platter all night, trying to satisfy our cravings for salty, smoky, fishy goodness. It's quite a task, considering it might be three months until the next party.

You might be thinking, with all of this elegant food, what else could we possibly want? Well, if you're one of my girls, you need a fabulous drink to go with it. And at these parties, the drink of choice is, of course, the desert dry vodka martini. When I say dry, I mean parched. Dry martinis, of course, are essential for quenching our thirst after consuming all those luscious, salty, caviar eggs. I set out an assortment of martini and cocktail glasses so the girls can choose their own. The serious business of picking out the perfect glasses excites us almost as much as shopping for shoes. And we adore shopping for shoes.

Over the years, our martinis have evolved. We used to use vermouth. Then we put the vermouth in a spray bottle and sprayed our glasses before adding the vodka. These days, our motto is, "Don't even pass the vermouth over the glass! Just pour the vodka!" Some of us like our martinis shaken (with tiny crystals of ice), while others like them stirred. Of course, I provide a delectable assortment of olives to accompany or drop into the martinis. We like olives stuffed with blue cheese, garlic, or hot peppers. After all, once the olives hit the vodka, isn't the drink considered a complete meal?

These dry martinis are standard at every caviar party and are, by far, our favorite drink. If you prefer, try some flavored martinis for the fun of it. In our group, there are usually one or two of us who decide to veer off the "desert dry" path and try something new. At a recent party, one of my girlfriends was all into pomegranates. She brought the juice and the seeds, and we all just watched to see what was going to happen next. After spending a few minutes at the bar, she appeared with a blush-pink martini, garnished with ruby-red seeds. That was the beginning of the end. For the rest of the night, she walked around with her pretty drink held high, just talking about how perfectly fabulous her martini was, and how she could legitimately drink all night, because she was consuming all antioxidants and no carbs. Oh, the drama!

You get the picture of what happens at our swanky caviar parties. I hope our crazy fun encourages you to host your own. Here are some final suggestions: keep the party intimate. Invite ten or so friends. Keep it simple: buy food that is already prepared so you have to cook as little as possible. Put out your prettiest plates, platters, glasses, and napkins. Dress up if you like that sort of thing; caviar deserves high fashion, after all. Most importantly, have fun and laugh all night with your best friends.

A SWANKY CHEESE TRAY

I really enjoy hosting hors d'oeuvre parties that feature beautiful cheese trays. Virtually everyone loves cheese, and developing each presentation inspires me to try new varieties and flavors. (As if I need a reason at all to indulge!)

There are several things to keep in mind when arranging a cheese tray. Most importantly: relax. You don't need to be a connoisseur or *maître fromager* to choose a handful of tasty items, nor should you feel compelled to serve a large selection. Depending on the size of my party, I usually go with three to six cheeses, each with a different texture and flavor. The key here is to offer a variety. Try to pick from among these groups: hard (such as a Parmesan or Pecorino); semifirm (such as Cheddar or Jarlsberg); semisoft (such as Gouda or Tilsit); soft-ripened (such as Brie or Pont l'Évêque); and blue (such as Gorgonzola or Stilton). In the end, be sure to buy what you like. There is no point in serving cheese you are not crazy about, simply because you think it's *chichi* or will make a good impression on your guests. If you're really uncertain about what to get, ask the person at the cheese counter in your local market. Better yet, go to a gourmet or specialty cheese shop, where the salespeople really know their products and will allow you to taste before you buy.

As for setting up the actual tray, I suggest serving some fruit alongside the cheese. Again, you don't need to go crazy here. It's easy to get carried away in the supermarket, filling lots of those little plastic bags, and suddenly you're at risk of displaying the whole produce section. This will only overwhelm the cheese you've worked so hard to assemble. Sliced pears, apples, strawberries, and grapes on the vine are beautiful with cheese, as are dried figs and dates. Choose one or two varieties of fruit and call it a day.

I happen to love olives, so I always have a variety of olive trays scattered around when I serve cheese. Nuts and crackers are nice additions, too. Again, keep it simple. These are hors d'oeuvres, not a last meal. The best way to learn about cheese is to visit wonderful specialty shops. The folks who handle hundreds of cheeses on a daily basis are very knowledgeable and can steer you in the right direction. For me, DiBruno Bros. in Philadelphia's Italian Market is sheer heaven. It is astounding how many cheeses (as well as olives, sausages, and olive oils) they are able to pack into their little shop. The aroma alone sends me over the edge as soon as I walk through the door. We all have our old stand-bys when it comes to cheese, but by branching out a bit, you just might find some new favorites.

To help you get started, here is an assortment of cheese I might serve at one of my parties: goat cheese, aged Gouda, Saint André, Boursin, and

Parmesan. I might serve all five if I'm hosting a large party. If the party is more intimate, I might put out only three. Remember to set out the cheese about thirty minutes to one hour before your guests arrive. Cold cheese is not only less flavorful than room temperature cheese, but semisoft and soft-ripened varieties, in particular, are best when served at their softest and smoothest.

I hope you serve some inviting cheese trays at your next party. Try some new selections, or begin with your favorites. The process might seem intimidating at first, but, really, it's not that deep. You might think the tray has to be just so. It doesn't. Honestly, so you know I'm serious, I personally don't need much to satisfy my cheese cravings. Sometimes, especially if the party is made up of me and a friend, a wedge of DiBruno Bros. buttery, triple-cream cheese—*Delice de Bourgone*—and a couple of spoons are all I need.

Bountiful
SEASONS

BOUNTIFUL SEASONS

I consider myself lucky to live in a part of the country where, every few months or so, the seasons change, bringing exciting newness to the landscape, to our daily routines, and, of course, to the table. Ever since I was little, I've looked forward to these changes. Winter's snow draped like blankets over rooftops and trees; spring's first flowers peeking shyly through the ground; summer's seemingly endless, lazy warm days; and fall's leaves setting the trees and the ground ablaze with color—I anticipated all of these scenes. I eagerly awaited the different foods we ate during each time of year, too. In fact, I still do. In the winter, pots of warming, thick bean dishes sit bubbling away on the stove, and juicy braised meats become succulent and luscious as they cook for hours in the oven. When spring comes, I glory in tender asparagus and crisp, fried soft-shell crabs. Summer brings gorgeously fresh black-eyed peas, sweet, juicy corn, and platters of creamy deviled eggs. Come fall, my kitchen basks in the aromas of spicy roasted chicken, thick stews, and sweet mashed yams.

Just like the landscape, the availability of certain foods changes with the seasons, constantly reminding me of the natural cycle of life. The problem is that this natural cycle is much less visible than it used to be. I remember when I was a kid growing up in Philadelphia, there were certain foods that were simply unavailable out of season. We might have been dreaming about juicy, sweet blackberries in October, but they were nowhere to be found. I had to wait until they started showing up on market shelves in the summer to get my fill. Nowadays, cartons of blackberries, along with lots of other fruits and vegetables, appear in supermarkets almost year-round. Not only is this produce outrageously expensive out of season, but it usually has little, if any, flavor. Sure, I could buy these items frozen. I know good quality frozen produce—even organic produce—is widely available these days. But I don't mess with that. I'd rather wait to eat it fresh. This means I have to go without particular foods some of the time, but that's really okay. My anticipation, and appreciation for them, increases in their absence. We've become accustomed to having so many foods available most of the year that we've for-

92

gotten what it feels like to look forward to them. In my opinion, there's just nothing better than buying fresh fruits and vegetables at their peak, and then eating them until I get my fill!

For me, it's just not that complicated. I eat what's in season and what's fresh. I also try to buy locally grown produce and naturally raised meat and poultry as often as I can. This way, I know I'm getting the highest quality and, therefore, the most flavorful ingredients possible. I try to stay away from big supermarkets as well. I'd much rather shop at farmers' markets and small local farm stands. I could spend the whole day going from one to the other, buying different things. I enjoy looking at the products, comparing them, and taking my time shopping almost as much as I enjoy going home and cooking. I think that's all part of the fun. I actually shop at least four or five times a week and I cook what I buy almost right away. The food I purchase remains fresh because I really don't store it for long. I hardly even bother with the freezer, either. It's really a shame how my freezer space goes to waste, but I don't need it. There's usually only a smoked ham hock or two, some salt pork, and maybe a bag of smoked turkey wings hanging out in there.

Now, don't get me wrong. there is nothing bad about supermarkets or storing and freezing food. I certainly understand that, for folks who don't like food shopping as much as I do or those who have small children, visiting a supermarket once or twice a week might make their lives easier. All I'm saying

is, if you have the chance to shop at a farmers' market, I think you'll really enjoy the experience. I know you'll appreciate the quality of food you find there. If a supermarket is your only option, though, just pay attention to what's in season and what looks and smells (and tastes, if you're allowed to sneak a taste) freshest. If, for example, you live in the Northeast, buying strawberries in December, as much as you might want them, isn't necessarily the wisest choice. The poor things have most likely been sitting in warehouses for weeks and are almost always devoid of flavor. The key is to try and buy the best food you can. You might have to be willing to, on occasion, just walk away and do without, rather than compromise on quality and flavor. You will be rewarded in the end, when you bite into an early summer strawberry and the ruby red sweet juice runs down your chin.

I admit I am fortunate. I was raised in a home where food really mattered and seasonal foods were celebrated. Even in 1960s Philadelphia, we had great neighborhood stores and markets, and my mother taught me how to shop. We went to the corner butcher together, where she explained how to order affordable and flavorful cuts of meat and poultry. She took me to local markets to buy fish and produce and showed me how to choose the best items. When I visited my grandparents in Virginia during the summers, my education continued. I gained an even greater appreciation of literally fresh-picked fruits and vegetables and fresh-caught

93

fish. I remember as a kid feeling grateful for each season's bounty and for my family's eagerness to celebrate it.

The following seasonal recipes are among my all-time favorites. Some pay tribute to the dishes of my youth, while others reflect my more recently developed styles and tastes. Each recipe is special to me, though, because it not only represents a certain time of year, but the emotions and stories I still associate with that season as well. Food, after all, isn't just about filling our tummies or responding to the weather. As the environment around us changes, the food we prepare and share with others can comfort, enliven, relax, or invigorate us. Once we understand this, we can really begin to appreciate the seasons' many bounties.

94

WINTER

For me, winter represents two completely different, but equally wonderful, types of eating. On the one hand, there is the festive, lavish sort of dining that takes place around the holiday table. Between the last week of November and January 2nd, I am on a holiday adrenaline high! Aside from shopping, decorating, and going to parties, I seem to be planning menus and throwing parties almost non-stop. And my holiday parties are no small affairs—we're talking numerous events with dozens of friends and family. I develop menus and cook for each and every one. We'll talk more about these traditional and elaborate favorites in the last chapter, but I wanted to mention this type of celebratory eating in order to contrast it with the winter dishes I focus on here.

On the flip side of the over-the-top, rich, and complex holiday foods I serve to "wow" guests are the much simpler meals that are meant to comfort, soothe, and quiet holiday-weary souls. I think of January and February as recuperative months, when I can retreat, relax, and recharge, and the recipes I prepare during these months reflect this simpler, slower mode. The weather at this time of year also calls for warming, satisfying food. Whether I'm homebound because of snow or it's just too cold to go out, I crave basic, feel-good dishes.

Most of the time, I like to make meals that require little attention and can just cook all day while I do other things, such as put decorations away, organize the house, take care of paperwork, or just watch a movie with friends. Dishes like stewed beans and braised meats are perfect for these occasions. They pretty much take care of themselves, fill the house with inviting aromas, and, when I am ready, comfort and satisfy my cold, weather-weary spirit.

Red Beans and Rice

I love all kinds of bean dishes. They are easy, inexpensive, and delicious one-pot meals that are as well suited for a family dinner as they are for a party of friends. Red beans are among my favorite dried beans. They are mild but also hearty and take well to pungent seasonings, such as the hot pepper flakes, garlic, onions, herbs, rich ham hocks, and spicy, smoky andouille sausages in this recipe. I particularly like these vibrant flavors, but you should use the ingredients you like best. I often set a pot of beans to cook with whatever delicious remnants of past meals I find in the fridge. Utilizing leftovers in this way makes the dish even more economical.

The main thing to remember when cooking beans is to stir the pot occasionally to prevent the beans from burning or sticking to the bottom of the pan. This is particularly important if you're cooking on an electric stove, as the burners often cause hot spots on the pan. The other thing is to watch that the beans don't get too dry during cooking; you will need to add water or stock every so often to keep the beans just submerged. Occasionally stirring and adding water to the beans will ensure that they are evenly cooked, perfectly tender, and delicious.

I always like serving some kind of bread with beans, and I think cornbread is just about the perfect choice. Sweet and moist, with a dense but cake-like consistency, it pairs perfectly with spicy, hearty red beans.

Serves 8

1 pound dried red beans

2 ham hocks (about ½ pound each), scored or cracked, or 1 pound smoked turkey butts, cut into about 1-inch pieces

1 large yellow onion, peeled and chopped

1 teaspoon cayenne pepper

2 sprigs fresh thyme

3 dried bay leaves

4 cloves garlic, peeled and chopped

1 teaspoon dried red pepper flakes, or to taste

2 andouille sausages (about ½ pound), cut into 3-inch pieces

Seasoned salt & black pepper

4 cups cooked white rice, for serving

Cornbread, for serving (see page 130)

At least 8 hours before serving the dish, pick through the beans and remove any small stones or dried bits. Place the beans in a large saucepan or Dutch oven and pour in enough cold water to cover by about ½ inch. Add the ham hocks, onion, cayenne, thyme, bay leaves, garlic, red pepper flakes, and sausages, and season with seasoned salt and pepper. Bring to a boil over medium-high heat, and continue to boil, stirring frequently, for about 20 minutes. Reduce the heat to low and stir the beans again. Cover and simmer, stirring occasionally to prevent the mixture from burning, until the beans are tender and the juice is starting to thicken, about 8 hours. (The beans will be very soft, appearing almost overcooked and ready to burst, but that's what you want.) Add more water as necessary just to keep the beans covered throughout the cooking process.

To serve, remove the bay leaves and thyme sprigs. Spoon rice into individual bowls, ladle the red beans overtop, and serve with cornbread.

Turkey Wings

I ate a lot of turkey wings growing up and still enjoy them today. They are meaty, filling, and delicious and cost practically pennies a serving. This recipe is as suited to weeknight family suppers as it is to weekend gatherings. Roasting turns the skin golden brown and crispy in no time, while the meat remains juicy and tender. Make a bit of gravy with the pan drippings, serve the wings and gravy over rice, and I just know you'll be content to relax and nibble away for some time. This method is straightforward and easy, but if you want, you can prepare this dish in a slow cooker. Simply toss everything but the flour and water into the pot and cook on low for 6 to 8 hours. Stir in the flour and water toward the end to thicken the juices.

Serves 8

8 turkey wings

2 teaspoons black pepper

2 teaspoons granulated garlic

2 teaspoons seasoned salt

4 ribs celery, chopped

½ onion, peeled and chopped

4 carrots, peeled and chopped

1 tablespoon all-purpose flour

½ cup water or Chicken Stock
   (see page 36)

Cooked white rice, for serving

Preheat the oven to 350°F.

Season the turkey wings with pepper, granulated garlic, and seasoned salt, rubbing enthusiastically. Spread the celery, onion, and carrots evenly in a medium roasting pan and arrange the seasoned wings on top. Roast for about 1 hour, or until the wings are golden brown and the vegetables are softened and caramelized.

Remove the roasting pan from the oven and lift out the turkey wings, setting aside momentarily to keep warm while making the gravy. Sprinkle the pan drippings and vegetables with flour, stirring with a wooden spoon until the mixture is pasty, and set over medium heat. Drizzle in the water or stock, stirring constantly, and simmer until thickened to a medium gravy consistency. Return the turkey wings to the pan and coat with the gravy. To serve, arrange the turkey wings and gravy on a large platter and serve the white rice on the side.

97

Stewed Navy Beans

I just can't help but smile and relax when I think about this dish. A steaming bowl of creamy stewed navy beans makes me happy any day of the week and at any time of year, but it is especially comforting in the winter, when all I want is something warming and satisfying. I remember playing outside in the snow as a little girl and seeing the kitchen window glowing and foggy from the steaming pot of beans cooking on the stove. Even then, I knew that I was happiest in the warm, fragrant kitchen. For me, this dish will also always represent Saturday night supper, especially in my pre-restaurant days when my family spent most Saturdays at home cleaning all day or fooling around with one hobby or another. I put the beans on the stove and, except for visiting the pot to give it a stir every so often, I pretty much left them alone. All day, the delicious aroma of those beans cooking made our stomachs growl, and we couldn't wait to sit at the table and dig in. A day can't get much better than that.

These beans are wonderful on their own, but they are even better with hearty bread or buttermilk biscuits, as I have suggested here. Serve the biscuits on the side, or set a biscuit in your bowl and ladle the creamy beans overtop. If you want to add a bit of spice to the dish (and I always do), sprinkle some dried red pepper flakes over the beans; they will warm you up even more.

Serves 8

1 pound dried navy beans

4 ham hocks (about ½ pound each), scored or cracked, or 2 pounds smoked turkey legs or wings, roughly chopped

1 cup finely chopped yellow onion

¼ teaspoon dried oregano

¼ teaspoon dried thyme

2 dried bay leaves

1 tablespoon finely chopped garlic

2 quarts Chicken Stock (see page 36)

1 teaspoon seasoned salt

Buttermilk Biscuits, for serving
  (see page 179)

At least 8 hours before serving the dish, pick through the beans and remove any small stones or dried bits. Place the beans in a large saucepan or Dutch oven and pour in enough cold water to cover by about ½ inch. Add the ham hocks, onion, oregano, thyme, bay leaves, garlic, stock, and seasoned salt and bring to a boil over medium-high heat. Continue to boil, stirring frequently, for about 20 minutes. Reduce the heat to low and stir the beans again. Cover and simmer, stirring occasionally to prevent the mixture from burning, until the beans are tender, the juice is starting to thicken, and the ham hocks are beginning to fall apart, about 8 hours. (The beans will be very soft, appearing almost overcooked and ready to burst, but that's what you want.) Add more water or stock as necessary just to keep the beans covered throughout the cooking process.

To serve, remove the bay leaves. Pour the beans and whole ham hocks into a large serving bowl (or cut the meat from the ham hocks and stir into the beans) and spoon into individual bowls. Serve with biscuits.

99

Braised Oxtails

I first developed a fondness for oxtails during my travels to Jamaica, where they are served often. These small, bony cuts of meat traditionally came from oxen, but now come more regularly from cows. I sometimes find that folks are uncertain about trying oxtails. Maybe the name frightens them off, or they confuse them with other offals (innards and extremities), for which many of us have acquired a taste. Whatever the reason, I suggest giving them a try, especially in a flavorful recipe like this one.

For me, this dish represents the best of winter comfort food. Because the meat on oxtails is tough, it requires long, moist cooking, and braising is just the thing to make it tender. I extend the preparation time by marinating the oxtails overnight with flavorful herbs, aromatics, wine, and stock. Taking the time to marinate the meat is worth it. The oxtails develop a lot of flavor this way, even before the low and slow braising process, enhancing the dish all the more. In the end, the meat will be so sweet and tender that it will fall off the bone, and the braising liquid, which becomes the sauce, will be rich, slightly thickened, and, oh, so satisfying.

Serves 6 to 8

6 pounds oxtails

1 tablespoon seasoned salt

1½ teaspoons black pepper

1½ teaspoons granulated garlic

8 to 10 cloves garlic, peeled and chopped

½ cup chopped fresh flat-leaf parsley

4 sprigs chopped fresh thyme

1 medium onion, peeled and quartered

½ red bell pepper, cored, seeded, and cut into 1-inch pieces

½ yellow bell pepper, cored, seeded, and cut into 1-inch pieces

2 cups red wine

2 cups Beef Stock (see page 35)

1 tablespoon all-purpose flour

2 tablespoons water

At least 8 hours before cooking the oxtails, combine the oxtails, seasoned salt, pepper, granulated and fresh garlic, herbs, onion, peppers, wine, and stock in a large roasting pan. Cover with plastic wrap and set aside in the refrigerator to marinate for at least 8 hours or overnight.

The next day or when you are ready to proceed with the dish, preheat the oven to 350°F. Remove the marinated oxtails from the refrigerator and set aside (still covered in the roasting pan) to warm to room temperature, about 20 minutes. Remove the plastic wrap from the roasting pan and transfer directly to the oven. Braise the oxtails until the meat is very tender and begins to fall off the bone, about 2 hours.

Carefully remove the oxtails from the roasting pan. Combine the flour and water in a small bowl, stirring until smooth to form a slurry (thickener). Bring the liquid in the roasting pan to a boil over high heat and drizzle in about three-quarters of the slurry, stirring constantly until the sauce begins to thicken to a loose gravy consistency. Add the remaining slurry if necessary. Reduce the heat to medium and return the oxtails to the pan to coat with the sauce.

To serve, arrange the oxtails, sauce, and vegetables on a large serving platter or spoon onto individual plates.

Braised Beef Short Ribs

These rich, tender, succulent ribs are perfect for the cold weather months when we all crave comforting, warming dishes. Although the ribs take some time to cook, the dish comes together quickly, leaving you free to do whatever else is on your day's schedule while they braise. If you really want some free time, or want to come home after a busy day's work to melt-in-your-mouth ribs, you can braise the ribs in your slow cooker. To do so, follow the directions in the first paragraph, place the remaining ingredients in the slow cooker, and simmer on the low setting for about 8 hours.

Serves 4 to 6

1 tablespoon canola oil

6 pounds beef short ribs, cut into
   1-rib pieces

Seasoned salt & black pepper

About 1/3 cup all-purpose flour, for coating

3 medium onions, peeled and chopped

4 large cloves garlic, peeled
   and finely chopped

2 cups Barbecue Sauce (see page 57)

1 1/2 cups Beef Stock (see page 35)

2 tablespoons Worcestershire sauce

2 teaspoons chopped fresh thyme

1 pound baby carrots, peeled

2 tablespoons water

Heat the oil in a large saucepan or Dutch oven over medium-high heat. Pat the short ribs dry, season on all sides with seasoned salt and pepper, and coat lightly with flour, reserving 1 tablespoon of the flour. Add the ribs to the pan, about 4 or so at a time, and brown on all sides. Set each batch aside in a shallow pan or bowl while completing the rest.

Reduce the heat to medium and add the onions to the pan, sautéing until golden brown. Stir in the garlic and sauté until softened. Add the barbecue sauce, stock, Worcestershire sauce, and thyme and bring to a boil over high heat. Add the ribs and any juices that accumulated in the pan to the sauce and reduce the heat to low. Cover and simmer for 30 minutes.

Stir in the carrots, cover, and simmer until the ribs are very tender and the meat is falling off the bones, about 3 to 3 1/2 hours.

Remove the short ribs to a bowl, leaving just the braising liquid and vegetables in the pan. Combine the water and the reserved 1 tablespoon of flour in a small bowl, stirring until smooth to form a slurry (thickener). Bring the braising liquid to a boil over high heat and drizzle in about one-third of the slurry, stirring constantly until the sauce begins to thicken to a loose gravy consistency. Add the remaining slurry if necessary. Reduce the heat to medium and return the ribs to the pan to coat with the sauce.

To serve, arrange the ribs, vegetables, and sauce on a large platter, or spoon into individual bowls.

Curried Goat

I fully admit that this is an unusual dish and that some of you might be crinkling your noses at it. I just had to include it, though. Not only is curried goat one of my Jamaican favorites, it also represents how Jamaicans, like traditional Southern cooks, have learned to prepare delicious and nutritious meals with whatever ingredients are fresh and available. Like chickens, fish, and oxen, goats are plentiful in Jamaica. Many of us might consider the meat of a lesser quality because it is bony and gristly, but when cooked low and slow, it becomes really flavorful and tender.

This is my favorite way to prepare goat, with lots of vibrant, spicy ingredients. Rice is the best accompaniment, too, as it soaks up the delicious sauce and balances the heat in the dish. As you see, this recipe serves a lot of people. Although curried goat is easy to make, it requires some planning and additional market stops, so I usually wait until I have a crowd for dinner to prepare it.

Goat meat is sold pre-cut or cracked and is almost always available frozen in Jamaican markets. It is sometimes sold fresh in ethnic markets as well, or you can ask your butcher to order it for you. I heartily recommend you try goat meat, but if you wish, you can certainly prepare this dish with chicken instead. Just be sure to cook the chicken for only one hour, rather than the three hours the goat requires.

Serves 8 to 10

1½ cups canola oil

5 pounds fresh goat

1 onion, peeled and quartered

8 cloves garlic, peeled and chopped

3 tablespoons mild curry powder

5 medium potatoes, quartered

2 green bell peppers, cored, seeded, and quartered

1 Scotch bonnet chili pepper, cored, seeded, and finely chopped

2 sprigs fresh thyme

4 plum tomatoes, cored and quartered

1 tablespoon seasoned salt

1½ teaspoons black pepper

Cooked white rice, for serving

Heat the oil over medium-high heat in a large saucepan or Dutch oven. Add the goat meat and sauté until well browned on all sides. Reduce the heat to medium, add the onion and garlic, and sauté until softened and golden brown. Stir in the curry powder and cook, stirring frequently, until fragrant, about 1 minute.

Add the potatoes, peppers, thyme, tomatoes, seasoned salt, and pepper, stirring to combine, and cover. Reduce the heat to low and simmer, stirring occasionally, until the meat and all of the vegetables are tender, about 3 hours.

To serve, arrange the rice on a serving platter and spoon the curried goat overtop.

SPRING

If winter is my time for quiet reflection and retreat, spring is my season for breaking out! By March, I've had it with the cold and I'm tired of feeling so confined. Spending several months buried beneath heavy coats, hats, and gloves really cramps my style, and as much as I enjoy being at home, by spring I need to get out and feel free again.

As spring approaches, every fiber in my body responds and I start to get really excited. I watch the trees intently for new buds. I look for the flowers to start popping up through the earth. And most importantly, I begin driving by my favorite farmers' markets to see if they've opened for business.

Sometimes, I stop the car and go in only to be disappointed. "No, not yet, Delilah," the owner will say. "Maybe next week." Oh, I feel so dejected! At that point, I seek out whatever farm stand *is* open or head to Reading Terminal Market in Philadelphia just to console myself.

Eventually, these markets come alive and, I'm telling you, it doesn't matter what they're selling—I'm buying. "Spring is coming now; I'm in!" I say to myself. From then on, I'm at the markets regularly—three, four, or five times a week—hanging around, talking to people, and buying whatever is fresh.

The dishes I make in the spring often vary according to the weather. Where I live in the

mid-Atlantic, the days and evenings can remain pretty chilly and rainy for a time and then suddenly turn really dry and warm. Regardless of whether I'm serving warm soup, crispy fried fish, or grilled chicken, all of my food relies on the same thing: fresh, vibrant ingredients.

Every spring, I find myself doing the same thing—gazing in wonder at all the gorgeous new life around me and wishing I could bottle it forever. Of course, I can no sooner do this than have access to an endless supply of spring ingredients. The only thing to do is take advantage of the season's every exhilarating moment and tasty recipe. Like the brilliant land-scape, the availability of spring produce fades before we know it, so we need to be ready to jump into action and plunge into this most miraculous of seasons.

Sweet Potato-Ginger Soup

Sweet potatoes are, of course, a Southern favorite, and they are once again the star of the show in this creamy, mildly spicy, slightly sweet soup. All of the spices here complement sweet potatoes, but the vibrant flavor of the fresh ginger is the most important. This soup could easily be served in the cool fall months, but to me, the bright, spicy ginger represents the freshness of spring.

Serves 4

2½ tablespoons butter

1 cup finely chopped yellow onion

½ cup finely chopped carrot

¼ cup fresh finely chopped ginger

2 pounds sweet potatoes, peeled and
  cut into ½-inch cubes

⅛ teaspoon ground cinnamon

⅛ teaspoon freshly grated nutmeg

⅛ teaspoon ground allspice

4 cups Chicken Stock (see page 36)

1 cup heavy cream

1 tablespoon dark brown sugar, packed

½ teaspoon salt

Melt the butter in a large saucepan over medium-high heat. Add the onions and carrots and sauté until softened. Add the ginger, sweet potatoes, cinnamon, nutmeg, and allspice, stirring constantly until the sweet potatoes begin to soften and the spices are aromatic, about 2 to 3 minutes. Add the stock and bring to a boil. Reduce the heat to medium low and simmer for 30 minutes.

Purée the soup using a hand-held immersion blender, or in several batches using a conventional blender. Return the soup to the saucepan and whisk in the cream, brown sugar, and salt.

To serve, ladle into bowls or serve in a soup tureen.

Potato Salad with Herbs

I prepare and adore all kinds of potato salads. I like this one because it is lighter than mayonnaise-based potato salad and features fresh, flavorful herbs and pungent scallions. You could certainly use regular vinaigrette here, but I like the perky, full flavor of Caesar dressing. This colorful and satisfying potato salad is sure to please friends and family at any spring luncheon or dinner.

Serves 4 to 6

5 pounds medium red-skinned potatoes
$1/2$ cup chopped fresh dill
$1/2$ cup chopped fresh flat-leaf parsley
$1/3$ cup chopped scallions
Caesar Dressing (see page 59)
Salt & black pepper

Place the potatoes in a large saucepan or medium stockpot, fill with enough cold salted water to cover by about $1/2$ inch, and bring to a boil over high heat. Reduce the heat to medium and simmer until the potatoes are just tender, about 15 minutes. Drain the potatoes and when they are cool enough to handle, cut them into quarters.

Combine the potatoes, herbs, and scallions in a large bowl. Pour in the dressing, tossing gently to combine, and season with salt and pepper. Set in the refrigerator to chill, if desired.

Serve in a large serving bowl.

Turkey and Crab Salad

I came up with this salad about twenty-five years ago when I was deep into gourmet cooking. Back then, "gourmet" was all about light dishes, featuring colorful, innovative combinations of flavors and textures. One day when I was playing around in the kitchen, I decided to try this pairing of turkey and crab. It was a hit from the start and I have been making it ever since. This is a fresh, delicate, and yet, substantial salad. In my opinion, it is most tastefully and beautifully presented on tender, mildly flavored, bright green Boston lettuce leaves.

Serves 4 to 6

2 pounds roasted turkey, cut into
   1-inch pieces

2 scallions, trimmed and chopped

1 rib celery, sliced on the bias into
   1/2-inch-thick pieces

1/2 small onion, peeled and finely chopped

1/4 teaspoon seasoned salt

1/8 teaspoon black pepper

1 1/2 cups mayonnaise

1/2 teaspoon cayenne pepper

1 tablespoon roughly chopped fresh
   flat-leaf parsley

1 pound jumbo lump crabmeat

1 head Boston lettuce, cored and leaves
   separated, for serving

Combine all of the ingredients except the crabmeat and lettuce in a large bowl, tossing gently until well mixed. Gently fold in the crabmeat.

To serve, arrange leaves of Boston lettuce on a serving platter or on individual plates and spoon the salad overtop.

Fried Soft-Shell Crabs

I am known for having many favorite foods, but soft-shell crabs are more than just one of my favorites. To me, they are truly special. In the first place, they are unique because they are seasonal. Soft-shell crabs begin to appear in markets usually in April and are generally available through mid-September. To my mind, though, they are at their peak (at least in the mid-Atlantic region) early in the spring. You can buy them off-season frozen, but since they are not at their best this way, why bother? As with all seasonal products, I like to wait until the crabs are freshest. All of this anticipation makes them even more of a treat. When I see the soft-shells sitting on top of the seafood counter, I know spring has arrived.

I do love eating soft-shell crabs, but the reason they are really special to me is because they remind me of some of my happiest summer days in Virginia. My first encounter with soft-shell crabs was in Richmond at Abe's Bar and Grill on North Avenue. My cousin Linda and I went there often when I was in town for the summer. First, we'd go to the barbershop on the corner where our Uncle Dick and her dad, my Uncle Evan, worked. We never stayed long—only just enough time to hit 'em up for money so we could go to lunch. Then we'd bop on down to Abe's. No matter how sunny and hot it was outside, Abe's was always really dark and mysterious. Of course, we were only teenagers at the time so we had to bypass the bar. We didn't care, though. Acting all grown up, we'd swagger over to a booth on the other side of the room and drink our favorite limeade in the most mature and lady-like fashion we could muster.

One day, Linda suggested we order soft-shell crabs. At fourteen, I had no idea what they were. They for sure weren't plentiful in 1960s Philadelphia. "What in the world is a soft-shell crab?" I asked. Noticeably shocked at my ignorance, Linda's eyes widened, and in her more mature sixteen-year-old voice, she declared, "You eat the whole thing, Lila!" "What do you mean you eat the whole crab?" I responded, completely startled. I had absolutely no idea what she was talking about. But, having always looked up to my cousin, I followed her lead and ordered the crab—and my life was forever changed.

From then on, we religiously went several days a week to Abe's with two things in mind: limeade and soft-shell crabs. In fact, we were so focused that we didn't even care about tattling on Linda's older brother, Milton, who, underage at just eighteen, used to sit at the bar and drink in the afternoon. He would get really upset with us, thinking we went to Abe's to spy on him. We paid him no mind at all, though. "We aren't thinking about you, Milton!" we'd say defiantly, as we strode toward our regular booth. And we really weren't; we were there for the soft-shells.

Even today, all these years later, I stop for soft-shell crabs when I visit Richmond in the spring and early summer. Abe's is long gone, but remembering those wonderful lunches with Linda always makes the soft-shells, wherever I order them, all the more delicious and special.

This recipe is very simple and basic so as to highlight the freshness and natural sweetness of the crabs. When you're in the mood for soft-shells, you really need little else on the plate. If you want to serve a side or two, though, a green salad and corn on the cob do nicely.

Serves 4

1 cup buttermilk

¼ cup hot sauce

4 cups Fish Flour (see page 34)

8 soft-shell crabs, cleaned

About 2 cups canola oil, for frying

Hot sauce, for serving

Combine the buttermilk and hot sauce in a shallow pan. Pour the fish flour into a second shallow pan. Coat each crab first with the buttermilk mixture, then dredge in the fish flour, coating well and gently shaking off any excess flour.

Heat the oil in a large sauté pan or skillet over medium-high heat. (There should be about ½ inch of oil in the pan.) To check if the oil is hot enough, sprinkle a bit of fish flour into the oil. If the flour sizzles right away, the oil is ready. Carefully place 2 or 3 crabs at a time in the pan, sautéing about 2 to 3 minutes on each side until crisp. Remove to a paper-towel-lined baking sheet to drain and keep warm while sautéing the remaining crabs. Add more oil to the pan if necessary.

To serve, arrange 2 crabs on each plate and serve with hot sauce on the side.

Grilled Shellfish with Vegetables

This is definitely one of my most favorite dishes, not only because it's delicious, but also because it's impressive and just plain fun. The greater number and variety of fresh, colorful ingredients I can pile on the grill, the better, so I like to have a crowd of about six to ten people who will happily consume the numerous platters of food I present.

The greatest thing about this dish is that it's a little different each time I make it. I prepare it in the summer, fall, and spring, so what I throw into the mix often depends on the time of year. I'll include a variety of tomatoes in the summer, sweet potatoes in the fall, and asparagus in the spring. I'll just pick up whatever's in season and looks freshest at my local market.

This recipe is certainly delicious and works well, but I hope you use it more as a rough outline rather than a strictly defined template. The most important part of a dish like this is to add what you like. Use Yukon gold or purple potatoes, throw in shallots, pile on quartered apples or pears, choose littleneck or cherrystone clams, or replace the shrimp with freshwater prawns. You get the idea. Whatever array of ingredients you choose, I guarantee that when the platters hit the table, your guests' eyes will pop open like saucers, and you'll know it's a winner.

One technical thing to keep in mind: place a fish grilling mesh on the grill for this recipe. You can usually buy them at seafood markets and at some hardware stores. The mesh allows you to cook everything evenly on the grill without fear that bits and pieces will fall through the grill bars. What a tragedy that would be. Depending on the number of folks you're serving, I also suggest piling the fish and vegetables on several platters so everyone around the table can reach what they want. In addition, I like to place smaller bowls near each guest's plate for discarding shells and such.

Serves 8

1 onion, peeled and quartered

1 red bell pepper, cored, seeded, and quartered

1 green bell pepper, cored, seeded, and quartered

1 yellow bell pepper, cored, seeded, and quartered

1 orange bell pepper, cored, seeded, and quartered

2 potatoes, quartered

2 heads garlic, halved widthwise

1/2 bunch fresh flat-leaf parsley, stemmed

Prepare a hot grill.

Combine the onion, peppers, potatoes, garlic, parsley, beer, clam juice, salt, pepper, stock cubes, and oil in a large bowl, tossing to coat.

Place a large fish grilling mesh on the grill. Spread the seasoned vegetable mixture on top, arrange the seafood over it in an even layer, and cook for about 10 minutes. Add the tomatoes, corn, asparagus, and okra, cover the grill, and cook until the vegetables are tender and the seafood is fully cooked, about 10 minutes. (The clams and mussels will have opened, and the shells of the shrimp, crab, and lobster will be bright red.)

1 (12-ounce) bottle beer

1 (8-ounce) bottle clam juice

1 tablespoon salt

2 teaspoons black pepper

2 cubes Knorr's Seafood Stock

1 cup canola oil

24 jumbo shrimp, deveined and shells on

25 clams, scrubbed

1 bag mussels, scrubbed and debearded

8 to 10 baby lobster tails

4 large pieces Dungeness crab legs

6 plum tomatoes, cored and quartered

4 to 5 ears corn, husked and broken in half

16 stalks asparagus, ends trimmed

16 pieces okra, trimmed

To serve, *discard all clams and mussels that remain closed* and arrange the vegetables and shellfish on large platters or on tables covered with newspaper.

115

Jerk Chicken

Okay, I admit it. There are some dishes that just make me crazy—a totally obsessed eater with a one-track mind. Yup, that's me around jerk anything: fish, pork, or chicken. There is just nothing like it. I first had jerk chicken in Jamaica about thirty years ago, and I have been a fanatic ever since. I mean, this is serious. After my first taste of the succulent, smoky, spicy meat, I craved it. So much so, in fact, that now, as soon as my feet hit the ground in Jamaica, I simply must have it.

My favorite place to get jerk in Jamaica is a roadside stand called Scotchies. It is literally an open-air shack on the side of a dirt road in Montego Bay, Jamaica. Behind it, a few guys tend to a huge grill that is really nothing more than a large cinder block pit. Additional cinder blocks sit in the fire and support long pieces of pimiento wood (wood from the evergreen tree that produces allspice). It is this wood that gives jerk its truly unique character. The chickens are grilled directly on top of it, having first marinated in a rub of spices, hot peppers, and aromatics. Jamaicans originally used variations of this rub, called jerk seasoning, to preserve meat and poultry. Now they mostly use it to flavor the meat—and taunt visitors like me!

From the moment I arrive on the island until the minute I leave, I'm craving, and trying to get my hands on jerk. On my way to the hotel and back to the airport, I stop at Scotchies. Then, almost every day in between, I find a way to take a cab back to the stand to get more. I'm telling you, I don't care what the cab costs—I'm going.

On a recent trip, I was on my way back to the airport when my fellow passenger and traveling companion Patti LaBelle, asked me, "Are we stopping at Scotchies?" "Heck, yeah!" I said. "We'll get to the airport smelling like smoke," she fretted. "You stay in the car. I'll go get it!" I wasn't going to let a little smoke get in the way of a final treat.

This recipe is about as close to Jamaican jerk as I can get. Pimiento wood isn't available here in the States, so we will never get the real taste of the Caribbean. We can still make a pretty good jerk, though. The secret is to use really fresh ingredients, especially spices. You know I don't often use freshly grated nutmeg outside of baking, but it truly makes a difference in this recipe. Most jerk is served dry, without sauce, as I suggest here. Sometimes, though, it is presented with finely chopped hot peppers as a condiment or with a hot pepper sauce, similar in consistency to a thin barbecue sauce. If you want a sauce or condiment, go for it. As for me, just hand me the chicken right off the grill and I'll take care of business.

Serves 8

2 teaspoons freshly grated nutmeg

2 teaspoons ground cinnamon

1 tablespoon ground coriander

1 teaspoon whole cloves

At least 8 hours before grilling the chicken, combine all of the ingredients (except the chickens) in a medium bowl. Place the chicken pieces into one large zip-top bag (or divide between two smaller bags) and add the combined seasonings. Seal the bag(s), shake to coat all of the chicken pieces, and set in the refrigerator to marinate for at least 8 hours or overnight.

2 teaspoons ground allspice

1 teaspoon black peppercorns

3 dried bay leaves

6 scallions, trimmed and roughly chopped

1 large onion, peeled and roughly chopped

3 Scotch bonnet chili peppers, cored,
   seeded, and roughly chopped

8 sprigs fresh thyme, stemmed

6 cloves garlic, peeled and roughly
   chopped

1/2 cup fresh lime juice

1 cup soy sauce

2 tablespoons sugar

1/2 cup canola oil

2 whole chickens (about 3 pounds each),
   cut into 8 pieces each

The next day or when you are ready to proceed with the dish, prepare a hot grill. (If possible, use a combination of wood charcoal and soaked mesquite or hickory wood chips for the best flavor.) Arrange the marinated chicken pieces on the grill, cover, and cook, turning once, until well browned and fully cooked, about 30 to 40 minutes.

To serve, arrange the chicken pieces on a large serving platter.

Red Snapper with Caramelized Yams

This simple but elegant dish brings together two of my favorite foods: red snapper and yams. The delicate, flaky fish pairs beautifully with the naturally sweet yams, which become even more flavorful when caramelized. Evocative of the Caribbean as well as the South, this dish comes together quickly, and is sure to please even the most carnivorous of dinner guests.

A note about preparation: I call for cooking the fillets in two batches using one pan and finishing them on a baking sheet in the oven. If you choose this method, be sure to handle the fish carefully, as it is extremely delicate. Use a large spatula or fish spatula to transfer the fillets if possible. In the case that you have enough ovenproof pans to do so, however, I would recommend cooking all of the fish on the stove at once—four fillets in each pan—and then transferring the pans directly to the oven to finish cooking. This way, you need not worry so much about moving the fish and risk breaking the gorgeous fillets.

Serves 4

2 large yams

½ cup vegetable oil

10 tablespoons butter

8 red snapper fillets (about 6 ounces
    each), tails on (optional)

Salt & black pepper

2 tablespoons light brown sugar, packed

Chopped scallions, for garnish

Thinly sliced carrots, for garnish

Place the yams in a medium saucepan, cover with cold water, and bring to a boil over medium-high heat. Reduce the heat to a simmer and cook until the yams are just tender, about 15 minutes. Drain and set aside to cool slightly. When the yams are cool enough to handle, peel and slice into about ¼-inch-thick rounds. Set aside momentarily.

Preheat the oven to 350°F.

Heat ¼ cup of the vegetable oil and 3 tablespoons of the butter in a large sauté pan over medium-high heat. Season the snapper fillets with salt and pepper and place 4 fillets in the pan, skin sides down. Cook until the skin is golden brown, about 3 minutes, turn the fillets, and cook again for about 3 minutes more. Carefully remove the fillets to a large lightly oiled baking sheet. Discard any browned bits and oil left in the pan and heat the remaining ¼ cup of oil with 3 more tablespoons of butter over medium-high heat. Cook the remaining 4 fillets in the same manner and arrange them on the baking sheet with the others. Place in the oven and roast the fillets until fully cooked, about 8 to 10 minutes.

Meanwhile, melt the remaining 4 tablespoons of butter along with the brown sugar in a large sauté pan over medium-high heat. Season the yam rounds with salt and pepper, arrange in the pan, and cook until browned and caramelized, about 3 minutes on each side. Remove the yams to a paper-towel-lined plate to drain.

To serve, arrange several yam rounds on each plate, set 2 snapper fillets on top, and garnish with scallions and carrots.

Turkey Loaf with Mushrooms and Caramelized Onions

I like serving turkey loaf most any time of the year, but I think it is delicious in the spring when the days are filled with warm sun and the evenings are still a bit brisk. This dish is a great alternative to traditional meatloaf and, really, turkey works just as well. You can use all white meat if you like, but I suggest combining dark and white meat. The dark meat adds flavor and prevents the loaf from becoming too dry. The addition of sautéed mushrooms and onions gives this delicious but modest dish a special touch. The turkey loaf has a lot of flavor on its own, but mushrooms and onions dress it up a bit. Of course, if you want to increase the comfort level of this dish even more, just serve a helping of mashed potatoes on the side.

Serves 6 to 8

TURKEY LOAF

5 pounds ground turkey (about 2 pounds
 dark and 3 pounds white meat)

6 cloves garlic, peeled and chopped

2 tablespoons chopped fresh flat-leaf parsley

1 teaspoon chopped fresh thyme

4 extra large eggs

2 cups dry breadcrumbs

1 tablespoon seasoned salt

1 teaspoon black pepper

1 green bell pepper, cored, seeded, and
 chopped

2 tablespoons Dijon mustard

2 tablespoons Worcestershire sauce

MUSHROOMS AND ONIONS

2 tablespoons canola oil

2 Spanish onions, peeled and thinly sliced

Salt & black pepper

2 cups sliced shiitake mushrooms

¼ cup chopped fresh flat-leaf parsley

Preheat the oven to 325°F.

To make the turkey loaf, combine all of the ingredients in a large bowl, mixing gently so as not to overwork the turkey. Place the mixture on an oiled baking sheet and shape into a rectangular loaf, measuring about 9 x 5 inches. Bake until completely cooked, about 1 hour.

Meanwhile, make the mushrooms and onions. Heat the oil in a large sauté pan over medium heat. Add the onions, season with salt and pepper, and sauté, stirring occasionally, until softened and light golden brown. Add the mushrooms and continue to sauté, stirring occasionally, until softened and browned. Add the parsley and toss to combine.

To serve, arrange slices of turkey loaf on a large platter and spoon the mushrooms and onions overtop.

Mashed Potatoes

These mashed potatoes make for a perfect spring side dish. They are prepared with delicate red-skinned potatoes and feature the bright flavors of fresh herbs and scallions.

Serves 6

3 pounds red-skinned potatoes,
   cut into about 1-inch pieces

1½ cups milk

¼ pound (1 stick) butter

½ teaspoon black pepper

Salt

1 tablespoon chopped fresh flat-leaf parsley

1 tablespoon chopped fresh dill

1 tablespoon chopped scallions

Place the potatoes in a large saucepan or medium stockpot, fill with enough cold salted water to cover by about ½ inch, and bring to a boil over high heat. Reduce the heat to medium and simmer until the potatoes are just tender, about 15 minutes.

Meanwhile, heat the milk and butter in a small saucepan over medium heat just until the butter is melted.

Drain the potatoes, return them to the pan, and mash them until smooth using a fork or potato masher. Stir in the warm milk and butter and add the pepper. Season with salt and fold in the herbs and scallions.

Serve immediately in a large bowl.

Veal Chop with Bourbon Applesauce and Pecan Wild Rice

Even though I have been preparing this recipe for years, I still think of it as a special treat. Veal is expensive, so I usually make it for guests when the evening calls for an impressive meal. As elegant as this dish is, though, it is pretty simple to prepare. You just need to think ahead a bit and organize yourself. While one component of the meal is cooking or keeping warm, you want to be preparing another. The idea is to have everything ready to serve at the same time.

Keep in mind that the applesauce is not really a sauce, but rather a chunky, saucy compote. It requires only minutes of cooking and should be done by the time the veal is ready to come out of the oven. In order to accomplish this modest juggling act, I suggest that you have all of the applesauce components ready to go (apples chopped, ingredients measured, etc.), so that you can toss them in the pan as soon as you have finished frying the veal. I admit that as much as I adore veal, cooking it does require planning as it is best served as soon as it's ready.

Serves 8

PECAN WILD RICE

2 tablespoons butter

½ cup finely chopped onion

3 cups wild rice, rinsed

9 cups water

1½ teaspoons salt

½ teaspoon black pepper

3 cups coarsely chopped toasted pecans

VEAL

About 4 cups vegetable oil, for frying

8 veal rib or loin chops,
   about 1¼-inch-thick, bone in

Salt & black pepper

To make the rice, melt the butter in a large saucepan over medium-high heat. Add the onion and sauté until softened. Stir in all of the remaining ingredients (except the pecans), raise the heat to high, and bring to a boil. Reduce the heat to medium-low, cover, and simmer until the rice is fully cooked, tender, and most of the liquid has been absorbed, about 30 to 45 minutes. Drain any excess water, stir in the pecans, and set aside to keep warm while preparing the veal.

Preheat the oven to 250°F.

To make the veal, heat about 1 cup of the oil in a large saucepan or Dutch oven over medium-high heat. (There should be about ¼ inch of oil in the pan, and it will appear to shimmer on the surface when it is ready.) Season the veal chops on both sides with salt and pepper, place about 2 or 3 of the chops in the pan, and brown on each side for about 5 minutes, or until *nearly* cooked to desired doneness. Place the chops on a baking sheet and brown the rest of the chops, about 2 or 3 at a time, adding more oil as needed. Reserve the pan and set the veal in the oven to finish cooking while preparing the applesauce.

APPLESAUCE

1½ cups finely chopped shallots

6 cups finely chopped Granny Smith apples

6 cups finely chopped McIntosh apples

2¼ cups bourbon

6 cups Beef Stock (see page 35)

2 tablespoons chopped fresh thyme

12 tablespoons butter, chilled
    and cut into small cubes

Salt & black pepper

To make the applesauce, pour out and discard all of the oil from the reserved pan, leaving a thin film of oil in the pan. Set the pan over medium heat, add the shallots and apples, and sauté until softened, stirring frequently. Pour in the bourbon to deglaze, stirring with a wooden spoon to loosen any browned bits from the bottom of the pan. Add the stock and thyme and bring to a simmer. Incorporate the butter a few cubes at a time, stirring constantly, until the liquid has slightly thickened and is glossy. Season with salt and pepper.

To serve, place a veal chop, wild rice, and applesauce on each plate.

SUMMER

When the vibrancy of spring has relaxed into the ease of summer, all is well in my world. This is when I am happiest and feel truly myself. Summer for me means freedom, and I am all about that. I just love being outdoors, and when the weather is warm, I can stay out virtually all day. My schedule becomes increasingly flexible, allowing me to take time off from work to travel and visit more with friends. And the food—oh, the food! Cooking in the summer is about freedom, too. Not only do the long days offer many opportunities for cooking and eating with friends and family, but the seemingly endless supply of fresh ingredients also gives us many delicious reasons to do so.

The best thing about summer produce is that it enhances fresh fish, meat, and poultry, while requiring very little from the cook. Of course, you have to wait until fruits and vegetables reach their seasonal peaks, but it's totally worth it. I know that my desire to hang around farmers' markets is somewhat unusual, but this is how I find the best ingredients at just the right time. I try to only buy hard-shell crabs, for example, when they are heavy with meat late in the summer. I'll wait for watermelon, too, and only eat it at the peak of ripeness. Now when I say I love watermelon, I mean I'm a nut about the stuff. But I will walk right past it in the stores if it's not sweet or juicy enough. Why bother? When the watermelons are ready, though, I'll load the car with a whole bunch, go home, and eat an entire quarter of a large melon myself.

It's the same way with corn, cherries, or peaches. Where I live, the best peaches appear in late August. I'll buy peaches earlier in the season, but then I only eat them grilled. They are still pretty firm at that point so they hold up well when cooked. Grilling also caramelizes the natural sugars, ultimately making them sweeter. When peaches reach their peak, though, I am all about eating them out of hand and making juicy cobblers. I don't need to do much to a cobbler when I use ripe fruit. A little butter, sugar, crumbly topping, and I'm done.

Summer menus call for no-fuss cooking, which is easy when you start with fresh, flavorful ingredients. I've included a variety of recipes in this chapter, from a quick black-eyed pea salad to a long-cooking barbecued brisket. Sometimes a fast dish makes life easier, and other times you want to throw a meal in the oven to do its thing for several hours while you play. It all depends on how you feel. Once again, if you choose the best ingredients possible, you can't go wrong—especially in the summertime. Get out in the sunshine, share some good food and drink with people you love, and enjoy some much-deserved freedom.

Salad with Cider Vinaigrette and Poached Pears

This salad is delicious any time of year, but I seem to make it a lot during the summer. It features a combination of complementary textures and flavors: succulent, sweet pears; tender, mild lettuce; creamy, musky blue cheese; crisp, rich pecans; and tart vinaigrette. Serve it for lunch or as a salad course with dinner.

Serves 8

POACHED PEARS

4 Bosc pears

1 cup white wine

2 cups water

2 tablespoons sugar

½ vanilla bean, split

1 strip lemon peel, about 3 inches long
   and 1 inch wide

1 strip orange peel, about 3 inches long
   and 1 inch wide

1 small stick cinnamon

CIDER VINAIGRETTE

¼ cup apple cider vinegar

½ cup extra-virgin olive oil

1 shallot, peeled and finely chopped

Salt & black pepper

SALAD

1 head Boston lettuce, cored and leaves
   separated

¼ pound blue cheese, crumbled

½ cup pecan pieces or roughly chopped
   pecans, lightly toasted

To make the poached pears, peel the pears, leaving the stems intact. Combine the remaining ingredients in a large saucepan and bring to a boil over high heat. Reduce the heat to low, place the pears in the liquid, and cover with a piece of cheesecloth or small plate to keep the pears submerged. Gently simmer until the pears are just tender, about 20 to 25 minutes. Remove from the heat and set aside, allowing the pears to cool to room temperature in the poaching liquid.

To make the vinaigrette, whisk together the vinegar, oil, and shallot in a medium bowl and season with salt and pepper.

To make the salad, toss together the lettuce, blue cheese, pecans, and vinaigrette in a large bowl.

To serve, slice each poached pear in half lengthwise and carefully remove the cores. Divide the salad among 8 plates and top each one with a pear half.

Grilled Corn on the Cob

No wonder summer is my favorite time of year—it is the season for corn, and I am crazy about corn. For purists like myself, eating it hot off the cob is the best. There is just nothing like biting into an ear of perfectly cooked corn, the kernels cracking between your teeth and bursting with sweet juice in every bite. What is better than that?

Boiled or steamed corn is fine, but I think grilling it is even better. By grilling the ears in the husks (with the silk removed), the kernels become just tender and develop a roasted flavor, while remaining protected from the high heat. As I suggest in this recipe, I like brushing the ears with a little butter and seasoning them with some salt and pepper, but that's it. There is no need to get fancy here. If the corn is fresh and sweet, it surely doesn't require anything else. Once you've had grilled corn, you might never want to cook it on the stove again.

Serves 6

6 ears fresh corn, husks on
12 tablespoons (1½ sticks) butter
Salt & black pepper

Prepare a hot grill.

Carefully husk the corn, keeping the husks attached at the stems and removing the silk. Rub each ear of corn with 2 tablespoons of butter, pull the husks back up around the buttered corn, and place on the grill. Turn the ears every 2 to 3 minutes until well browned, about 10 to 15 minutes total.

To serve, pull back the husks from the hot corn, season with salt and pepper, and pile on a serving platter.

Fried Green Tomatoes

Thanks to Fanny Flagg's novel, Fried Green Tomatoes at the Whistlestop Café, *and the 1991 movie of the same name, even folks who are generally unfamiliar with Southern food know about fried green tomatoes. No doubt about it, they are quintessentially Southern. Tomatoes grow plentifully in many parts of the country, but rather than waiting to be overwhelmed by an abundance of ripe tomatoes, we take advantage of many of them when they're still green. After all, how many sliced or stewed tomatoes or how much fresh salsa can a person eat?*

Under-ripe green tomatoes are altogether different from ripe, sweet, juicy tomatoes. Really firm and tart, they are only good prepared two ways: fried and pickled. I like them both, but the slightly salty golden crust and crisp green fruit of a fried tomato are enough to make any southerner swoon. They are extra special, too, of course, because we can only enjoy them during the summer. And do we ever!

Serves 6 to 8

About 4 cups canola oil, for frying

2 large eggs

4 cups milk

4 cups all-purpose flour

⅛ teaspoon granulated garlic

½ cup seasoned salt

1 tablespoon black pepper

6 to 7 large green tomatoes, cored
   and cut into ½-inch-thick slices

Heat about 2 cups of the oil in a large sauté pan over medium-high heat. (There should be about ½ inch of oil in the pan, and it will appear to shimmer on the surface when it is ready.)

Meanwhile, whisk together the eggs and milk in a large shallow pan. Combine the flour, granulated garlic, ¼ cup of the seasoned salt, and pepper in a second large shallow pan. Coat the tomato slices first with the egg mixture and then dredge them in the flour mixture, coating well.

Carefully place the tomatoes, about 5 or 6 slices at a time, in the hot oil and fry on both sides until golden brown. Set on a paper-towel-lined baking sheet to drain and keep warm while frying the remaining slices. Add more oil to the pan as necessary.

To serve, sprinkle with the remaining seasoned salt and arrange on a serving platter.

Fried Okra

Okay, let's just say it up front: this is the vegetable on the table that no one wants to eat. I know it. You're thinking, "It's yucky; it's slimy." Well, all I can say in response is that if this is what you think of okra, you've never eaten it properly cooked, and certainly never cooked by a southerner. All this talk about slime makes me laugh, actually. Okra only acquires this texture when it is overcooked, and, in truth, it is probably the only vegetable we don't overcook in the South! We know that it breaks down and gets mushy very quickly, so we are careful about adding it to dishes at just the right time to keep it crisp. Okra is the last ingredient to go into a gumbo, for example. If I'm sautéing okra, I actually take the pan off of the heat before adding it and give it only a few tosses. Okra really is that delicate.

It is because okra is fragile that it works so well fried. We give the okra a good tasty coating, which protects it, and fry it in hot oil so it cooks quickly. When prepared correctly, fried okra is as crisp and delicious on the inside as it is on the outside.

Serves 8

About 6 cups canola oil, for frying

½ cup buttermilk

½ cup cornmeal

1 cup all-purpose flour

1 tablespoon granulated garlic

2 tablespoons seasoned salt

¼ teaspoon cayenne pepper

2 pounds fresh okra, trimmed

Heat the oil in a large saucepan over medium-high heat. To check if the oil is hot enough, sprinkle a bit of flour into the oil. If the flour sizzles right away, the oil is ready.

Pour the buttermilk into a shallow pan. Combine the cornmeal, flour, granulated garlic, 2 teaspoons of the seasoned salt, and the cayenne pepper in a second shallow pan. Coat the okra slices first with the buttermilk and then dredge them in the cornmeal mixture, coating well.

Carefully place the okra, about 4 or 5 pieces at a time, into the hot oil and fry until golden brown. Set on a paper-towel-lined baking sheet to drain and keep warm while finishing the remaining slices.

To serve, sprinkle with the remaining seasoned salt and arrange on a serving platter.

129

Cornbread with Strawberry Butter

Let's face it, cornbread is good anytime of year. I have been making this recipe forever, and it's always a hit for breakfast, snacking, and in breadbaskets at dinner. In keeping with Southern tradition, I like my cornbread sweet, moist, and dense. Of course, it's always even more delicious spread with butter. In the summer, I like to serve large squares of warm cornbread with homemade strawberry butter made from sweet, juicy strawberries. I'm sure that once you try this cornbread recipe, you won't use any other.

Makes two 8 x 8-inch pans

STRAWBERRY BUTTER

¼ pound (1 stick) butter, at room
    temperature

3 very ripe fresh strawberries,
    hulled and chopped

1 tablespoon confectioners' sugar

CORNBREAD

¼ pound (1 stick) butter, melted

2 cups yellow cornmeal

2 cups all-purpose flour

1 cup sugar

2 tablespoons baking powder

1 teaspoon salt

1½ cups milk

4 eggs

To make the strawberry butter, combine the butter, strawberries, and sugar in a medium bowl and mash with a fork until incorporated but still chunky with bits of butter and strawberries. Set aside at room temperature while preparing the cornbread. (Store the butter refrigerated in an airtight container for up to 1 month.)

Preheat the oven to 350°F. Coat two 8 x 8-inch square pans with canola oil.

To make the cornbread, combine all of the ingredients in a large bowl, mixing until smooth. Pour into the prepared pans and bake until a wooden skewer inserted in the centers comes out clean, about 40 minutes. Set on wire racks to cool in the pans for about 20 minutes before turning out of the pans.

To serve, slice the cornbread into squares and serve with strawberry butter.

Deviled Eggs

No doubt about it—deviled eggs are always a hit. To me, they epitomize old-fashioned, comforting finger food. The thing is, despite their simplicity, they are really a lot of work to prepare. I guess this is why they are such a treat and folks devour them at parties. Everybody loves them, but few people make them regularly. I'll spend hours making platters of deviled eggs, only to see them disappear in a matter of minutes! My friends are shameless about it, too. As soon as they walk through the door, they ask, "Are you making deviled eggs?" I tell them, "Why don't you just wait and see?"

I have been making deviled eggs for so many years, I have acquired quite a collection of deviled egg plates. You're probably thinking that buying these specialty plates is just another of my excuses to purchase more china. I admit, you're partially right. Deviled eggs are so grand, though, that they deserve to be presented beautifully. I have round plates, oval plates, egg-crate-shaped plates—it's crazy. Recently, I saw a round aqua-colored egg plate that sat—get this—on a pedestal! Now that's taking deviled eggs to another level. But you know, it makes sense. Deviled eggs are usually the center of attention. Why not show them off? As I was looking at that pedestal, my adrenaline running from excitement, I was saying to myself, "Delilah, do not get that plate! Goodness knows you don't need yet another one." (I didn't get the plate, but I still might go back to the store. . . .)

Regardless of how many egg plates you have or how you wish to present your deviled eggs, I know you'll like this recipe. You will notice that I call for eighteen eggs, but the recipe only makes twenty-four halves. There are several reasons for this. First, I really pile the yolk mixture into the whites, so I need the extra yolks. Secondly, sometimes the whites break up too much during the peeling process and are unusable. Also, the truth is, I dip my finger so many times into the tasty yolk mixture, nibbling—I mean testing—as I'm making it, I need to account for the loss by cooking extra eggs. I can't help but eat two or three anyway before they even hit the table, so the more I make the better. You'll see. You just try keeping your hands off these tempting morsels.

Serves 6

18 extra large eggs, at room temperature

1/8 teaspoon salt

1 teaspoon yellow mustard

1 teaspoon Dijon mustard

1 teaspoon hot sauce

1 teaspoon seasoned salt

1/4 teaspoon cayenne pepper

1 tablespoon sweet relish

1/4 cup mayonnaise

Place the eggs in a large saucepan, cover with cool (not ice-cold) water, and add the salt. Bring to a boil over high heat and boil for 3 minutes. Reduce the heat to low and simmer for another 15 minutes. Carefully drain the water out of the pan and run the eggs under cool running water while they are still in the pan. Fill the pan with cool water and set aside for about 5 minutes to cool the eggs completely.

Drain the eggs, peel, and split in half widthwise. Place the egg yolks in a medium bowl and set the egg whites on a work surface. Mash the yolks with a fork and add the remaining ingredients, mixing until smooth.

OPTIONAL GARNISHES

Paprika

Crumbled bacon

Chopped dill

Chopped chives

Caviar

Fill the egg whites generously with the egg yolk mixture, covering the surfaces of the whites completely. (You might have a few extra egg whites using this method, but the idea is to pile the filling very high.)

To serve, arrange the deviled eggs on a serving platter or deviled egg plate and garnish as desired.

Corn and Crab Chowder

I don't think you can go wrong with this chowder. It is great for lunch or dinner and is always a hit at my parties. Virtually everyone loves corn and crab and the two make a perfect pair. Naturally sweet, slightly crunchy corn complements the mild sweetness of the tender crabmeat, and the delicate aromatics in this dish highlight them both. Simply serve this chowder on its own, or garnish it with some chives and cornbread croutons. The chives add a bit of vibrancy and freshness, and the croutons are a crunchy, delicious play on the corn theme.

Because corn is so prominent here, I, of course, suggest you wait until summer to make this chowder so you can find the freshest, most flavorful ears available. I buy corn exclusively from my local farmers' markets, and I hope you can do the same. Not only do I like to support local growers, but the kernels on these ears are also much sweeter and more tender than those enclosed in the tired-looking husks I usually see in large supermarkets.

Serves 4

STOCK

4 ears corn, husked

2 tablespoons vegetable oil

1 large carrot, peeled and roughly chopped

1 rib celery, roughly chopped

1 medium yellow onion, peeled and
  roughly chopped

3 cloves garlic, peeled and smashed

2 sprigs fresh thyme

1 teaspoon black peppercorns

1 teaspoon salt

2 quarts water

CHOWDER

1/2 pound bacon, chopped

6 tablespoons butter

1 1/2 cups finely chopped yellow onion

3/4 cup finely chopped celery

To make the stock, cut the corn kernels off of the cobs, set aside in a bowl, and reserve the cobs.

Heat the oil in a large saucepan over medium-high heat. Add the carrot, celery, onion, garlic, thyme, peppercorns, and salt and sauté until the vegetables are softened. Add the water and reserved corncobs and bring to a boil over high heat, skimming off any foam that rises to the surface. Reduce the heat to medium-low and simmer until reduced by half to about 4 cups, about 1 to 1 1/2 hours. Strain through a fine mesh strainer, discarding the solids, and reserve.

To make the chowder, heat a large saucepan or Dutch oven over medium-high heat, add the bacon, and cook until golden brown. Using a slotted spoon, remove the bacon and set on paper towels to drain. Pour all but about 1 tablespoon of the rendered bacon fat out of the pan.

Add 2 tablespoons of the butter to the pan and melt with the bacon fat over medium-high heat. Add the onions, celery, garlic, cayenne pepper, thyme, and salt, and sauté, stirring frequently, until the vegetables are softened. Sprinkle in the flour, stirring to form a paste (roux), and cook for

1 ½ teaspoons finely chopped garlic

¼ teaspoon cayenne pepper

1 sprig fresh thyme

½ teaspoon salt

3 tablespoons all-purpose flour

1 cup heavy cream

2 tablespoons chopped fresh flat-leaf parsley

1 pound jumbo lump crabmeat, for serving

½ cup Cornbread Croutons
    (see page 60), for garnish

Chopped chives, for garnish

about 2 minutes. Stir in the reserved stock and corn kernels and bring to a boil over high heat. Reduce the heat to medium-low, partially cover, and simmer, stirring occasionally, about 20 minutes.

Remove the pan from the heat and stir in the bacon, cream, parsley, and remaining 4 tablespoons of butter. Set over medium-low heat and cook at a bare simmer for about 10 minutes.

To serve, remove the thyme sprig, spoon the crabmeat into bowls, and ladle the chowder on top. Garnish with croutons and chives.

Sea Scallops with Black-Eyed Pea Salad

Where would Southern cuisine be without black-eyed peas? I simply cannot imagine. Also known as black-eyed suzies and cowpeas, they are as important to the Southern table as grits or okra. They find their way into numerous dishes, the most famous, of course, being Hoppin' John—a spicy combination of peas and salt pork served with rice on New Year's Day.

Although southerners are quite familiar with fresh peas, I fear that many in the North have only encountered the dried, bagged variety that sit on the bottom of most supermarket shelves. This is really a shame! Sure, dried peas cook up fine, but, oh, there's nothing like fresh black-eyed peas! And I should know. I've spent many hours shelling peas, starting when I was just a little girl on my grandparents' farm.

This salad is a far cry from rich Hoppin' John, but because it is light and fresh, it is perfect for summer. I really suggest using fresh black-eyed peas if you can find them. They are such a treat. They are, however, admittedly difficult to find—or at least available for only a very limited time—outside of the South, so you might have to resort to using dried black-eyed peas. If this is the case (and, actually, this applies to fresh as well), be sure to cook them just until tender; you don't want them to be so soft that the skins are peeling off or they are mushy. The peas should be tender but still firm so they stay whole when you toss them with the other ingredients.

As for the scallops, well, these sumptuous, delicate morsels are the perfect complement to the spices and herbs in this salad. The dish comes together quickly and easily, making it just right for a light summer lunch or supper.

Serves 8

SALAD

5 cups cooked fresh black-eyed peas, or
　1 (1-pound) bag dried black-eyed peas,
　cooked

1/2 cup plus 2 tablespoons sherry vinegar

1/2 cup olive oil

1/2 cup finely chopped red onion

1/2 cup finely chopped red bell pepper

3 tablespoons finely chopped scallions

2 tablespoons finely chopped jalapeño
　pepper

At least 5 hours before serving the dish, make the salad. Toss all of the ingredients in a large bowl, cover, and set aside in the refrigerator for at least 4 hours, stirring occasionally. Remove the salad from the refrigerator at least 30 minutes before serving to warm to room temperature.

When you are ready to proceed with the rest of the dish, make the scallops. Heat half of the oil in a large sauté pan over medium-high heat. Season the scallops on both sides with salt and pepper, place half of the scallops in the pan, and sauté on each side for about 1 1/2 minutes until golden brown and still tender in the centers. (Scallops overcook very quickly so watch them carefully.) Remove the scallops from the pan and set aside to keep warm. Heat the rest of

2 tablespoons finely chopped
  fresh flat-leaf parsley

1 ½ teaspoons finely chopped garlic

1 tablespoon hot sauce

¾ teaspoon seasoned salt

½ teaspoon black pepper

SCALLOPS

¼ cup canola oil, divided

24 sea scallops (about 2 pounds)

Salt & black pepper

the oil in the pan and repeat the process, sautéing the remaining scallops in the same manner.

To serve, toss the salad one more time, spoon onto individual plates, and top each salad with 3 scallops.

Lobster Stuffed with Crab and Bay Scallops

If you want to impress your guests, you can never go wrong with lobster. This dish, featuring lobster, crab, and scallops, is sure to be a success, and although it might look complicated, it is pretty easy to prepare. To make the going even easier, buy already cooked lobsters and proceed with the recipe from there. Maybe you are a little squeamish about boiling live lobsters, or perhaps you just want to save time. Whatever your reason for doing so, buying cooked lobsters will get you out of your apron sooner, and in no time you'll be sitting at the table with a gorgeous dish.

Makes 4 servings

LOBSTER

2 large live lobsters
(about 2 to 3 pounds each)

STUFFING

1 tablespoon canola oil

1 pound bay scallops, cooked

1 cup crushed buttery crackers
(about 15 crackers), such as Ritz

2 pounds jumbo lump crabmeat

1 1/2 tablespoons chopped fresh
flat-leaf parsley

2 teaspoons chopped fresh tarragon

1 teaspoon chopped fresh thyme

2 teaspoons fresh lemon juice

1/4 teaspoon seasoned salt

1/4 teaspoon black pepper

1/2 cup plus 2 tablespoons clarified butter,
divided (see *Chef's Note*)

Preheat the oven to 425°F.

Fill a large stockpot three quarters full with salted water and bring to a boil. Drop the lobsters into the water, cover the pot, and boil for about 7 minutes. Lift out the lobsters using tongs and place immediately in a large bowl of ice water.

When the lobsters are cool enough to handle, drain the ice water, and begin working with the lobsters one at a time. Set a lobster on a cutting board back side down. Using a sharp chef's knife, cut through the middle of the body from head to tail, forming 2 identical halves. Remove the pink coral and any green tomalley, reserving for another use or discarding. Remove and discard the stomach sac from the back of the head, the black vein running from head to tail, and any spongy gray tissue. Place the lobster halves on a baking sheet while repeating the process with the remaining lobster. Arrange all 4 halves on the baking sheet and set aside while preparing the stuffing.

To make the stuffing, heat the oil in a large sauté pan over medium-high heat. Add the scallops and sauté for about 1 1/2 minutes, tossing once or twice, until they just begin to turn opaque. Remove them to a large bowl and add the crushed crackers, crabmeat, parsley, tarragon, thyme, lemon juice, salt, pepper, and 1/3 cup of the butter, folding gently to combine.

SALAD

About 4 cups mixed greens,
   such as mesclun, dandelion
   greens, and watercress

3 tablespoons olive oil

1 tablespoon Champagne or
   white wine vinegar

Black pepper

Divide the stuffing evenly among the 4 lobster halves, filling any empty cavities and covering the tail meat with stuffing. Drizzle with the remaining butter and roast until the stuffing is golden brown, about 10 to 12 minutes.

To make the salad, combine the greens in a large bowl, toss with oil and vinegar, and season with pepper.

To serve, arrange some salad on each plate and top with half a lobster.

CHEF'S NOTE: Clarified butter (also called drawn butter or *ghee*) is easy to prepare. Because it is free of milk solids, it has a higher smoking point than regular butter (meaning it doesn't burn as quickly), has a longer shelf life, and a lighter flavor. To prepare it, slowly melt unsalted butter in a saucepan. Gently simmer until the white milk solids have sunk to the bottom of the pan and the clear, clarified butter remains on top. Skim any foam that rises to the surface, carefully pour the clarified butter into a jar, and store in the refrigerator.

139

Steamed Blue Crabs

Almost everyone loves crab, but as far as steamed whole crabs go—either you don't touch 'em or you love 'em. People who can't be bothered with steamed crabs (you know who you are!) complain that they require just too much time and energy for so little reward. They want the crab, but they don't want to do the work. Folks who love whole crabs, however, are crazy, not only about the flavor of the incomparably sweet meat, but the whole eating routine as well. They'll sit for hours with a pile of crabs, cracking, picking, and sucking away at the shells for the teeniest drop of juice or most miniscule piece of meat. In addition to this admirable patience, the truest connoisseurs also have all kinds of serious rituals. Some only like male crabs (jimmies), while others prefer females (sooks). Some pick all the claws off, pile them up, and eat them first. Others do the same with the bodies. Still other folks painstakingly suck all of the meat and juice out of the tediously slender legs, while some just throw them out. The variety of routines is as great as the number of hours these people can sit in one place.

Most of the crabs we eat in the mid-Atlantic region come from the Chesapeake Bay area and are available throughout the summer. In my opinion, the meatiest and most flavorful crabs are caught from late August to early September. Outside of the summer season, most crabs are likely coming from Louisiana, where they are heavy and full of meat most of the year.

I do hope you have some steamed crab lovers in your midst. This really is a fun and easy recipe, and nothing says summer like cracking open a pile of crabs with some ice-cold beer and good friends.

Serves 4

2 (12-ounce) bottles beer

½ cup apple cider vinegar

4 cups water

24 live Maryland blue crabs,
  preferably large jimmies

2 cups Old Bay seasoning

3 dried bay leaves

Pour the beer, vinegar, and water into a large stockpot. Add half of the crabs, sprinkle with 1 cup of Old Bay, and place the bay leaves on top. Arrange the rest of the crabs over the seasonings and sprinkle with the remaining 1 cup of Old Bay. Cover and bring to a boil over medium-high heat. Reduce the heat to medium and simmer until the crabs are bright red, about 14 to 16 minutes.

Set a large colander in a large bowl and drain the crabs, reserving the steaming liquid.

To serve, arrange the crabs on a large serving platter and pour the steaming liquid into small bowls for dipping.

Roasted Pork Ribs

There are many ways to make and serve pork ribs, and the method you choose often depends on where in the country you live. The ribs can be roasted dry, with a rub, or wet, with a sauce. Northerners usually like sauce all over the place, whereas southerners usually like their ribs drier so they can really taste the meat. Regardless of how you prepare them, though, all perfectly roasted pork ribs are cooked low and slow, and the final product should be super tender, succulent, and flavorful. I just have to mention here that we are talking about straight slabs of pork ribs—no fussy baby back ribs, please! Those are for nibbling at cocktail parties, not serious eating.

The following recipe combines the best of the North and the South; the ribs are flavored with a dry rub and served with barbecue sauce. These ribs are delicious served as I suggest, simply sliced and dipped in sauce. If you want to go the extra mile and experience a real Southern favorite, make yourself a rib sandwich. I know, you're thinking, "What about the bones? Sandwich? What?" Here's what you do: Take a piece of home-style white bread and place six ribs on top. Smother them with sauce and place another piece of bread over them. Now you have what looks like a sandwich, but you're not going to eat it that way. You only did all this to get the sauce on the bread. So, take the top piece of bread in one hand and a rib in the other and alternate bites of each. Then, when you're all done with that, you get to eat the top piece of bread that has been soaked with sauce. What a finish! That's a rib sandwich.

Although this recipe requires some planning (the ribs marinate for at least eight hours), it is easy, and the dry rub of house seasoning makes the ribs really tasty. If you want to give the ribs an additional punch of flavor, try smoking them in the oven. First soak some wood chips in water, bourbon, or whiskey. Drain the chips, scatter them evenly in a shallow pan or heatproof bowl, and set them on the lowest rack or floor of the oven during the roasting process. The smoky sweetness of the meat is totally addictive. Whether you smoke them or not, I'm sure these ribs will become one of your favorite summer meals.

Serves 8

2 slabs pork ribs
House Seasoning (recipe follows)
Barbecue Sauce (see page 144), for serving

HOUSE SEASONING
1 cup kosher salt
¼ cup black pepper
¼ cup granulated garlic
½ cup paprika
1 tablespoon plus 1 teaspoon dry mustard
2 teaspoons cayenne pepper

At least 8 hours before roasting the ribs, remove any excess fat from the pork ribs and place them on a baking sheet. Combine all of the ingredients for House Seasoning in a bowl, mixing well. Rub the seasoning generously on the ribs, cover with plastic wrap, and set in the refrigerator to marinate for at least 8 hours or overnight.

The next day or when you are ready to proceed with the dish, preheat the oven to 300°F.

Arrange the marinated slabs of ribs on a clean baking sheet and roast until well browned and tender, about 2 hours.

To serve, cut the slabs into individual ribs, arrange on a serving platter, and serve with barbecue sauce on the side.

142

Roasted Beef Ribs

These ribs are truly delicious any time of the year. They are great for cool weather dinners, when you want easy, hearty dishes, and they are equally good for warm weather meals that call for no-fuss preparations. You can pretty much just throw them in the oven to do their thing all afternoon, and then serve a big platter of them outdoors or pack them up for a picnic.

Serves 8

2 tablespoons salt

2 tablespoons brown sugar

1 tablespoon granulated garlic

1 teaspoon dried thyme

1 tablespoon chili powder

2 slabs beef ribs, each cut in half

Barbecue Sauce (see page 144), for serving

At least 8 hours before roasting the ribs, stir together the salt, sugar, garlic, thyme, and chili powder in a small bowl. Place each half slab of ribs in a zip-top bag and divide the combined seasonings among them. Seal the bags, shake to coat all of the ribs, and set in the refrigerator to marinate for at least 8 hours or overnight.

The next day or when you are ready to proceed with the dish, preheat the oven to 275°F.

Arrange the ribs in a single layer in a roasting pan and roast until well browned and tender, about 3 hours.

To serve, arrange the ribs on a serving platter and serve with barbecue sauce on the side.

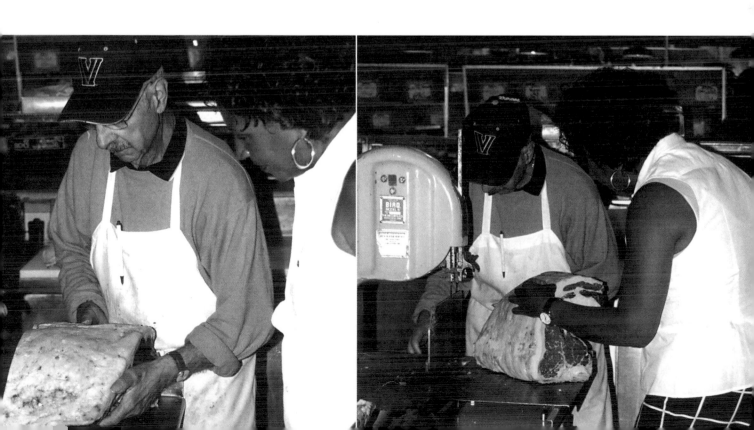

Barbecued Beef Brisket

This is down-country cooking at its best. Just thinking about this dish puts me in mind of warm summer days, picnics, and relaxing with friends around the table. Barbecued brisket is the perfect warm weather meal, because although the oven is involved, the meat cooks low and slow, requiring almost no fuss. It virtually takes care of itself. Now, when I say slow, we're talking in the true Southern don't-rush-me-now sense of the word. First, I marinate the brisket for a day to soak up lots of flavor, and then I like to cook it for a good eighteen hours to ensure it is as flavorful and tender as possible. Thinly sliced brisket served on soft hamburger buns with barbecue sauce—a summer meal can't get better than that.

Serves 6 to 8

BRISKET

5 pounds beef brisket

6 cups Lawry's Caribbean Jerk Marinade

Soft bread rolls, for serving

BARBECUE SAUCE

⅓ cup canola oil

4 onions, peeled and chopped

1 cup coarsely chopped garlic

1 (28-ounce) can tomato puree

3¾ cups apple cider vinegar

3½ cups water

2½ cups brown sugar, packed

1½ cups chili powder

1½ cups tomato paste

½ cup Worcestershire sauce

½ cup chopped celery

½ cup yellow mustard

½ cup black pepper

1 cup corn syrup

At least 24 hours before cooking the brisket, place the brisket in a small roasting pan and rub liberally with the marinade. Cover and set in the refrigerator to marinate for about 24 hours. (You can also marinate the brisket in a zip-top bag.)

When you are ready to proceed with the dish, preheat the oven to 225°F. Remove the marinated brisket from the refrigerator and set aside to come to room temperature, about 30 minutes.

Cover the roasting pan with foil and roast the brisket until very tender, about 18 hours.

Meanwhile, to make the barbecue sauce, combine all of the ingredients in a large saucepan and bring to a simmer over medium-high heat. Reduce the heat to low and simmer, stirring occasionally, for about 2 hours. Set aside and reserve until the brisket is done.

To finish the brisket, remove from the oven and set aside, covered, to rest for about 15 minutes.

To serve, slice the brisket into very thin pieces, arrange on a serving platter, and serve with soft rolls and barbecue sauce on the side.

144

Sautéed Dandelion Greens

Dandelion greens are very special since they are only available for a short while in the spring and summer (depending on where you live). They have a pleasant, slightly bitter flavor and a gorgeous, delicate consistency, which I preserve by cooking them quickly. Fresh, fast, and flavorful, sautéed dandelion greens make for the perfect summer side dish.

Serves 4

8 strips bacon, chopped

4 pounds dandelion greens

Salt & black pepper

Heat a large sauté pan over medium heat, add the bacon, and cook until browned and crisp. Pour out and discard all but about 2 tablespoons of rendered fat from the pan.

Place the pan back over medium heat, add the dandelion greens, and season with salt and pepper (keeping in mind the bacon is already salty). Toss just until the greens are wilted.

Serve the greens immediately on a serving platter.

Sweet Iced Tea

There are many wonderful things that distinguish the South from the rest of the country, but the Southern obsession for sweet tea has to be near the top of the list. For those of you who have never tried the real thing, you're probably thinking, 'I've had sweet tea. What makes this so special?' Well, honey, when I say sweet, I mean curl-your-toes, makes-you-want-to-run-around-the-block sweet! Why do you think we brew the tea so strong and pour it over so much ice? I have to say, it's truly wonderful.

I have added lemon slices and mint to this recipe, making the already delicious tea even more flavorful and refreshing. I really hope you try it. Just don't expect to sleep anytime soon after drinking a glass or two.

Makes about 10 cups

10 cups water

6 teabags black tea

2 cups sugar

1 lemon, sliced

1 bunch fresh mint, stemmed

Bring the water to a boil in a large saucepan. Remove from the heat and add the teabags and sugar, stirring to dissolve the sugar. Set aside to steep until cool.

To serve, remove the tea bags from the tea, place the lemon slices and mint in a large pitcher, and stir in the cooled tea. Pour the tea into tall glasses over ice.

Pineapple, Ginger, and Peach Smoothie

This smoothie is delicious and easily varied to suit your taste and mood. The following recipe serves as a refreshing drink or snack anytime of day. For a quick, healthy breakfast, I like to substitute one cup of peach yogurt for the pineapple juice. When I want more of a treat, I will substitute one cup of peach sorbet instead. Sometimes, when I start down this road, I end up going all out, and in addition to the sorbet, I add dark rum to the mix. Now, that's a smoothie!

Makes about 4 cups

1 cup pineapple juice

½ fresh very ripe pineapple, peeled and roughly chopped

2 tablespoons Ginger Syrup (available in gourmet or specialty food stores)

4 peaches, peeled, pitted, and roughly chopped

2 cups ice

Combine all of the ingredients in a blender and purée until smooth. Serve in tall glasses.

Strawberry Lemonade

I came up with this recipe over twenty years ago and have been selling it at my restaurants and serving it at parties ever since. One of the keys to really good lemonade is getting all the juice and pulp out of the lemons. Rolling the lemons firmly against a table before slicing and squeezing them will help with this. I usually leave all the lemon pulp and pieces of strawberries in the lemonade and don't even bother to remove the lemon seeds. Whether you do the same is up to you. You can strain all of this out, just as you can add more or less sugar and water to suit your taste. I do recommend, though, that you pour the lemonade over lots of ice to make it really refreshing. In addition, for that extra zing on a warm summer evening, add a splash of whiskey, bourbon, or rum. It doesn't get any more laid-back than that.

Makes about 8 cups

Juice of 12 lemons

1 pint very ripe strawberries,
  stemmed and mashed

2 cups sugar

About 4 cups water

Combine the lemon juice, strawberries, and sugar in a large pitcher, stirring to dissolve the sugar. Stir in the water, adding more or less to taste.

Serve in tall glasses over ice.

147

FALL

Right off the bat, I'll admit that fall is a tricky time of year for me. I know, I know—colorful trees, spicy apple cider, turkey, and all. But come September and October, I'm still dealing with the fact that I can't drive the car with the top down as much, I have to put my T-shirts away, and I need to start storing the patio furniture. Most of all, though, I mourn the closing of my favorite summer farm stands. As the summer wanes, I run around like a crazy woman trying to buy up the last of the season's produce before the markets are barren and gone. I'm really a sad case. Even the market signs reading, "Thank you for a great season. See you in the spring!" cause a lump in my throat. Tragic. It's just that I'm at a low point coming off a high of having the best of summer's fruits and vegetables.

But once I collect myself and resolve to take my sweaters out of their cedar chests, the adrenaline of fall kicks in. I start to get excited about Halloween and Thanksgiving and look forward, of course, to warming, soul-satisfying foods. Some farmers' markets do remain open year-round, and I am thankful for their piles of colorful apples, pears, sweet potatoes, squash, dark leafy greens, and pumpkins. I start to crave these foods when the air turns brisk and the jewel-colored leaves are scattered everywhere. I also begin to yearn for comforting dishes that are rich with full-flavored character, such as fish stew, spicy roasted chicken, and roasted leg of lamb.

These recipes call me back indoors and satisfy my appetite, which seems to naturally grow at this time of year. They put me in mind of warm, cozy, candle-lit dining rooms, and inviting tables draped with heavy linens and set with substantial flatware. Although I do love sitting around a sumptuous table, I also enjoy feasting on flavorful fall dishes in more casual settings. With a glass of wine in one hand and a plate of food, a fork, and a linen napkin in the other, I'll often walk right past the dining room table and plunk myself down in front of a roaring fire in the living room.

I regard fall as a transition time between the easy, breezy days of summer and the festive madness that overtakes us right after Thanksgiving. For all my initial crankiness, it really is a beautiful season, colored not only by busy routines, but also a return to the warmth of the table. I hope these recipes inspire you, as they do me, to pull out a sweater and get back to the stove.

Fish Stew

This flavorful stew is a light, Southern take on heavier, richer versions more traditionally found in the mid-Atlantic and the North. It is perfect for the cooler months when we crave something slightly spicy, warming, and hearty. It is also well suited to warmer seasons, though, because it is filled with fresh vegetables and flavored with stock rather than cream. This recipe is healthy and comes together in less than two hours, making it suitable any time of year.

Serves 6

1½ pounds redfish fillets or other firm
    white fish, such as snapper or grouper

2 tablespoons Cajun seasoning

⅓ cup canola oil

⅓ cup all-purpose flour

1 cup chopped celery

1 cup chopped onion

½ cup chopped green bell pepper

1 tablespoon chopped jalapeño pepper

2 dried bay leaves

1 tablespoon finely chopped garlic

2 cups chopped plum tomatoes

2¾ cups prepared seafood stock
    or clam juice

¾ teaspoon salt

¼ teaspoon cayenne pepper

¼ cup chopped scallion

2 tablespoons chopped fresh
    flat-leaf parsley

Cut the fish fillets into 3-inch pieces and season with 1 tablespoon of Cajun seasoning. Place in a shallow pan, cover with plastic wrap, and set aside in the refrigerator while preparing the rest of the dish.

In a large heavy-bottomed saucepan or Dutch oven, stir together the oil and flour to form a paste (roux). Place over medium heat and simmer, stirring gently with a whisk or wooden spoon, until the roux becomes a milk chocolate-brown color, about 15 to 20 minutes. Stir in the celery, onions, and peppers and continue to simmer, stirring frequently, for 6 to 7 minutes. Add the bay leaves and garlic and cook for about 2 minutes more. Add the tomatoes, stock, salt, cayenne pepper, and the remaining 1 tablespoon of Cajun seasoning. Reduce the heat to medium-low and gently simmer, stirring frequently, until a thin film of oil appears on the surface, about 30 minutes. Add the seasoned fish fillets, scallions, and parsley to the stew and simmer until the fish is done and flakes easily with a fork, about 5 minutes.

To serve, remove the bay leaves and ladle the stew into individual bowls or serve in a soup tureen.

Trout with Tomato-Brown Butter

Southerners love fish and seafood, and during my visits to Virginia when I was little, we ate a lot of trout caught in local streams. In my opinion, trout is at its best when simply fried with a light crunchy coating of seasoned cornmeal. I use mostly yellow cornmeal in my cooking, but I like using white here because it is more delicate in flavor and color. To this traditional preparation, I have added my own flair with a bit of tomato-brown butter. No sauce goes better with trout than the nutty, full flavor of brown butter, and the addition of finely chopped oven-dried tomatoes gives it a refreshing zing.

Serves 4

TROUT

2 cups white cornmeal

1 teaspoon salt

½ teaspoon black pepper

8 rainbow trout fillets
(4 to 6 ounces each), skin on

About 2 cups canola oil, for frying

TOMATO-BROWN BUTTER

½ pound (2 sticks) butter

½ tablespoon sherry vinegar

½ cup oven-dried tomatoes, finely
chopped (see *Chef's Note* page 153)

¼ cup finely chopped fresh
flat-leaf parsley

Salt & black pepper

Preheat the oven to 300°F.

Stir together the cornmeal, salt, and pepper in a shallow pan. Season the trout with additional salt and pepper and dredge in the cornmeal, coating well and gently shaking off any excess.

Heat the oil in a large sauté pan or skillet over medium-high heat until very hot. (There should be about ½ inch of oil in the pan.) To check if the oil is hot enough, sprinkle a bit of cornmeal into the oil. If the cornmeal sizzles right away, the oil is ready. Carefully place 2 fillets in the pan at a time, frying on each side for about 2 minutes until golden brown. Set the browned fillets aside on a baking sheet while preparing the remaining trout. Arrange the rest of the fillets on the baking sheet, place in the oven, and bake until just cooked, about 5 to 6 minutes.

Meanwhile, to make the tomato-brown butter, melt the butter in a large sauté pan over medium-high heat. Continue to simmer the butter (watching it carefully and lowering the heat if necessary to prevent it from burning) until it begins to foam, turns golden brown, and develops a nutty aroma. Remove from the heat, stir in the vinegar, oven-dried tomatoes, and parsley, and season with salt and pepper.

To serve, arrange 2 fillets on each plate and spoon the tomato-brown butter overtop.

Cod with Black-Eyed Peas

This dish is perfect for fall, as it's filled with rich flavor, varied textures, and is oh, so satisfying. I have already mentioned that fresh black-eyed peas are one of my favorite summer foods, but I admit dried peas do work well here. Combined with the likes of onion, garlic, bacon, hot peppers, oven-dried tomatoes, and goat cheese, they serve as a flavorful and comforting bed for the roasted cod.

Serves 4

BLACK-EYED PEAS

2 cups dried black-eyed peas

1 onion, peeled and quartered

1 dried bay leaf

1 whole clove

1/2 teaspoon black pepper

1/2 teaspoon salt

COD

1/4 cup vegetable oil

4 cod fillets (about 6 to 8 ounces)

Salt & black pepper

ASSEMBLY

1/4 pound bacon, cut into 1/4-inch pieces

1 cup chopped yellow onion

1 1/2 tablespoons chopped garlic

2 fresh red Thai chile peppers, stemmed
  and chopped

16 oven-dried tomatoes
  (see *Chef's Note*, page 153)

1 cup chopped scallions

To make the black-eyed peas, pick through the peas and remove any small stones or dried bits. Place the peas in a large saucepan or Dutch oven and pour in enough cold water to cover by about 1/2 inch. Add the remaining ingredients and bring to a boil over medium-high heat. Reduce the heat to low and stir the beans again. Cover and simmer, stirring occasionally, until the beans are tender, about 1 hour. Remove from the heat, drain, and set aside.

Preheat the oven to 350°F.

To make the cod, heat the oil in a large sauté pan over medium-high heat. Season the cod fillets with salt and pepper, place in the pan, and cook until browned on the first side. Turn the fillets, place in the oven, and roast until fully cooked, about 10 minutes.

Meanwhile, to assemble the rest of the dish, heat a large sauté pan over medium-high heat. Place the bacon in the pan and cook until browned and crisp. Using a slotted spoon, remove the bacon to a paper-towel-lined plate to drain. Reduce the heat to medium, add the onion and garlic to the hot bacon drippings, and sauté until softened. Stir in the Thai chiles and sauté until tender. Fold in the tomatoes, scallions, thyme, drained bacon, and black-eyed peas and

2 teaspoons chopped fresh thyme

½ pound goat cheese, crumbled
    or cut into small pieces

Salt & black pepper

Chopped fresh flat-leaf parsley, for garnish

cook for about 5 minutes. Remove from the heat, stir in the goat cheese, and season with salt and pepper.

To serve, divide the black-eyed pea mixture among four plates, set a cod fillet on top, and garnish with parsley.

CHEF'S NOTE: Sun-dried tomatoes add texture and flavor to a variety of dishes, but rather than purchase them already prepared, I like to dry my own tomatoes in the oven. Simply slice plum tomatoes lengthwise and arrange them cut sides up on a baking sheet. Sprinkle with salt, pepper, and sugar and dry in a 150°F oven for about 3 hours. Once they cool, store them in airtight containers. Kept in a cool, dry area, they will remain fresh and flavorful for several months.

Fried Lobster Tail with Corn, Okra, and Tomatoes

This dish is my Southern version of traditional steamed lobster tail. As if lobster tail weren't delicious enough, I fry it, making it even more decadent. I find the accompanying vegetables are just the ticket to round out the meal, too. They are light and fresh and complement the richness of the lobster.

This dish is terrific for entertaining, because you can marinate the lobster tails several days ahead without worry. The following recipe makes two servings, but you can certainly increase the amounts for a larger party. I suggest, though, that you keep the gathering as intimate as possible so you can assemble the plates quickly and serve the lobster tails hot and crispy.

Serves 2

1 cup buttermilk

2 teaspoons hot sauce

2 raw lobster tails, shelled

1½ tablespoons butter

1 cup fresh corn kernels

½ cup chopped tomatoes

¼ cup Shrimp Stock (see page 37)

1 teaspoon granulated garlic

Salt & black pepper

About 3½ cups canola oil, for frying

1 cup all-purpose flour

½ teaspoon seasoned salt

4 to 5 pieces okra, trimmed and sliced into
   1-inch-thick pieces (about ½ cup)

Stir together the buttermilk and hot sauce in a medium bowl. Add the lobster tails, turning to coat, cover, and set aside in the refrigerator to marinate for at least 10 minutes.

Melt the butter in a medium sauté pan over medium heat, add the corn, and sauté for about 1 minute. Stir in the tomatoes and sauté for about 1 minute more. Pour in the stock and add about ½ teaspoon of the granulated garlic. Season with salt and pepper and simmer until thickened. Remove from the heat and set aside while finishing the lobster.

Heat the oil in a large saucepan or skillet over medium-high heat. (There should be about 1 inch of oil in the pan.) To check if the oil is hot enough, sprinkle a bit of flour into the oil. If the flour sizzles right away, the oil is ready.

Combine the flour, seasoned salt, and the remaining ½ teaspoon of granulated garlic in a shallow pan. Remove the marinated lobster tails from the buttermilk and skewer them lengthwise with 2 wooden skewers. (This will prevent them from curling during the frying process.) Dredge the tails in the flour, coating them liberally, and carefully place them in the pan of oil. (The oil should rise about halfway up the sides of the tails.) Fry until golden brown, carefully turn

155

the tails using the ends of the skewers, and fry on the second sides until golden brown. When the lobster tails are well browned, cover the pan and cook for an additional 5 minutes. Drain the lobsters on paper towels and carefully remove the skewers.

To finish the vegetables, set them again over medium heat and bring to a simmer. Add the okra, toss a few times, and remove from the heat. (You want to cook the okra very quickly until it is just tender to prevent it from becoming mushy.)

To serve, divide the vegetables between 2 plates and place a lobster tail overtop.

Spicy Roasted Chicken

I serve chicken frequently to friends and family, so I am always thinking about new ways to prepare it. This recipe for roasted chicken is really very basic, but I add some pizzazz with lots of fresh herbs, spices, garlic, and lemon. To give it even more flavor, I like to marinate the chicken overnight in all of these vibrant ingredients so they fully penetrate the skin and the flesh. You don't have to marinate the chicken for this long, but it does make it extra special.

The great thing about roasting chicken is that it's easy and always works. You really don't need any fancy equipment here. A large, straight-sided pan or roasting pan will do the trick (no rack required). You don't even need a thermometer. As long as the juices are running clear and the bird is golden brown, you are good to go.

The chicken alone is enough to satisfy me, but for the most comforting of fall dinners, I suggest rounding out the meal with sides of Mashed Sweet Potatoes and Roasted Brussels Sprouts (see page 162).

Serves 4

3 sprigs fresh rosemary, stemmed

1 tablespoon seasoned salt

1 teaspoon black pepper

6 cloves garlic, peeled and roughly chopped

1/4 cup canola oil

1 teaspoon lemon pepper

Juice of 1 lemon

2 teaspoons paprika

2 sprigs fresh thyme, stemmed

1 whole chicken (about 4 pounds)

At least 8 hours before roasting the chicken, stir together all of the herbs, spices, and aromatics in a small bowl. Rub the chicken liberally inside and out with the seasoned mixture, place in a large zip-top bag, and set in the refrigerator to marinate for at least 8 hours or overnight.

The next day or when you are ready to proceed with the dish, preheat the oven to 350°F.

Place the marinated chicken in a small roasting pan and roast until fully cooked, well browned, and the juices run clear, about 1 hour.

To serve, carve the chicken and arrange on individual plates with mashed yams and Brussels sprouts.

Roasted Leg of Lamb with Peaches and Mint

Whenever I prepare lamb, I feel like I'm making a really special meal. Lamb is just that way. Whether I prepare chops, a roast, or racks, I know that dinner will not only be delicious, but that I will want to sit up a little straighter in my chair and eat with a bit more reverence. It is that wonderful.

This dish is perfect for fall. The sweet and savory flavors complement the lamb and one another, creating what really becomes a warming and comforting one-dish meal, perfect for a brisk autumn evening.

Serves 8

1 tablespoon butter

6 peaches, 3 peeled, pitted, and roughly chopped and 3 halved and pitted

5 shallots, 1 peeled and finely chopped and 4 peeled and left whole

9 cloves garlic, 1 peeled and finely chopped and 8 peeled and left whole

½ cup chopped fresh mint

Salt & black pepper

1 leg of lamb (about 5 pounds), boned and butterflied

½ cup canola oil

2 springs fresh thyme

4 medium red-skinned potatoes, quartered

Preheat the oven to 375°F.

Heat the butter in a medium sauté pan over medium heat. Add the chopped peaches, finely chopped shallots, and finely chopped garlic and sauté for about 1 minute. Remove to a medium bowl and add the mint, tossing to combine. Season with salt and pepper and set aside to cool to room temperature.

Place the lamb on a work surface, butterflied side facing up, and generously season with salt and pepper. Mound the chopped peach mixture along one of the long sides of the lamb and roll the lamb over the mixture into a cylinder, tucking in the ends as you go. Set the lamb seam side down, tie with 5 pieces of twine at 2- to 3-inch intervals down the length of the roll, and then tie lengthwise to secure the ends.

Heat the oil in a medium roasting pan over high heat. Place the lamb in the pan and sear on all sides until well browned. Surround the lamb with the remaining peach halves, whole shallots, whole garlic cloves, thyme sprigs, and potatoes. Roast the lamb to medium rare (about 140°F.) or to desired doneness, basting occasionally with pan drippings, about 1 to 1¼ hours. Remove and discard the thyme sprigs. Cover the pan loosely with foil to rest the lamb and keep warm for about 10 minutes.

To serve, remove the twine from the roast and slice into about ½-inch-thick pieces. Arrange the lamb slices on a serving platter and surround with the roasted shallots, garlic, and peaches.

158

Porterhouse Steak

I only eat three kinds of steak: rib eye, filet mignon, and porterhouse. All are wonderful for different reasons, but if you really want to "wow" your guests or family, the porterhouse is your best bet. To my mind, no presentation is more impressive than a plate of this perfectly browned and glistening oversized steak. Cut from the large end of the short loin, porterhouse steak is composed of meat from both the tenderloin and the top loin. This is why it is so expensive.

You will notice that I haven't included any side dishes in this recipe. Fries, of course, are a natural pairing with porterhouse, and if you want 'em, go for it. Frankly, whatever else you're serving is not that important. It's all about the steak, baby. In fact, there won't be any room for a side dish anyhow. The steak will take up the whole plate.

I just have to say this: do not even wave a ketchup bottle over the same plate as this steak. If you do, you will—in my opinion—ruin this so-gorgeous-as-to-knock-you-out piece of meat.

Serves 6

6 porterhouse steaks
  (about 16 ounces each)
¼ cup olive oil
2 tablespoons chopped fresh thyme
2 tablespoons onion powder
2 tablespoons chopped garlic
Black pepper

Place the steaks on baking sheets. Rub both sides of each steak with oil, thyme, onion powder, and garlic and season with pepper. Cover with plastic wrap and set in the refrigerator for about 1 hour. Remove the steaks and set aside to warm to room temperature for about 20 minutes.

Preheat the broiler.

Place the steaks on a broiler pan and broil on each side for about 3 to 5 minutes (for medium rare), or to your desired doneness.

Serve immediately on individual plates.

159

French Fries

Ever since I was little, French fries have been my favorite food. I grew up making fresh-cut fries for my school friends during our lunch breaks, and I still prepare them every chance I get. I like the combination of Russet and sweet potatoes in this recipe, but you can certainly use all of one or the other if you wish. As far as condiments go, I know ketchup is the all-American favorite, but I prefer tangy, more vibrant accompaniments, such as vinegar, aioli, or hot sauce.

Serves 4

2 large Russet potatoes, sliced lengthwise
   into ¼-inch-thick strips
2 large sweet potatoes, sliced lengthwise
   into ¼-inch-thick strips
2 quarts canola oil
Salt & black pepper
Ketchup, vinegar, aioli, or hot sauce,
   for serving

Place the potatoes in a large colander and rinse with cold water until the water runs clear. (This will remove surface starch.) Place the potatoes in a large bowl, cover with cold water, and set aside in the refrigerator for at least 30 minutes. (You can also store the potatoes like this for up to 2 days.)

Heat the oil in a heavy 5-quart stockpot or large Dutch oven over medium-high heat. (The oil will appear to shimmer on the surface when it is ready.)

Drain the potatoes, place them on a paper-towel-lined baking sheet, and pat with additional towels to dry *completely*. Carefully place a handful of potatoes into the oil and fry until barely colored and slightly soft. (They are only blanched, not fully cooked, at this point.) Remove the potatoes using a large slotted spoon and place on a paper-towel-lined baking sheet to drain while continuing with the remaining potatoes. Allow the blanched potatoes to rest for about 10 minutes.

To finish the fries, place a handful of blanched potatoes into the oil, now frying until golden brown, crisp, and slightly puffed. Remove the fries using a large slotted spoon, season with salt and pepper, and place on a paper-towel-lined baking sheet to drain and keep warm while continuing with the remaining potatoes.

Serve the fries hot on a large platter accompanied by your preferred sauce.

Fried Plantains

I came to appreciate plantains during my trips to Jamaica, where they are plentiful and served frequently. Known as "cooking bananas," they are less sweet than the common yellow banana, and can be cooked when firm and green, or ripe and brown. For savory dishes like this one, I prefer to use firm, green variety.

Because fried plantains have a potato-like flavor and consistency, they are a delicious alternative to French fries. Pair them with burgers, steaks, and poultry dishes, as well as with my Jamaican favorites, Curried Goat (see page 104) and Jerk Chicken (see page 116).

Serves 8

About 2½ cups vegetable oil, for frying
4 firm, green plantains, peeled and sliced
  on the bias into ¾-inch-thick pieces
Salt

Heat the oil in a large sauté pan over medium-high heat. (There should be about 1 inch of oil in the pan, and it will appear to shimmer on the surface when it is ready.) Add about one-quarter of the plantain pieces at a time and fry until golden brown. Remove to a paper-towel-lined baking sheet to keep warm while frying the remaining slices and sprinkle with salt. Add additional oil to the pan as necessary.

Serve warm on a platter.

161

Mashed Sweet Potatoes

To me, mashed sweet potatoes are the quintessential fall side dish. The natural sweetness of the sweet potatoes pairs perfectly with spicy ginger and fragrant nutmeg. Serve them with roasted chicken or pork and you have a delicious and comforting meal.

Serves 4

3 large sweet potatoes, peeled
   and cut into large pieces
3 tablespoons butter, at room temperature
1 teaspoon ground ginger
1/4 teaspoon ground nutmeg
Salt & black pepper

Place the sweet potatoes in a large saucepan, fill with enough cold salted water to cover by about 1/2 inch, and bring to a boil over high heat. Reduce the heat to medium and simmer until the yams are just tender, about 15 minutes.

Drain the sweet potatoes, return them to the pan, and mash them until smooth using a fork or potato masher. Stir in the butter, ginger, and nutmeg and season with salt and pepper.

Serve immediately in a large bowl.

Roasted Brussels Sprouts

A recipe can't get any easier than this. It comes together in no time and is great with roasted meat or poultry. I know a lot of folks stay away from Brussels sprouts due to their slightly bitter flavor, but roasting mellows their bitterness, caramelizing and crisping the outer leaves, while making the inner leaves deliciously tender.

Serves 4

1 pound Brussels sprouts, stem ends trimmed
1/4 cup canola oil
Salt & black pepper

Preheat the oven to 375°F.

Toss together the Brussels sprouts and oil in a large bowl and season with salt and pepper. Spread evenly on a baking sheet and roast until tender and golden brown, about 20 minutes.

Serve hot in a serving bowl.

Dirty Rice

I admit I'm not a big rice person, but I do love dirty rice. Just give me the pan of rice and a spoon and I'm happy. In this version, which makes a great fall side dish, I rely on the Cajun tradition of using chicken gizzards and pork, in addition to a whole host of aromatic vegetables, herbs, and spices. The pork adds a lot of intense, rich flavor, but you can easily make this rice without it. Use ground beef or turkey if you prefer. When opting for the turkey variation, I suggest using chicken livers along with the gizzards. Because turkey is lean, you will need to boost the flavor somewhat and add some additional richness.

Serves 8

1 pound chicken gizzards

2 tablespoons vegetable oil

2 tablespoons all-purpose flour

1 pound ground pork

1 cup chopped onion

½ cup chopped green bell pepper

½ cup chopped celery

4 cups cooked white rice

2 teaspoons salt

½ teaspoon cayenne pepper

¼ cup chopped scallions

¼ cup chopped fresh flat-leaf parsley

1 tablespoon chopped fresh thyme

Place the gizzards in a medium saucepan, add water just to cover, and bring to a boil. Reduce the heat to low, cover, and simmer gently until fully cooked, about 1 hour. Drain the gizzards, reserving the broth, and chop finely.

Combine the oil and flour in a large saucepan, stirring to form a paste (roux). Cook over medium heat, stirring frequently, until dark chocolate brown in color, about 8 to 10 minutes. Stir in the pork and cook until browned, stirring occasionally, for 5 to 6 minutes. Add the onion, pepper, and celery and cook until the vegetables are softened, another 5 to 6 minutes. Add the chopped gizzards, stirring to combine. Pour the reserved gizzard broth into a measuring cup and, if necessary, add enough water to make 1 cup of liquid. Add the broth and rice to the pan, stirring to combine. Toss in the remaining ingredients and cook until the rice is heated, about 3 minutes.

Serve hot in a serving bowl.

163

Catherine's
TABLE

CATHERINE'S TABLE

My grandmother Catherine Howard was a true Southern lady. She and my grandfather lived modestly in the same house in Richmond, Virginia, for nearly 50 years and she worked hard all of her life. But for all of her frugality and down-to-earth sincerity, Catherine was a proper Southern woman in the most traditional sense. She carried herself in the same graceful manner as the most genteel and well-to-do Southern ladies of her day and tended to her home with great pride and attention to detail. In the South, keeping a clean, well-organized house and providing tables of nourishing, beautifully presented food are as important as practicing good manners and knowing proper etiquette. My grandmother not only excelled in all of these areas, but she taught me to appreciate them as well.

I started spending summers with Catherine when I was just a little girl. Both sets of my grandparents lived in Virginia, and every summer my parents shipped off me and my sister Paula from Philadelphia to visit them for weeks at a time. Although we had fun at my maternal grandparents' farm in King Queen County, I have to admit I always liked staying with Catherine best. My mother, after all, is the youngest of thirteen children, most of who

remained in the area to raise their families. Although everyone always welcomed us warmly, we felt like (and really were!) the outsider city kids from up North. Come to think of it, I'm sort of surprised anyone noticed us at all. We were just three more little ones in the mix of literally dozens of kids and extended family. Of course, our grandmother was always glad to see us. But especially since we were the youngest of the bunch, we just knew she must have been thinking, "Oh, more grandchildren. Okay, get in line with the rest of 'em!" Who could blame her? My father, on the other hand, has only one younger sister, Lilly, who is only a few years older than I am. So when Paula and I visited Catherine and my grandfather, there were only three little ones in all to attend to. And did they ever! They doted on us and gave us lots of special treatment. It's no wonder Paula and I always wanted to stay with them.

Summers in Richmond were magical. As Catherine's first and oldest grandchild, I was always close to her and looked forward to spending as much time with her as possible. She was a busy woman, though. In addition to tending to her own home, she worked full time as a housekeeper for the Parker family in the suburbs. Much of what I learned about keeping house, setting a table, and cooking, I learned during those summers, as I watched my grandmother seamlessly care for two households. When I was very little, she sometimes took me to work with her. I loved tagging along and following her around that big beautiful house. The Parkers were wealthy society folks. I remember thinking their fancy Thunderbird convertible was one of the prettiest cars I had ever seen, and it was always a treat to play with their three lovingly groomed little dogs.

My grandmother took care of the house and tended to the cooking while Mrs. Parker attended social events, such as bridge games and golf outings at the local club. Sometimes Mrs. Parker hosted card games and teas at the house, and my grandmother assisted with these affairs, as well. She prepared beautiful trays of tea sandwiches and refreshments and set up the dining room or living room with all kinds of sparkling tableware. I loved watching her choose china, glasses, silver, and carefully pressed tablecloths and napkins from the Parkers' cabinets and then arrange them in just the right way. Occasionally, my grandmother permitted me to practice doing this myself. While keeping a close eye on me, she let me play with some of the tableware and invent my own dreamy place settings. These were the days I enjoyed most at the Parkers' house. I loved pretending I was hosting my own fancy affairs with tea and cakes. I remember looking forward to the day when I, too, would have such

pretty things of my own and be able to arrange them as perfectly as did my grandmother.

Although my grandmother worked all day at the Parkers' house, she somehow managed to care for her own home with equal care and attention to detail. In traditional Southern fashion, this meant not only keeping the house in tip-top shape, but also providing three meals a day for the family whether she was at home or at work. Now, here's the thing: I'm not talking about just keeping the refrigerator stocked and making sure there was cereal for breakfast. I mean the woman set the table and prepared full meals twice a day for breakfast and dinner. She even made sure we had a proper lunch every day. She always left a little something like tuna salad and a pot of soup—light dishes to nibble on until dinner.

Summers in Richmond meant carefree weeks filled with delicious food. Good cooking was everywhere, from the local tavern, to the neighborhood bar, to the seemingly endless platters served up at family gatherings. In the end, though, my happiest food memories center on my grandmother's table. It was a sight unlike any other I have ever experienced since! In case you're envisioning a cozy kitchen table set for simple down-home Virginia meals—well, get that scene right out of your mind! My grandmother would never have stood for that. She always served breakfast and dinner on a formally set dining room table, complete with linens, decanters, multiple glasses, silver, china, serving dishes—the works! My grandmother received many

168

of these pieces from the Parkers, who periodically wanted to make space in their cabinets for new items. This happened many times over the years, so she obtained quite a collection of tableware.

My grandmother believed it was important for me to learn at an early age how to properly set a table, so she allowed me to assist her. I loved every minute of it! I'd go into the buffet and retrieve her folded and pressed linen, lace, or damask tablecloths and napkins from the second drawer. Then I'd carefully take the pieces she wanted out of the various cabinets and arrange them on the table just as she had instructed. Of course, there were never any jars or bottles of condiments on her table. Every sauce, relish, mustard, jam, preserve, pickle, and spread had its own china or glass bowl, and I set those out, too. She did, though, make two exceptions to this rule. One was

the jar of homemade Concord grape jam. To this day, I don't know why my grandmother served it in the jar, but she did. Maybe she figured it was so delicious and gorgeous it didn't require any gussying up. My grandfather basically mandated the other exception. Even though there were enough pretty glasses in the house to stylishly hydrate the neighborhood, he insisted on drinking his iced coffee out of a Ball mason jar. Why, I have no idea. I'm sure my grandmother wasn't thrilled about this, but I never do recall her making a fuss. Every item on my grandmother's table was important, but it was only fully set when we placed the jar of grape jam next to the basket of biscuits and the jar of iced coffee beside my grandfather's plate.

If setting this table was a production, you can just imagine what the food was like. My, my, my! How

my grandmother kept up with all this, I just don't know. Every morning, she was in the kitchen by 5:00 a.m. making breakfast. She needed to start early because this was our biggest meal of the day and she had so many dishes to prepare. Of course, nobody cooks like this anymore. In fact, the spread my grandmother presented on a daily basis was probably akin to what most folks only enjoy these days at Sunday dinners or on the holidays. My grandmother was a traditional Southern lady, though, who grew up in an era when a big breakfast was the main meal of the day. It was supposed to carry you through most of a day's work.

Even as times changed, my grandmother continued making these enormous and wonderful meals. During the summer, when my sisters and I visited, we kept busy with chores and working in the garden. It was important to my grandmother that, before she went out to work, we all had a substantial breakfast. It certainly was that—and more! There was sausage, bacon, corn, fried chicken, homemade jam, juice, biscuits, grits, and the dishes went on and on. I can still remember as a little girl being asleep upstairs and smelling my grandmother's biscuits baking at 6 o'clock in the morning. The aroma would downright wake me out of a sound sleep! I just couldn't stay in bed. I'd creep downstairs and sit with my grandmother as she moved about the kitchen, rolling dough, dredging chicken, and frying bacon.

My grandmother kept to the same routine every day. She prepared these wonderful breakfasts, went off to work, and then came home and served up a similarly abundant dinner. We sure ate our fill in the mornings, but the evening meals were often more extravagant. Because we weren't rushing off to work or chores, we could take our time—which really meant we were able to eat even greater amounts of her wonderful dishes! Oh, to think of it now. We had so much fun.

After setting the table and preparing the meal, the next task was fitting ourselves around the table. This was always quite a feat. Not only was my grandmother's table too big for the dining room, it competed for space with the china cabinet, buffet, two sideboards, and a furnace that were also squeezed in there. The dining chairs practically butted right up against all this furniture, so once we squeezed into our seats, we could hardly move. If we had forgotten anything in the sideboards at that point, well, it was too darned bad. Nothing was coming out of those drawers, that's for sure! The thing is, there really was no reason to get up. Everything we possibly could have wanted was on that table. There were platters of fried fish and smothered chicken; dishes of pickled watermelon; compotes filled with preserves; pitchers of peach wine; and pedestals of rich cake. We sat around that table and ate as though our days were numbered. After we picked at our last piece of chicken and scraped the bowls of preserves clean, we just had to sit. Well, for one thing, we were stuffed. But besides that, we couldn't move our chairs away from the table!

As I got older, I continued to travel to Richmond

whenever I could to visit my grandparents. Time was really kind to them. Even as they aged, they remained active and strong, and we were able to enjoy many more celebrations around that table. For my grandmother's 90th birthday, though, I thought it was high time to get her out of the house and honor her in a special way. I wanted her to know not only how much we all loved her, but also how grateful we were for her years of tender nurturing and generous nourishment. After thinking for a while about what we should do, I developed the perfect scheme.

When I was little, my grandmother often took me into town, where we'd walk on Broad Street by the Peabody Hotel. I remember looking up at its gorgeous façade, as my grandmother praised its Southern charm and explained how only the grandest affairs took place there. Of course, we could never go in, but I dreamed of what it was like inside—and I know she did, too. As her 90th birthday drew near, it became clear that there was only one place to host her party—at The Peabody. I didn't care what it cost and I decided we would invite everyone we could think of. My grandmother—this proper woman who lived her life as elegantly as the most genteel of Southern ladies—would finally not only have a look inside this grand hotel, but sit at the head of one of its most lavish dining room tables as well. I would make certain of it. On the day of the party, we took her by surprise as we walked her into the lobby. "Grandmom, look at where *we're* going," I told her. "Look at where *you* are!" After all those years of

gazing at the hotel from the street, she was overwhelmed at first to finally be inside. She relaxed soon enough, though. In fact, she sat at that huge dining table surrounded by family and friends with the grace and ease of a woman who knew she belonged there all along.

My grandmother passed away several years ago now, but I feel as though she is very much with me still. The memories I have of our time together are not merely comforting visions from the past; they have shaped my life in many ways and continue to be part of my present. As much as I have come to love the likes of caviar and Champagne over the years, I am still, and always will be, a crispy-fried-chicken, homemade-peach-preserves, please-pass-me-another-round-of-mashed-potatoes kind of girl deep in my soul. In truth, my grandmother taught me to appreciate all styles of cooking and eating. She might not have ventured too far from the traditional Southern table herself, but, oh, what a table it was! Just by watching my grandmother over the years, I learned that no matter what kind of food you make, as long as you cook it right, make sure it is as delicious as possible, and lay it out beautifully, it will make people happy and feel loved.

My grandmother's approach sure worked on me. I hope you will try these simple and basic recipes and, if the mood strikes you, serve them at the table as prettily as my grandmother did. I'm sure you will agree that they deserve as proper a setting as that.

Fried Chicken

I hardly know where to start with fried chicken. It's one of those dishes that has been important to me throughout my life, not only because my family enjoys it at nearly every gathering, but because I was practically weaned on the delectably crunchy, juicy stuff in my grandmother's kitchen.

During my summers in Richmond, it seemed fried chicken was always on the table in some form. My grandmother served it hot out of the pan for breakfast, cold as leftovers for lunch, and smothered with gravy for dinner. I often wondered why she took the trouble to fry up a huge batch of chicken every morning at 6:00 a.m., but then I realized she was planning ahead for future meals. One of my favorite summer lunches, in fact, was a sandwich of cold fried chicken (bones and all) on soft white bread.

I fixed these lunches myself, but on special occasions, my grandmother made fried chicken lunches for me. They were so delicious, I stayed up nights just thinking about them. Most of these occasions centered on church-sponsored day trips. Sometimes she'd go along and sometimes I went alone, but I always had my special lunch in tow. My grandmother would carefully pack fried chicken, white bread, and a fresh peach or slice of pound cake in a shoebox, and I'd sit on the bus with that box in my lap, counting the hours until I could open it up and start feasting. I was hardly as interested in where I was headed as in what awaited me in that box.

My grandmother's superior fried chicken set my standards pretty high. Needless to say, I am very fussy about how it's prepared and pride myself on frying outstanding chicken. I admit, though, it's not quite as good as hers. For one thing, I fry in oil, while my grandmother fried in lard, which gives the skin a dark brown color and extra crispy texture. Chicken fried in oil will be good, but it will never be as dark and rich as chicken fried in lard.

Most southern cooks marinate their chicken in buttermilk and hot sauce before frying. I suggest doing the same in this recipe, as it gives the chicken extra flavor and keeps it really tender as it cooks. Once the chicken has marinated, there are a few key things to keep in mind before and during the frying process. First, flour each piece right before it hits the oil. Don't let the pieces sit around in flour, or they will get soggy and refuse to crisp evenly.

Next, once the chicken is in the oil, do NOT play with it. Drop it in the pan and leave it alone. I have had to break my cooks of their desire to stir and fuss with the pieces as they bubble in the pan. The chicken does not need your help, thank you. "Get away from that fryer!" I yell. "Leave it. You've got to let it do its thing." Southern food is slow cooked, and fried chicken is no exception. Resist moving the pieces once they're in the pan, and for heaven's sake don't poke them. Buy yourself a good pair of tongs and leave the fork in the drawer. If you use a fork to turn the chicken, you'll pierce the skin, and all the juices will run out. You want to seal in all that tasty moisture, while creating a crunchy, golden brown outer coating. In addition, to ensure juicy and crispy fried chicken, add only a few pieces of chicken at a time to the pan to keep them from crowding. This will help maintain the hot oil temperature and allow for even cooking.

Whether you like eating fried chicken for breakfast, lunch, dinner, or as a snack, I hope you try this recipe. This is Southern comfort food at its best.

Serves 8

1 cup buttermilk

1 cup hot sauce

2 chickens (about 2½ pounds each), cut
into 8 pieces, at room temperature

6 cups canola oil, for frying

2 cups Chicken Flour (see page 34)

At least 8 hours before cooking the chicken, combine the but-termilk and hot sauce in a large zip-top bag. Add the chicken pieces, making sure they are completely coated, and set in the refrigerator to marinate for at least 8 hours or overnight.

The next day or when you are ready to proceed with the dish, heat the oil in a large skillet or saucepan. To check if the oil is hot enough, sprinkle a bit of chicken flour into the oil. If the flour sizzles right away, the oil is ready.

Meanwhile, place the chicken flour in a shallow pan and add the chicken pieces, dredging liberally and patting gently to remove any excess flour. Carefully place about 4 or 5 chicken pieces in the oil and fry on both sides, turning once, until golden brown and cooked completely. Remove from the pan and set aside on paper towels to drain and keep warm while frying the remaining chicken.

To serve, arrange the fried chicken on a large serving platter.

Smothered Chicken

*Smothered chicken is simply fried chicken cooked for a short time in onion gravy. My grandmother served this dish for break-
fast and dinner, often making use of leftover fried chicken.*

*At first, this might seem like a modest, nothing-to-it sort of recipe. It is pretty basic, I'll admit, but smothered chicken is hardly
simplistic. It was always one of the most important and beloved dishes on my grandmother's table. In addition to her outrageously delicious fried chicken, it features her onion gravy, which was a staple at every breakfast and dinner. A china gravy boat
of piping hot gravy was always within reach, ready for dipping biscuits or pouring over bacon or grits.*

*Onion gravy is so easy to make, I encourage you to prepare it not only for smothered chicken, but to serve it alongside
roasted chicken and turkey as well.*

Serves 8

ONION GRAVY

1 tablespoon canola oil

3 tablespoons butter

2 large Vidalia onions, peeled and chopped

3 tablespoons all-purpose flour

2 cups chicken broth

2 teaspoons seasoned salt

Black pepper

ASSEMBLY

Fried Chicken (see previous page)

Heat the oil and butter in a large sauté pan over medium heat
until the butter is melted. Add the onions and sauté until softened and golden brown. Sprinkle in the flour, stirring to make
a paste (roux), and continue to cook, stirring frequently, until
caramel colored. Add the broth, seasoned salt, and pepper and
simmer, stirring frequently, until thickened.

To assemble the dish, add the fried chicken to the pan and
coat with the gravy. Reduce the heat to medium-low and simmer for about 15 minutes.

Serve the chicken and gravy on a large platter.

177

Fried Butterfish

My grandmother served a lot of butterfish because they were plentiful in local waters and inexpensive. They are little critters (about eight ounces each) and filled with small bones. This is no fussy fillet dish. Once the heads are removed and the fish are butterflied and laid flat, you cook the whole thing, bones and all. For one thing, the bones are too darned small to pick out. And for another, cooking fish on the bone gives the flesh a lot more flavor.

My grandmother always described these fish as "fried hard," meaning not only are they crispy on the outside, but the bones become hard as well. Once this happens, the tender flesh separates from the bigger bones, and the smaller bones become crunchy and edible. This might seem like quite a process, but the whole joy of eating butterfish is picking around the bones to obtain as much tender flesh as possible. You have to work for every morsel, but you sure do appreciate it.

Serves 8

4 cups canola oil, for frying

2 cups Fish Flour (see page 34)

8 butterfish, butterflied and heads removed

Salt & black pepper

Heat the oil in a large sauté pan over medium-high heat. To check if the oil is hot enough, sprinkle a bit of flour into the oil. If the flour sizzles right away, the oil is ready.

Place the fish flour in a shallow pan. Set the butterfish flat on a work surface so both the fillets are exposed. Season with salt and pepper and dredge in the fish flour, patting gently to remove any excess flour. Carefully place about 4 or 5 fish in the oil and fry on each side for about 2 to 3 minutes until golden brown. Remove the fish to a paper-towel-lined plate to drain and keep warm while frying the remaining fish.

Serve hot on a large platter.

Buttermilk Biscuits

My grandmother baked a fresh batch of biscuits every day for breakfast and dinner. Thinking of it now, I don't know how she did it. We ate them so often, you might think we took them for granted or grew tired of eating the same thing every morning and evening. Neither ever happened, though. In fact, not only did we always look forward to eating biscuits, but my grandmother also taught us to treat them with great respect. It sounds sort of funny, I know, but this is how important they were to our meals. Sometimes my grandmother served biscuits in a china dish and other times in a basket. Regardless of the vessel, she always enclosed them in a crisp white linen cloth so they would remain warm and tender while sitting on the table.

Unlike some biscuits, my grandmother's were tiny, pop-in-your-mouth-type morsels. I could tear them up, easily downing three or four at a time. It's no wonder I always returned to Philadelphia at the end of the summer two sizes larger than when I arrived in Richmond! We ate biscuits plain, with butter, and with jam, and used them to sop up any stray drop of gravy left on our plates.

When I grew up, I returned many times to Virginia to try and learn my grandmother's secret for making these biscuits. She never used recipes, so I would stand next to her in the kitchen and try to write down ingredient amounts and dough making techniques that she just knew by heart. Her mind and hands held all of the information, but recipes were foreign to her. She could hardly convey the process for preparing something she baked every day for more than 50 years.

After decades of baking, I have come to make pretty good biscuits. My Aunt Lilly's biscuits come even closer to my grandmother's, though. Like my grandmother, Lilly still uses lard, which makes all the difference in the world. Butter makes a good biscuit, but lard makes them even flakier and more tender. I think you'll like this recipe, but if you want to use lard, go ahead.

179

Makes about 10 biscuits

3 cups sifted all-purpose flour

2 teaspoons salt

2 tablespoons baking powder

¼ pound (1 stick) unsalted butter, chilled and cubed

1 cup buttermilk

Preheat the oven to 325°F.

Combine the flour, salt, and baking powder in a large bowl. Using a pastry cutter or your fingertips, work the butter into the flour until the mixture resembles coarse meal. (It's alright if some pea-size pieces of butter remain visible.) Add the buttermilk and mix lightly to form a soft dough. (The dough should be gooey, but not wet.)

Turn the dough out onto a lightly floured work surface, sprinkle with additional flour, and roll to about ½ inch thick. Cut into 10 biscuits using a round cutter about 2 inches in diameter. Arrange the biscuits about 1 inch apart on a parchment-lined baking sheet and bake until risen and golden brown, about 15 minutes. Set on wire racks to cool.

Grits

Grits are a Southern staple, and my grandmother served them every morning for as long as I can remember. This is such a simple recipe, but that's what makes it so delicious. Milk, butter, grits, and a little salt and pepper are all you need to make a creamy, warming bowl of this perfect comfort food. Plate them up with a few spoonfuls of onion gravy, and you'll better understand the Southern love affair with this rich buttery mush.

Serves 8

2 cups milk

4 tablespoons butter

2 teaspoons salt

1 teaspoon black pepper

½ cup grits

Combine the milk, butter, salt, and pepper in a medium saucepan and bring to a boil over medium-high heat. Add the grits, pouring in a slow, steady stream and stirring constantly to prevent any lumps from forming. Reduce the heat to low and simmer, stirring frequently, until thickened, about 20 minutes.

Serve hot in a serving bowl.

180

Fried Corn

I really only eat corn on the cob and fried, and both require one simple thing: fresh corn. If I can't get fresh corn, forget about it. I'm not wasting my time. Fried corn is such a simple dish that only the freshest, sweetest summer corn will do. After you cut the kernels off the cobs, it is then important to scrape the cobs with the knife to extract as much juice as possible. This will not only give the dish extra flavor, but will help thicken it as well.

Serves 8

8 to 10 ears of corn, husked

¼ pound (1 stick) butter,
   or ½ cup rendered bacon fat

1½ teaspoons seasoned salt

1½ teaspoons black pepper

¼ cup milk

1 tablespoon all-purpose flour

Cut the corn kernels off the cobs (you should have about 5 cups of corn) and place in a large bowl. Once the kernels have been removed, scrape the cobs with a knife to gather any corn juice and add the juice to the kernels.

Melt the butter in a medium sauté pan over medium-high heat. Stir in the corn, any collected juice, salt, and pepper. Add the milk and simmer for about 30 seconds. Sprinkle the flour over the corn, stirring to incorporate, and simmer until the mixture thickens, about 1 or 2 minutes.

Serve immediately in a large serving bowl.

181

Fried Slab Bacon

My grandmother's breakfast table always included a platter of crisp slab bacon. The sound of it sizzling in a hot pan filled her kitchen in the early morning hours, and its smoky aroma lingered in the house for hours after we all got up from the table.

Unlike sliced bacon, slab bacon is sold as one big piece with the rind (skin) intact. Your butcher can slice it for you, or you can slice it yourself. Sometimes folks remove the rind, but my grandmother never did. That's part of what made her bacon so good. When she fried it, not only did the meat become really crisp, but the rind did as well, making each crunchy, salty bite even better.

Serves 8

1 pound slab bacon, sliced into ⅛-inch-thick strips.

Heat a large sauté pan or skillet over medium-high heat. Place one-third to half of the bacon strips in the pan (being sure not to crowd them), and fry on both sides until they are golden brown and crisp. Remove to paper-towel-lined plates to drain and keep warm while frying the remaining strips.

Serve hot on a platter.

Sausage Patties

These sausage patties are the perfect combination of pork, herbs, and spices. I particularly like to add sage, as my grandmother did, and red pepper flakes, which she did on occasion. You can shape these patties into any size you want, but my grandmother always made them preciously petite patties. A glistening platter of these sausage patties will be a welcome addition to any breakfast or brunch table.

Makes 12 patties

3 pounds ground pork

2 teaspoons dried sage

2 teaspoons ground fennel

2 teaspoons dried red pepper flakes

1 teaspoon black pepper

2 teaspoons seasoned salt

6 cloves garlic, peeled and chopped

1/4 cup chopped fresh flat-leaf parsley

About 1 cup vegetable oil, for frying

Preheat the oven to 175°F.

Combine all of the ingredients (except for the oil) in a large bowl, mixing well but being careful not to overwork the pork. Shape the mixture into 12 patties about 2 inches in diameter and 1 inch thick.

Heat the oil in a large sauté pan or skillet over medium-high heat. (There should be about 1/4 inch of oil in the pan, and it will appear to shimmer on the surface when it is ready.) Place about 6 patties in the pan and fry on both sides until well browned and fully cooked in the centers, about 10 minutes. Remove from the heat, arrange on a baking sheet, and set aside in the oven to keep warm while frying the remaining patties.

To serve, arrange the sausage patties on a large platter.

183

Fried Apples

My grandmother often prepared fried apples for breakfast. She was fussy about the apples she used and liked Granny Smith best for this dish. They hold their shape when cooked, and their fresh tart flavor remains bright even after they are caramelized with brown sugar and spices. Fried apples make for a flavorful side dish in general, but they are particularly wonderful when paired with salty, smoky items like the Slab Bacon and Sausage Patties we often enjoyed alongside them for breakfast (see previous page). That sweet/salty combination is always a winner.

Aside from the mixture of spices, this recipe gets its personality from the roughly sliced apples. This is not the time for peeled and fussily sliced, uniform apples. Leave the skins on, slice them, and cook 'em up. For additional flavor and to add even more character to this dish, substitute rendered bacon fat for half of the butter. Then, whether you're serving bacon or not, the apples will benefit from the meat's smoky saltiness.

Serves 8

4 tablespoons butter

8 Granny Smith apples, cored
   and roughly sliced

½ cup dark brown sugar, packed

1 teaspoon freshly grated nutmeg

⅛ teaspoon ground cinnamon

Salt & black pepper

Melt the butter in a large sauté pan over medium-high heat. Add the apples, sugar, nutmeg, and cinnamon and season with salt and pepper. Cook, stirring frequently, until the apples are caramelized, juicy, and softened but not mushy.

Serve hot on a platter.

Cheesy Scrambled Eggs

I love cooking eggs almost as much as I adore eating them. Although making egg dishes is hardly a complicated ordeal, it does require some practice. I happen to take the task pretty seriously.

These scrambled eggs come together quickly and easily, but I am very fussy about the final product. In my opinion, scrambled eggs should be cooked over low heat, and there should be no brown parts, please! They are to be yellow, fluffy, and moist, and if they are the least bit brown, you are sure to be on your way to flat, dry eggs. No thank you. To keep them from drying out, let alone browning, I suggest you turn the eggs out of the pan just before they are done. They will look a little too moist, but they will actually continue to firm up as they sit on the plate.

My grandmother often added cheese to her eggs, and this is how I like them best. You can certainly omit it if you want, but I promise you will be happy if you leave the recipe just as it is.

Serves 8

16 large eggs
1 cup grated mild yellow cheddar cheese
¼ teaspoon black pepper
¼ pound (1 stick) butter

Whisk the eggs in a medium bowl to break up the yolks. Add the cheese and pepper, whisking to incorporate.

Melt the butter in a large sauté pan over medium-low heat. Add the egg mixture and cook, stirring frequently with a wooden spoon or heatproof spatula, until the eggs form soft, creamy, fluffy curds. (*The eggs should not brown at all.*)

Serve immediately on a platter.

185

Pineapple Sherbet

Although most of my Richmond food memories center on my grandmother, pineapple sherbet puts me in mind of my grandfather. Throughout my childhood, he and I were pineapple sherbet buddies, and my fondness for the cold, creamy dessert has continued ever since.

Every day, my grandfather and I had the same routine. After dinner, I'd help my grandmother clean up in the kitchen for a few minutes, and then make my escape to the porch. It was there that my grandfather—or Smoky, as I called him, because he was so big and dark—sat, relaxing in the rocking chair. I'd saunter over to the porch swing opposite him, all cool and nonchalant, and just wait. No more than 30 minutes would pass before he'd speak. "Lila," he'd say, breaking the silence, "I want you to go up to High's and get me a quart of pineapple sherbet." Although he made the same declaration each night, Smoky spoke in an offhanded way that made this sound like a novel idea. I continued the ruse, answering, "Okay, Smoky," as I slowly brought the swing to a halt and stood up. He reached in his pocket for some money and handing it to me said, "And get yourself a pint, too." The smile he offered shattered our little charade, and I darted off like a shot down the street to High's Ice Cream.

Traveling as quickly as possible with my arms full of sherbet, I returned only minutes later. I handed Smoky his quart, returned to the swing with my pint, and the two of us consumed the entirety of our respective containers in silent bliss. To this day, I can still imagine my grandmother in the kitchen, surrounded by piles of dirty dishes and smiling to herself. She knew Smoky and I were bonding on the porch over pineapple sherbet.

Smooth and creamy with chunks of juicy pineapple, the sherbet Smoky and I savored every day on his porch was perfection. In fact, on my return trips to Richmond as an adult, I always visited High's for my regular pint. As soon as the first spoonful of sherbet hit my lips, I was a little girl again sitting on Smoky's swing. The year I returned to Richmond to find that High's closed, I cried. Then I found another place to get sherbet.

Although the following recipe did not come from High's, it is pretty good, if I do say so myself. Because it is so simple, you really must use very ripe pineapple and either fresh or high-quality canned pineapple juice. Share this sherbet with someone you love, and make some memories of your own.

Serves 8

2 cups Simple Syrup (see page 194)
½ cup chopped ripe pineapple
2 cups pineapple juice

Combine all of the ingredients in a large bowl and freeze in an ice cream machine according to the manufacturer's directions. The sorbet should be soft and smooth, not hard and icy.

Serve with a spoon!

Spiced Watermelon Rind

If you've never experienced spiced watermelon rind, you haven't enjoyed one of the greatest pleasures of summer. Now, I say this as a self-proclaimed watermelon addict. I love this melon and eat it in the summer every chance I get.

I guess folks came up with this recipe ages ago out of a desire to waste as little food as possible. Somewhere along the line, they determined all the watermelon rind they were discarding could be brined and spiced to make a tasty sweet pickle or chutney of sorts.

I don't know how this all came about, but I know my grandmother made this dish frequently. She served it, as she did most all condiments and pickles, in a pretty glass bowl that I recall always returned to the kitchen scraped clean.

Makes about 3 quarts

BRINING THE WATERMELON

4 cups cold water

1 cup salt

Rind of 1 medium watermelon, green skin
and pink flesh removed and cut into
about 1-inch pieces (about 6 cups)

SPICING THE WATERMELON

1 tablespoon ground ginger

1 teaspoon cayenne pepper

1 tablespoon whole cloves

1/4 cup salt

4 cups sugar

2 quarts cold water

1/4 cup lemon juice

1 lemon, thinly sliced

7 cups water

To brine the watermelon, combine the water and salt in a large container or bowl, stirring to dissolve the salt. Add the watermelon rind, cover, and set aside for 5 to 6 hours.

Drain the rind and rinse at least three times in cold water. Place the rind again in a large container or bowl, cover with cold water, and set aside for 30 minutes.

To spice the watermelon, drain the rind again and place it in a large saucepan. Sprinkle with ginger, add water just to cover, and bring to a simmer over medium heat, simmering until just tender, about 20 minutes. Drain the cooked rind, return to the saucepan, and add the remaining ingredients. Bring to a boil over medium-high heat, reduce the heat to medium-low, and gently simmer until the lemon slices and rind appear translucent, about 30 minutes. Set aside to cool completely.

Store the spiced rind in airtight containers in the refrigerator for up to 8 weeks.

Peach Preserves

I don't think my grandmother ever bought a jar of preserves in her life. Why should she have, when her yard was full of fruit trees? Thinking about it now, I doubt whether I was aware of how lucky I was to be able to go out back and pick a fresh peach right off the tree whenever I wanted. We certainly ate our fill of fresh peaches, and my grandmother also used them in pies, cobblers, and for preserves.

My grandmother's preserves were simple and wonderful, flavored only with lemon juice and sugar. This is really all you need to make delicious peach preserves, but I like adding some fresh ginger and nutmeg to spice them up a bit.

Makes 6 cups

3 pounds peaches

2 teaspoons finely chopped fresh ginger

2 teaspoons freshly grated nutmeg

5 cups sugar

⅔ cup lemon juice, or to taste

At least 8 hours before cooking the preserves, bring a large saucepan of water to a boil. Fill a large bowl about two-thirds full with ice water and set it next to the stove. Cut a small "X" in the rounded end of each peach. Place a few peaches at a time in the boiling water, blanching them for about 30 seconds. Remove the peaches and immediately set them in the ice water.

When the peaches are cool, peel and pit them, then chop them roughly into about 1-inch pieces, and place in a large bowl. Add the remaining ingredients, stirring to coat. Cover and set aside for at least 8 hours or overnight to macerate in the juices.

The next day or when you are ready to cook the preserves, place the peaches and juices in a large saucepan or Dutch oven and bring to a boil over high heat. Reduce the heat to low and simmer, skimming any foam that rises to the surface and stirring occasionally, until the preserves begin to set, about 30 to 40 minutes. They are ready when a candy thermometer placed in the simmering preserves reads 220°F., or when a small spoonful of preserves placed on a cold plate begins to set within about 15 seconds.

Remove the preserves from the heat, immediately spoon into sterilized jars, and seal. Set on wire racks to cool completely and store in the refrigerator.

189

Grape Jam

Just thinking about homemade grape jam makes me happy. Somehow, it seems to represent everything fun, easy, comforting, and sweet about my summers in Richmond. My grandparents grew trellises of Concord grapes in their backyard, and all summer the vines were filled with round jewels of purple fruit. I can still remember standing as a child underneath those trellises. The green leafy vines dripping with heavy bunches of grapes, the dappled sunlight spotting the ground at my feet, and the air thick with grape perfume—it was like being in a dreamy summer playhouse, where life was always perfect and beautiful.

Despite my best attempts to consume as many grapes as possible, those vines produced way more than any of us could eat. It seemed like my grandmother was constantly making grape jam to keep the fruit from going to waste, and I remember she often gave buckets of grapes away to neighbors as well.

My grandmother was a stickler about serving condiments in proper bowls, but for some reason, grape jam was an exception. I don't know why. Maybe she thought it was pretty enough in its own jar. Whatever the reason, we all did our best to empty those jars as quickly as possible. It actually wasn't that difficult, because we ate grape jam at every meal. There was always a jar on the table. Sometimes peach or pear preserves accompanied it, but the jam was always there.

My grandmother always made grape jam rather than jelly. Maybe it was a matter of time, and she didn't want to wait for hours while the juice dripped through a cheesecloth bag. Making jam was still a lot of work, though. She removed the seeds from every gosh-darned grape before cooking them down, skins and all, and then preserved the hot jam in sterilized jars.

Thick and full of fruit, I'd sit at the table with a buttered biscuit in one hand and a spoonful of jam in the other and think, "Here we go!" I can't imagine childhood memories get any better than that.

Makes 3 to 4 cups

6 cups seeded Concord grapes
2 cups sugar

Combine the grapes and sugar in a large saucepan or Dutch oven and bring to a boil over high heat. Reduce the heat to low and simmer, skimming any foam that rises to the surface and stirring occasionally, until the jam begins to set, about 30 to 40 minutes. It is ready when a candy thermometer placed in the simmering jam reads 220°F., or when a small spoonful of jam placed on a cold plate begins to set within about 15 seconds.

Remove the jam from the heat, immediately spoon into sterilized jars, and seal. Set on wire racks to cool completely and store in the refrigerator.

Pound Cake

As far back as I can remember, there was always a pound cake on hand in my grandmother's kitchen. Although it sat modestly on a plain cake plate beneath a glass dome, it was worthy of one of my grandmother's prettiest china platters. It sure was simple looking, but with its moist texture and buttery flavor, it was completely addictive. Baked in a tube pan, this golden cake sat proudly unadorned under that dome. My grandmother never fussed with glaze or confectioners' sugar. This was no show cake; this was an anytime cake. And I'll tell you, I ate it anytime. In fact, I ate it all the time, and that was the problem. "Girl, you've got to stop eating all day!" my grandmother would often declare. "How can I stop?" I always answered, my mouth filled with cake, biscuits, or fried chicken. There was so much good food around all the time, there wasn't enough collective willpower in Virginia to get me to put down the fork.

Ever since I was very little, I have had a unique passion for food. My sister Paula and I are complete opposites when it comes to eating. Even during those delicious summers in Richmond, Paula didn't much care about all the wonderful dishes that surrounded us everyday. She picked at the table and busied herself with other things, while I hung around the kitchen and counted the hours until the next meal.

Now, everyone with at least one taste bud likes pound cake. But Paula—she couldn't be bothered. I made up for this, though. I had my share and hers! I know you'll like this recipe, and—even if your interest in food is more like Paula's than

mine—I defy you to stop at just one slice.

Makes one 12-cup Bundt or tube cake

1 pound butter (4 sticks),
   at room temperature
3 cups sugar
6 large eggs
1 teaspoon vanilla extract
1 teaspoon lemon extract
Grated zest of 1 lemon
4 cups all-purpose flour
1/3 cup milk

Preheat the oven to 325°F. Butter and flour a 12-cup Bundt or tube pan.

Using a hand mixer (or an electric stand mixer fitted with the paddle attachment), beat the butter in a large bowl on medium-high speed until creamy. Add the sugar and continue beating until light and fluffy. Add the eggs, one at a time, beating well after each addition. Incorporate the extracts and lemon zest, beating until smooth. Reduce the mixing speed to low and slowly incorporate the flour, mixing until just combined and stopping several times to scrape the sides of the bowl. Add the milk, beating until smooth.

Pour the batter into the prepared pan and bake until the top is golden brown and a skewer inserted near the center comes out clean, about 1 hour and 20 minutes. Set on a wire rack to cool the cake in the pan for about 15 minutes. Turn the cake out of the pan and set on the rack to cool completely.

DELILAH'S EVERYDAY SOUL

Limeade

If there's one thing that takes me straight back to my childhood summers in Richmond, it's limeade. For some reason, this drink has never gained popularity in the North like it has in the South. I don't know why. It's the most refreshing, delicious combination of tartness and sweetness.

Actually, even I find it a little surprising that I love limeade as much as I do, considering one of my earliest memories of it is a rather unhappy one. I was all of six or seven years old, and my mother had recently delivered me to my grandparents' house for the summer. When she was in town, my mother used to take me to People's Drug Store, where we'd shop and sometimes get a bite to eat. This was the early 1950s, when drug stores sold as many ice creams and sandwiches as they did household and toiletry items. Back then, these local gathering places were outfitted with shiny soda fountains, spotless counters with comfy stools, and well-kept tables, where patrons could take a break from shopping and refresh themselves with a snack. When I was a little girl, People's was the spot in town. The menu was filled with delicious items, including barbecue pork sandwiches, cole slaw, fruit pies, and, of course, freshly squeezed limeade.

This one particular trip to People's began no differently than any other. Like Pavlov's dog drooling on cue, as soon as my mother and I entered the store, my desire for that sweet limey drink overwhelmed me. "Could I please get a limeade?" I begged my mother. Thinking she would order it for me as usual, I was surprised when she answered, "Sure, Delilah, go sit over there," and pointed me in the direction of the stools at the counter. Excitedly, I ran to a stool and climbed on it, deliriously happy to be sitting up high, my feet dangling beneath me. There were only a few other people sitting at the counter, so I knew the waitress would be over soon. I waited. 'Can she see me?' I wondered, 'Maybe she doesn't see me. It can't be long now.' I waited some more.

Finally, I saw her coming, shuffling in my direction, her bleached white apron practically gleaming. 'Alright!' I said to myself. 'It won't be long now.' I was just about to burst out my order, when she fired her words at me from across the counter: "Little girl, you can't sit here. Whatever you want, you have to go over there," and she motioned to the standing-only section. "Delilah!" my mother called to me, having noticed the confrontation. "Come over here, darling, and we'll get the limeade at this counter." My feet, now almost numb from dangling, hit the floor with a thud, and I ran, hardly feeling them at all, to my mother. Yes, I finally got my limeade that day. I think they must have left out some of the sugar, though. It was a little more sour than usual.

I guess my passion for limeade was just stronger than the likes of 1950s' social ignorance, and I grew up loving the stuff anyway. To this day, the very first thing I do upon driving into Richmond is get myself a limeade. People's has long since closed, so now I rely on Bill's Barbecue to hook me up. As soon as I get to Broad Street, I call my cousin, Linda, to tell her I'm in town. She immediately comes to meet me, and then we're off to start eating and drinking. Once at Bill's, we order pulled pork sandwiches with cole slaw, lemon chess pie, and, of course, limeade. I drink two or three large glasses back to back, while the waitress looks at me in astonishment. "She's from Philadelphia," Linda explains. "Don't pay her any mind." When the waitress leaves, Linda laughs at me and exclaims, "Lila! Girl, you better slow down." "What?" I respond smiling, lost in my limey bliss. I *admit that sometimes I smile not so much to be coy, but because I am completely and totally relaxed. It might have something to do with the Grey Goose that occasionally finds its way into our glasses of limeade.*

Every time I leave Richmond, I stop at Bill's to get more limeade for the road. This time, I order a full quart, "no ice," and a cup of ice on the side. It doesn't last long, but it keeps me going for a few minutes—at least until I get out of town. Richmond sure has changed over the years, but my love for limeade is sweeter than ever.

Makes 8 cups

Juice of 24 limes
About 10 cups seltzer water
Simple Syrup (recipe follows), to taste

SIMPLE SYRUP
2 cups sugar
1 cup water

Combine all of the ingredients in a large pitcher, stirring to blend. Serve in tall glasses over ice.

To make the syrup, combine the sugar and water in a medium saucepan, bring to a boil, and boil just until the sugar is melted.

Set aside to cool completely before using. Store the syrup in a sealed jar in the refrigerator or at room temperature.

Peach Wine

My summers in Richmond were filled with seemingly magical events. One of my favorites took place every year, but never on a particular day or at a specific time. Instead, it was long and drawn out, and demanded much patience, which is perhaps why it was so special. What was this incredibly exhilarating event? Why, the making of peach wine, of course!

Every summer, when the branches of the peach tree in my grandparents' back yard drooped heavily with fruit, I knew she would soon start making her annual batch of peach wine. She never picked peaches right off the tree, but waited until the really ripe peaches, bruised and too battered for pie, fell to the ground. It was then that she scooped them up and threw them into a large stoneware crock that stood in the corner of the kitchen. She collected fruit for weeks, periodically adding to the bubbling and fermenting peach mass, until she was ready to finally release the contents of the crock.

First, my grandmother strained the juice, discarding the tired-looking peels and pits that had worked so hard to produce the gorgeous golden liquid that remained. She then returned the juice to the crock, added sugar, yeast, and water, and left the mixture to ferment and do its thing all over again—this time for at least a month. I waited all summer for this process to end. I would visit that crock several times a week, lift off the cheesecloth lid, and ask, "Grandmom, is it ready yet?" Of course, her answer was always, "No, Delilah. Not yet."

At last, usually by late August, the crock was ready to offer up its spirited contents in thanks for our great patience. My grandmother would declare the wine fit to drink and would begin the final stages of this long summer journey. She lovingly and carefully strained the now pale golden wine, poured it into crystal decanters, and set the glittering vessels in their much-anticipated places on the dining room buffet. It was magical, watching those brown, bruised peaches transform into sparkling decanters of golden liquid. I begged for a taste, knowing that I was still too young for grown-up drinks. My grandmother always responded in the same way, though: "Sure, Delilah. It won't hurt you."

Although it was one of my favorite parts of the summer, decanting the wine was always bittersweet, as well. The decanters glistening grandly on the buffet announced the end of summer, and I knew I'd soon be headed back to Philadelphia to start school again. The promise of my northern transformation was never as magical as that of the peaches. When I returned home, though, scenes of Richmond kept me company. The joyful memories of my grandmother remained with me, as did the sweet flavor of her summer peach wine.

Makes about 1½ quarts

About 1 peck ripe peaches, pitted and roughly chopped (about 8 quarts)

Place the peaches in a large (at least 2-gallon) stoneware crock or stainless steel stockpot, cover with cheesecloth or a lid, and set in a cool, dry area for 3 weeks to begin fermenting.

Strain the fermented fruit, discarding the solids. Clean

6 cups sugar

2 (¼-ounce) packages active dry yeast

1 cup water

the crock or pot and pour in the strained juice. Stir in the remaining ingredients, cover again with cheesecloth or a lid, and set again in a cool, dry area for another 3 weeks, occasionally skimming any foam that rises to the top.

Carefully strain the wine and store in decanters.

197

FOOD *from* the COUNTRY

FOOD *from*
the COUNTRY

Every summer, my parents packed up the car and drove my sisters and me from Philadelphia to Virginia to visit family. Sometimes they dropped us off in Richmond to stay with my father's parents, and other times they traveled the extra distance to King Queen County to the farm where my mother grew up. My parents would stay for a few days and then return home, leaving my sisters and me to spend the next couple of months with seemingly endless numbers of aunts, uncles, and cousins.

I loved Richmond. My grandparents, Catherine and Smoky, lived in town. Yes, it was distinctively southern with its slower pace and old-fashioned traditions, but Richmond was not so very different from Philadelphia. There was still plenty of hustle and bustle to keep us occupied. My grandmother assigned daily chores around the house and in the garden, and we completed them as quickly as possible. It was summertime, after all, and my sisters and I looked forward to bopping around town, getting ice cream, and meeting with cousins and friends.

Visiting my grandparents' farm in rural Virginia was a different story altogether. In fact, especially when I was little, I felt like I wasn't just in a different state, but in a distant country. I still remember the long drive with my parents and sisters to the farm. My father liked to get a really early start. While it was still dark, my parents had us packed into the new de Soto, or canary yellow convertible Thunderbird with its super-duper hi-fi system, or whatever cool new car my father happened to be driving at the time. My sisters and I were still half asleep when we left Philadelphia to begin our nearly ten-hour drive south.

By late afternoon or early evening, we found ourselves in farm country. Fields of corn, melons, and fruit trees surrounded us for miles without a store or market in sight. It seemed hours since we had seen stoplights, sidewalks, and slick paved roads. When we made the final turn down the long driveway toward my grandparents' house, I felt sorry for my father's sassy, city-bred convertible, now spattered with bugs and kicking up dust, as it bounced and bumbled along the dirt road. I doubt if the cars ever recovered from the trauma.

When my father finally stopped the car and turned off the engine, I felt myself fully immersed in the newness of this world. Even late in the day, the sun was still hot and the occasional breeze offered little relief. City folks tend to think the country is quiet and peaceful. I was always struck, though, at how noisy it was. Birds were chirping, chickens were forever cackling in a seemingly annoyed frenzy, and the hum of a tractor was always within earshot.

Then, of course, there was the clamor of all the family. Driving up to my grandparents' house was like arriving in the center of a small town. There were folks everywhere, and when we arrived, they all came out to greet us, emerging from the house, the fields, and the gardens. Aunts, uncles, and cousins I hardly knew met us with great hugs, pats on the back, and laughter. I admit, especially in the beginning, I often felt like somewhat of an outsider. My sisters and I were, after all, mere visitors from up north. The family's sense of joyfulness and camaraderie was infectious, though, and I couldn't help but let myself be drawn into their daily celebration of everyday life.

Spending time on the farm sure gave me an appreciation of hard work and rural living. To be honest, as a kid, I would rather have been in Richmond snacking on pineapple sherbet from the corner store than doing farm chores. Being a city girl, I wasn't crazy about the country. Everything took more time and energy. Take, for example, something as simple as getting the mail. My grandparents only received the mail once a week, and in order to do so, one of the kids had to walk for several miles to the general store to retrieve it. That activity was never at the top of my list.

Then there were the sleeping arrangements. My grandparents' house didn't have separate bedrooms, so my cousins, sisters, and I all slept in a single large room on the second floor. Oh, did it get hot in the summer! The bathroom situation was also an issue for me, since, well, there wasn't one. We used an outhouse and bathed just once a week on Saturdays. This was a scene right out of the old days. Because the farm wasn't equipped with running water, we filled a large basin with boiled well water and then took turns bathing. Even as a little kid I wanted no part of that.

Despite my protestations, for at least a week or so each summer, my mother insisted that my sisters and I spend some time in the country with our grandmother, Nimmie Roane. (My grandfather had long since passed away, and although my grandmother remarried five times, hers was the authoritative presence on the farm.) It's not that I didn't want to be with my grandmother. In fact, I wanted to be with her more, but she was so busy with the goings-on of the farm that we never had much time together. It wasn't until years later, when she came up north to live with us during the winter, that my sisters and I were able to spend time with her and get to know her better.

During those summers, my grandmother Nimmie, who lived to be 95 years old, ran a disciplined household. She sure had years of experience—she raised twelve children in the farmhouse my grandfather built when they first married. My mother is the eleventh child of the twelve, so by the time my sisters and I showed up on the farm, Nimmie's organized work system was well in place.

My grandmother assigned chores to all of the kids depending on our size and age. When I was small, I sat on the porch for hours, shelling beans and black-eyed peas. As I grew taller, I picked corn and fruit. There was certainly enough work to go around. This was a self-sufficient farm, and the produce the family grew and the animals they raised were either consumed or sold at market. In addition to the fields of dandelion greens, melons, peas, beans, corn, and fruit trees on the property, the barns were filled with pigs, cows, and chickens. Blackberries grew wild around the property, and my uncles hunted for rabbit and fished local streams for porgies, croakers, and spots. The family didn't have much money, but they sure had an abundance of fresh ingredients.

The daily demands of farm life were so great that everyone looked forward to refueling and relaxing at mealtime. There was always lots of good food around, but we often had big eventful dinners like barbecues and fish fries, when tables were laden with fried chicken, ribs, fried fish, Smithfield ham, potato salad, collard greens, cornbread, and all kinds of desserts. Such dinners usually took place on Friday or Saturday nights. My aunts, uncles, and cousins gathered at the farm, and the women cooked while the men played cards and drank homemade corn liquor. Then we all ate until we were just too full for one bite more, or we had picked the platters clean.

Other memorable dinners took place in the churchyard after Sunday services. Distance between households and the demands of farm work prevented folks from visiting during the week, so church served as a central gathering place. Next to worshipping and praying together, this community had one thing on its collective mind: celebrating over food. And did they ever feast! This wasn't any old bring-a-picnic-basket-and-nibble affair. Families brought boxes and platters of fried chicken, salads, barbecued pork, cornbread, and loaves of white bread and arranged their delicious offerings on long tables.

All of the food was wonderful, but I particularly remember the enormous array of desserts. Blackberry pies, lemon chess pies, coconut pies, peach cobblers, coconut cakes, pineapple upside-down cakes, and the sweets went on and on. Each family had its own table, but the fun was bopping from one to the other and sharing dishes. There on the grass beneath the white church steeple, the community gathered for hours, eating, laughing, and visiting at what was indeed a spirited weekly thanksgiving.

As I now recall those summer days in King Queen County, I realize how lucky I am to have experienced them. I remember thinking as a child that the hot, work-filled days were grueling and sometimes uncomfortable. I longed to be back in Richmond or Philadelphia where life was easier. Now, though, I understand why my mother wanted me to experience some of how she lived as a girl. I might have arrived feeling like an outsider from the north, but I always left knowing that my appreciation of family traditions, communal celebrations, and impeccably fresh and lovingly prepared food connected me in an intimate way to my Virginia roots.

My early memories of summers on my grandmother's farm have remained with me all these years and inspired my passion for nurturing others through food. That's what cooking is, after all—caring for others and giving of oneself. My grandmother embodied this selfless spirit. Whether she was frying a huge cast iron pan of fish, baking blueberry pies, or teaching my cousins and me to shell peas on the porch, she was nourishing our bodies and our souls. I have come to understand that regardless of how little money or material things the family had, out there in rural Virginia, my grandmother made sure that everyone received his or her fill.

My Mother's Cold Plate Dinner

It's no wonder my mother is a wonderful cook. She grew up on her parents' farm in King Queen County, Virginia, the eleventh of twelve children, and was always surrounded by wonderful country cooking. Raising her own family in Philadelphia, my mother made dinner every night for my father, my sisters, and me, and we all sat together at the table. My parents both worked—my father had two jobs—so the dinner hour was an important time for all of us to talk and reconnect. One of my favorite meals was this cold plate dinner. My mother prepared it almost every Friday or Saturday night. It was always a treat, because it featured some of my favorite foods. What's more, she served it with potato chips. Even the plates my mother used for this meal were special. They resembled old-fashioned luncheon plates, fashioned with separate sections for each item.

This cold plate is as simple as nothing, really, but it makes for an easy and delicious dinner any night of the week.

Serves 8

2 heads iceberg lettuce,
  2 tomatoes, cored and thinly sliced
16 Deviled Eggs (see page 132)
2 pounds thinly sliced pastrami
8 dill pickle spears, or 1 small jar butter pickles
Potato chips, as needed

Core the heads of lettuce and separate the leaves. Place some lettuce leaves on each plate and set tomato slices on top. Divide the remaining ingredients among the plates, arranging them as you wish.

  Serve chilled.

Poached Pear Salad

My mother prepared this salad frequently, and ever since I was a child, it has been one of my favorites. It's so easy, it's ridiculous. Poached pears, lettuce, and mayonnaise—that's it. My mother used canned pears and sometimes peaches, which are delicious, too. I give a recipe here for succulent poached pears (substitute peaches if you like), but there is absolutely no shame in using canned fruit. I grew up on the stuff and loved it.

Serves 8

PEARS

8 Bosc pears

2 quarts water

1/4 cup sugar

1 cup honey

Juice and zest of 2 lemons

Juice and zest of 2 oranges

1 tablespoon roughly chopped fresh ginger

1/2 teaspoon whole cloves

2 cardamom pods, or about 1 teaspoon
  cardamom seeds

1 star anise

ASSEMBLY

2 heads iceberg lettuce,
  cored and leaves separated

1 cup mayonnaise

To make the poached pears, peel the pears, leaving the stems intact. Combine the remaining ingredients in a large saucepan and bring to a boil over high heat. Reduce the heat to low, place the pears in the liquid, and cover with a piece of cheesecloth or small plate to keep the pears submerged. Gently simmer until the pears are just tender, about 20 to 25 minutes. Remove from the heat and set aside, allowing the pears to cool to room temperature in the poaching liquid.

To assemble the salad, slice each pear in half and remove the cores. Divide the lettuce among 8 plates, set 2 pear halves on top, and place a dollop of mayonnaise on top of each pear.

Serve immediately.

Johnny Cakes

Johnny cakes are as well known in the North as they are in the South. Also called hoe cakes, these simple griddlecakes are essentially cornmeal pancakes. They are delicious served with syrup, but my favorite way to eat them is alongside Fried Salt Herring.

Serves 6

1 cup all-purpose flour

2 cups yellow cornmeal

1 tablespoon plus 1 teaspoon sugar

2 teaspoons salt

2 eggs, lightly beaten

2 cups milk

Vegetable shortening, for frying

Stir together the flour, cornmeal, sugar, and salt in a medium bowl.

Whisk together the eggs and milk. Whisk in the flour mixture until smooth.

Heat about 1 tablespoon of shortening in a large sauté pan or skillet over medium-high heat. Using about 2 heaping tablespoons of the batter for each cake, fry about 4 or 5 johnny cakes at once in the pan until golden brown, about 2 minutes on each side. Remove to a plate to keep warm while frying the remaining cakes. Add additional shortening to the pan as needed.

Serve warm on a large platter.

Fish Fry

There were always lots of folks around my grandparents' house. The farm was their workplace as well as their home, so it was forever jumping with people. On Friday or Saturday nights, however, when our family hosted a fish fry, things really heated up. In keeping with tradition, the women cooked while the men smoked and played cards over glasses of whiskey and homemade corn liquor. The guys weren't the only ones having fun, though. Even as they minded numerous cast iron skillets of splattering oil and fish, the women chatted and socialized, too. Mostly, they communed about local events and issues and complained about the fellas in the other rooms drinking too much moonshine.

The celebration kicked into high gear once the ladies set out the food buffet-style on long tables. Platters of fish, huge bowls of potato salad and collard greens, pans of cornbread, stacks of soft white bread, and bottles of hot sauce sure tested the legs on those tables over the years. Everyone grabbed a plate, loaded it up with food, and sat themselves down to eat. Folks spread out all over the place, throughout the house, on the porch, on the lawn—wherever they could find a bit of empty space.

The fish we fried on the farm included croakers, porgies, and spots—relatively small, firm-fleshed white fish that the men fished out of local streams. I have suggested them here, but use whatever mild, white fish you like best. Salads and breads of virtually every kind pair well with fried fish. For a down-home meal like the ones we enjoyed, though, you can't go wrong with creamy potato salad, rich collard greens, cornbread and white bread, and, of course, hot sauce. (Moonshine is optional.)

207

Serves 20

Vegetable oil, for frying

About 4 cups Fish Flour (see page 34)

Salt & black pepper

10 croakers (about 1 pound each), butterflied and heads removed

10 porgies or sea breams (about 8 ounces each), butterflied and heads removed

10 spots (about 1 pound each), butterflied and heads removed

Potato Salad (recipe follows), for serving

Collard Greens (recipe follows), for serving

Cornbread (see page 130), for serving

Sliced white bread, for serving

Hot sauce, for serving

Heat the oil in one large skillet or several smaller sauté pans or skillets over medium-high heat. (There should be about ½ inch of oil in the pan(s).) To check if the oil is hot enough, sprinkle a bit of fish flour into the oil. If the flour sizzles right away, the oil is ready.

Place the fish flour in a large shallow container. Set the fish flat on a work surface so both fillets of each fish are exposed. Season with salt and pepper and dredge in the fish flour, patting gently to remove any excess flour. Carefully place as many fish in the pan(s) as will comfortably fit without crowding and fry on each side for about 2 to 3 minutes until golden brown. Remove the fish to a paper-towel-lined baking sheet to drain and keep warm while frying the remaining fish.

Serve hot on a large platter with potato salad, collard greens, cornbread, white bread, and hot sauce on the side.

Potato Salad

24 medium red-skinned potatoes, cooked,
 peeled, and cubed

1 bunch celery, trimmed and finely chopped

2 Spanish onions, peeled and finely chopped

2 green bell peppers, stemmed, cored, seeded,
 and finely chopped

4 carrots, peeled and grated

1 cup sweet relish

¼ cup yellow mustard

10 hard-cooked eggs, peeled and roughly chopped

4 cups mayonnaise

2 tablespoons sugar

Salt & black pepper

Combine all of the ingredients in a large bowl,
season with salt and pepper to taste, and toss gently.

Transfer the salad to a serving bowl and serve
chilled or at room temperature.

Collard Greens

Serves 20

5 smoked turkey wings, cracked at the joints
 and skins split to expose the meat

1 tablespoon dried red pepper flakes

2 tablespoons salt

1 tablespoon black pepper

2 quarts water

3 bunches fresh collard greens, stemmed
 and roughly chopped

4 bunches fresh turnip greens, stemmed
 and roughly chopped

4 bunches rape greens (broccoli raab),
 stemmed and roughly chopped

4 bunches mustard greens, stemmed
 and roughly chopped

Combine the turkey wings, red pepper flakes, salt,
pepper, and water in a large stockpot and bring to a
boil over high heat. Reduce the heat to medium-low
and simmer until the turkey meat is tender and
begins to fall off the bones, about 45 minutes.

Add the greens, stirring frequently at first to
incorporate into the liquid. Reduce the heat to
low, cover the pot, and simmer until the greens are
very tender and most of the liquid has evaporated,
about 3 hours.

To serve, pour the greens, residual cooking liquid, and turkey (bones and all, if desired) onto a
large platter.

208

Fried Salt Herring

My sisters and I used to beg my mother to make fried salt herring. It was one of our favorite Saturday breakfasts, and she'd serve it with grits, scrambled eggs, and johnny cakes. Although frying the fish didn't take long, my mother had to spend some time preparing the herring beforehand.

Salt herring, as the name suggests, is very salty as it is preserved in salt. It first requires rinsing, and then must be soaked in water to extract much of the salt. The soaking time varies, but my mother used to set it aside for about two days, changing the water periodically.

Whenever I saw my mother coming home from the market with burlap bags of salt herring, I knew we were in for a treat. Crispy and succulent, fried salt herring is delicious on its own or with the tasty dishes my mother served alongside it.

Serves 8

8 salt herring fillets (about 8 ounces each)

About 2 quarts canola oil, for frying

2 cups Fish Flour (see page 34)

Grits (see page 180), for serving

Cheesy Scrambled Eggs (see page 185), for serving

Johnny Cakes (see page 206), for serving

Rinse the herring fillets in cold water. Place them in a large container, cover with cold water, and soak for about 48 hours, changing the water four times.

Heat the oil in a large saucepan or Dutch oven over medium-high heat. Check if the oil is hot enough by sprinkling a bit of fish flour into it. If the flour sizzles right away, the oil is ready.

Place the fish flour in a shallow dish. Drain the fillets, dry with paper towels, and dredge in the fish flour, patting gently to remove any excess flour. Carefully place the fillets in the oil and fry until golden and crisp, about 5 minutes. Drain on a paper-towel-lined plate.

Serve the herring fillets with grits, scrambled eggs, and johnny cakes.

Chicken and Dumplings

Food doesn't get more country than chicken and dumplings. We ate this dish a lot on the farm given that there were always chickens running around. It's really a nothing-to-it meal, but it is so comforting and satisfying. The major work is completed once the chicken is cooked. The dumplings then come together lickety-split, and transform into soft, billowy clouds as they cook in the rich, flavorful broth.

Serves 6

CHICKEN

1 chicken (about 3 pounds)

4 cups water

2 cups Chicken Stock (see page 36)

1 carrot, roughly chopped

1 medium onion, cut into quarters

1 rib celery, roughly chopped

1 teaspoon seasoned salt

1/4 teaspoon black pepper

DUMPLINGS

2 cups all-purpose flour

1/2 teaspoon baking soda

1/2 teaspoon salt

3 tablespoons vegetable shortening

1 cup buttermilk

Place the chicken in a large saucepan or Dutch oven, add the remaining ingredients, and bring to a boil over medium-high heat. Reduce the heat to low, partially cover, and simmer until the chicken is fully cooked, about 1 hour. Remove chicken and set aside to cool. Strain the broth, discarding the solids, and reserve.

Remove the chicken meat from the bones, tearing into bite-size pieces and discarding the skin. Set the chicken aside.

To make the dumplings, combine the flour, baking soda, and salt in a large bowl. Using a pastry cutter or your fingertips, work the shortening into the flour until the mixture resembles coarse meal. (It's alright if some pea-size pieces of shortening remain visible.) Add the buttermilk and mix lightly to form a soft dough. (The dough should be gooey, but not wet.) Turn the dough out onto a lightly floured work surface and knead only a few times to bring the dough together. Roll the dough to about 1/4 inch thick. For drop dumplings, pinch off about 1 1/2-inch pieces of dough. For rolled dumplings, cut the dough into 2-inch squares.

To assemble the dish, bring the reserved broth to a boil in a large saucepan or Dutch oven over high heat. Reduce the heat to medium and maintain at a simmer. Drop the dumplings into the simmering broth, moving them gently to keep them separated. Simmer until they are puffed and fully cooked, about 10 minutes. Add the chicken to the broth and dumplings and simmer until the chicken is heated.

Braised Rabbit

By the time I was born, my maternal grandfather, James Roane, had long since passed away. My mother recounted many sto-ries about him over the years, though, that offered a glimpse of his colorful Southern personality.

My grandfather's hunting expeditions often made for great tales. During the fall, especially, he was fond of hunting rabbits in the woods surrounding the farm. Just about every two weeks, he'd take off early in the morning with four other fellas to scout out and conquer the quick-footed fluffy creatures. Sure enough, by sundown, the group returned victorious. As the men emerged from the woods with their floppy trophies in tow, the twelve Roane kids and bands of others looked on excitedly to determine which of the guys had acquired the greatest spoils from the day's events.

At this point, the hunt now officially over, the women took command, skinning and preparing the rabbits for the big dinner that was to follow. Sometimes they fried the rabbits and other times they cooked up rich rabbit stews. Of course, the rabbit dishes were always set out with all the trimmings: collards or other greens, mashed potatoes or baked sweet potatoes, string beans, gravy, and several desserts.

This recipe is based on the rabbit stews my grandmother often prepared. This rich one-dish meal comes together easily and is deliciously flavored with an array of vegetables, aromatics, and herbs. I think my grandfather Roane would approve.

Serves 8

3 tablespoons oil

1 cup plus 2 tablespoons all-purpose flour

Seasoned salt & black pepper

2 whole rabbits, each cut into 8 pieces

2 cups thinly sliced onions

1 cup chopped parsnip

1 cup chopped carrot

1½ pounds white button mushrooms,
   thinly sliced

2 tablespoons chopped garlic

¼ cup chopped sweet potato

1 tablespoon chopped fresh thyme

2 dried bay leaves

Salt

Heat the oil in a large Dutch oven or small roasting pan over medium-high heat. Stir together the 1 cup flour, seasoned salt, and pepper in a shallow pan. Season the rabbit pieces with additional seasoned salt and pepper and dredge in the flour, patting gently to remove the excess flour. Place half of the rabbit pieces skin sides down in the oil and brown on each side for about 3 to 4 minutes. (The rabbit will not be fully cooked at this point.) Remove the browned pieces to a plate, place the remaining rabbit pieces in the pan to brown, and remove them from the pan momentarily.

Add the onions to the pan and sauté until softened. Stir in the parsnips, carrots, mushrooms, garlic, sweet potatoes, thyme, and bay leaves and season with salt and additional pepper, if desired. Add the stock and browned rabbit pieces, raise the heat to high, and bring to a boil. Reduce the heat to medium-low, cover, and simmer, occasionally skimming any

4 cups Chicken Stock (see page 36)

2 tablespoons butter

1 tablespoon finely chopped fresh
   flat-leaf parsley

fat and foam that rise to the surface, until the rabbit is very tender, about 30 minutes.

Remove the rabbit from the pan. Knead together the butter and remaining 2 tablespoons of flour in a small bowl to make a paste (*beurre manié*). Drop small bits at a time into the simmering liquid and vegetables, stirring frequently until slightly thickened. Return the rabbit pieces to the pan, simmer for about 3 minutes more, and stir in the parsley.

To serve, arrange the braised rabbit on a large platter.

Country Pork Ribs

When we think of ribs, we usually think barbecue, but these are slightly different. Roasted with a flavorful mixture of stock, garlic, seasoned salt, onions, and peppers, they are simple and succulent. This recipe comes together quickly, and the ribs roast for less than two hours, making them a perfect addition to weeknight and weekend meals.

Serves 4 to 6

4 pounds country-style pork ribs

1 cup water

½ cup Chicken Stock (see page 36)

8 cloves garlic, peeled and chopped

1 tablespoon seasoned salt

2 teaspoons black pepper

1 large onion, peeled and sliced

2 green bell peppers, stemmed, cored, seeded, and sliced

Preheat the oven to 350°F.

Arrange the ribs in a large roasting pan or on a large baking sheet. Stir together the water, stock, garlic, seasoned salt, and pepper in a large bowl. Add the onion and peppers, tossing to combine. Pour over the ribs and roast until the ribs are very tender, about 1½ to 2 hours.

To serve, slice the ribs and arrange on a large platter

Braised Pork Chops with Mashed Potatoes

We ate a lot of pork on my grandparents' farm, as it was plentiful and always fresh. There are many ways to cook pork chops, but I really like braising them. By cooking the chops in a flavorful liquid along with lots of aromatics, herbs, and spices, the meat remains tender and succulent. This dish is comforting and filling and pairs well with potatoes. I like creamy mashed potatoes best, prepared, of course, with cream and butter. You can lighten them up with milk if you wish, but for that authentic country quality, treat yourself to the good stuff.

Serves 4

PORK CHOPS

1 cup canola oil

4 center-cut pork chops, about
   1 1/2 inches thick

Seasoned salt & black pepper

1 cup thinly sliced yellow onions

2 large Granny Smith apples, cored and sliced

1 tablespoon chopped fresh rosemary

2 teaspoons finely chopped garlic

2 tablespoons light brown sugar, packed

1/4 cup brandy

1/2 cup apple cider

1 1/4 cups Chicken Stock (see page 36)

2 tablespoons chopped fresh flat-leaf parsley

MASHED POTATOES

3 pounds potatoes, peeled and
   cut into 1 1/2- to 2-inch pieces

1 cup heavy cream

4 tablespoons butter

1 teaspoon salt

1/2 teaspoon black pepper

Heat the oil in a large saucepan over medium-high heat. Season the pork chops with seasoned salt and pepper and place them in the pan, browning on each side for about 4 minutes. Remove them from the pan and set aside momentarily.

Add the onions to the pan and sauté until softened and lightly browned. Toss in the apples, rosemary, and garlic, sautéing until the apples are slightly softened. Stir in the brown sugar and brandy and bring to a simmer, stirring with a wooden spoon to loosen any browned bits on the bottom of the pan. Pour in the cider and stock, bring to a simmer, and return the pork chops to the pan. Reduce the heat to medium-low, cover, and simmer until the chops are fully cooked and very tender, about 30 minutes.

To make the potatoes, place them in a large saucepan or medium stockpot, fill with enough cold salted water to cover by about 1/2 inch, and bring to a boil over high heat. Reduce the heat to medium and simmer until the potatoes are just tender, about 15 minutes.

Heat the cream, butter, salt, and pepper in a small saucepan over medium heat just until the butter is melted.

Drain the potatoes, return them to the pan, and mash them until smooth using a fork or potato masher. Gradually add the warm cream mixture, stirring until incorporated.

To finish the pork chops, stir in the parsley just before serving. Arrange the pork chops on a platter and serve with mashed potatoes on the side.

Smithfield Ham

You have to be totally crazy about food to take on the process of preparing a Smithfield ham. Of course, I am, which is why I've included this recipe. The ham requires a number of long and involved steps, but for those of us who consider it to be the absolute best of all country-cured hams—and there are a lot of us—they are totally worth it.

Smithfield hams are special. For one thing, to receive this distinctive name, they must come from Smithfield, Virginia. There, these hams are dry-cured, seasoned, hickory smoked, and aged anywhere from six months to two years. This elaborate process results in a ham that is dry, lean, dark in color, rich in flavor, and salty as the dickens. In this state, it is most similar to pro-sciutto, and some folks eat it like they do this prized Italian salt-cured, air-dried ham. Personally, I think this is a bit much. The ham is so salty, it will downright dry up your taste buds. Much more often, therefore, people cook Smithfield ham, which is where the extended process comes into play.

First, the ham needs to soak, preferably for about 24 hours, in order to remove much of the salt. Then, after draining it, the ham simmers in more water for an additional eight hours. The final stage takes place in the oven. The skin and fat are removed, and the ham is roasted for another hour-and-a-half or so until it is beautifully browned. Lest we waste one bit of this gorgeous beast, let's return to the skin. I arrange the skin on a baking sheet and roast it along with the ham. Once the ham is done, I crank up the oven temperature and continue to cook the skin until it transforms into the light, crispy snack we southerners lovingly call cracklings. That's when the party begins. I admit, I love Smithfield ham, but when the cracklings are ready, I don't think twice about the ham; I just want the skins. Most times, the cracklings don't even make it to the table, let alone onto a platter. Even my finicky sister, Paula, steps in at this point and starts nibbling. Just wait—you think potato chips are addictive!

Cooking Smithfield ham takes quite some time, but once it's done, it lasts for weeks. Keep in mind the ham weighs about sixteen pounds to start. It loses some of that weight during cooking, but afterwards it's still heavy as sin, and you only eat thin slivers of it at a time. My grandparents might have prepared two Smithfield hams a year, which is saying a lot, because they always had armies of folks to feed. These days, I usually prepare one Smithfield ham a year, most often at Christmastime, when my house is filled with friends and family and I host a lot of parties.

There are many ways to eat this delicious ham. Slice it thin and eat it plain. Serve it with syrup or molasses. Put it on biscuits or in sandwiches made with white bread, mayonnaise, and sliced tomatoes. No matter how you enjoy it, you can't get a more authentic taste of the country than Smithfield ham.

Serves "an army"

1 Smithfield ham (about 14 to 16 pounds)

Place the ham in a large container and cover with cold water. Cover and set aside in a cool area or in the refrigerator for 24 hours.

Remove the ham and set it in a large stockpot or high-sided roasting pan. Pour enough water in the pot/pan to nearly cover the ham and bring to a boil over medium-high heat. Reduce the heat to medium-low and simmer for 8 hours.

Remove the ham from the water and set aside until it is cool enough to handle.

Preheat the oven to 350°F.

Trim all the skin off of the slightly cooled ham and arrange on a baking sheet. Remove and discard most of the surface fat from the ham. Place the ham in a large roasting pan. Roast the baking sheet of pork skin along with the ham until the ham is well browned, about 1½ hours.

Remove the ham from the oven, raise the oven temperature to 400°F., and continue roasting the skin until golden brown and crisp, about 20 to 30 minutes more.

To serve, place the ham and pork skins (cracklings) on separate platters and slice the ham thinly.

Blackberry Pie

Blackberries are probably my favorite food on earth. I snack on them just about everyday, and actually keep a pint on the passenger seat of my car, as I drive around doing my errands. Of course, I also adore blackberry pie. It was a staple at my grandparents' house since blackberries grew wild around the farm. While the other kids were helping with chores, I used to wander off to pick blackberries. I liked to be alone, and, besides, even as a little kid I could do this on my own. Blackberry bushes grow low to the ground, so getting my fill was never an issue.

This is an easy pie to make and it beautifully showcases summer's perfectly ripe berries. Just be sure to gently toss together the filling components so as to keep the berries whole. Blackberries are really delicate and tend to break apart easily. By treating them with care, you will prevent the filling from cooking down to mush, and, instead, the pie will be full of big pieces of berries.

Makes one 9-inch pie

PIE CRUST

Pie Dough (see page 222)

FILLING

6 pints fresh blackberries

2 cups sugar

1 tablespoon ground cinnamon

1 teaspoon ground nutmeg

1 tablespoon vanilla extract

Grated zest of 1/2 lemon

ASSEMBLY

1/4 pound (1 stick) butter,
  cut into small cubes

To make the crust, divide the dough in half, reserve one half for later use and roll out the other half on a lightly floured work surface to about a 12-inch circle. Fit into a 9-inch pie plate, crimp the edges, and set in the refrigerator to chill for at least 25 minutes.

Preheat the oven to 350°F.

To make the filling, combine all of the ingredients in a large bowl, tossing gently to combine.

To assemble the pie, pour the filling into the chilled pie crust, dot with butter, and bake until the crust is golden and the filling is thick and bubbly, about 45 to 50 minutes. Set on a wire rack to cool completely before serving.

Coconut Custard Pie

This pie is for coconut lovers only. Based on a traditional custard pie, I pack it with freshly grated coconut and spice it with the tiniest bit of nutmeg for good measure. The final result is nothing fancy, but it will do you proud every time.

Makes one 9-inch pie

PIE CRUST
Pie Dough (see page 222)

FILLING
4 large eggs

²/₃ cup sugar

¼ teaspoon salt

2 teaspoons vanilla extract

2½ cups half-and-half, scalded

1 fresh coconut, cracked, peeled,
  and grated (about 3 cups)
  (see *Chef's Note*, page 227)

¼ teaspoon freshly grated nutmeg

To make the crust, divide the dough in half, reserve one half for later use and roll out the other half on a lightly floured work surface to about a 12-inch circle. Fit into a 9-inch pie plate, crimp the edges, and set in the refrigerator to chill for at least 25 minutes.

Preheat the oven to 450°F.

To make the filling, whisk the eggs in a large bowl until smooth and slightly foamy and stir in the remaining ingredients.

Pour the filling into the chilled pie crust and bake for 10 minutes. Reduce the temperature to 325°F. and bake until the filling is just firm, about 30 to 40 more minutes. Set on a rack to cool completely.

Serve at room temperature or chilled.

220

Lemon Chess Pie

Every self-respecting Southern cook has at least one recipe for chess pie in her files. This rich, creamy dessert has absolutely no pretense. A basic custard pie, the filling is often flavored with brown sugar, vanilla, or lemon juice, as I have used here.

Although chess pie is simple to make, southern cooks—as they sometimes do—get carried away with the sugar. Now, when I say these pies are sweet, I mean oh-Lord-please-don't-kill-me sweet! I ate a piece of lemon chess pie at Bill's Barbecue in Richmond, Virginia, one day that had so much sugar in it, I was sure diabetic shock was in my immediate future. My Aunt Emily, however, makes perhaps the best lemon chess pie I have ever tasted, and I have based this recipe on hers. The perfect balance of sweet, tart, rich, and creamy, this pie is just right for a summer picnic or afternoon snack.

Makes one 9-inch pie

PIE CRUST

Pie Dough (see page 222)

FILLING

2 cups sugar

2 large eggs

4 tablespoons butter, melted

¼ cup evaporated milk

1 tablespoon grated lemon zest

¼ cup lemon juice

1 tablespoon all-purpose flour

1 tablespoon yellow cornmeal

¼ teaspoon salt

To make the pie crust, divide the dough in half, reserve one half for later use and roll out the other half on a lightly floured work surface to about a 12-inch circle. Fit into a 9-inch pie plate, crimp the edges, and set in the refrigerator to chill for at least 25 minutes.

Preheat the oven to 400°F.

Line the pie shell with aluminum foil, fill with dried beans or pie weights, and bake for 5 minutes. Remove the foil and weights and bake until light golden brown, about 2 more minutes. Set aside to cool completely on a wire rack.

Reduce the oven to 350°F.

Combine the filling ingredients in a large bowl, whisking until smooth. Immediately pour into the cooled pie shell and bake until the filling is firm, about 50 minutes. Set on a wire rack to cool completely.

Refrigerate for 1 hour before serving.

Peach Cobbler

Could there be a more sincere summer dessert than peach cobbler? Prepared with only the sweetest, ripest peaches, it doesn't need much more than a little sugar, butter, some spices, and a squeeze of lemon. The peaches are the stars of this show.

Cobblers often just have a top crust, but I prefer to make mine like a large double-crust pie, cloaking the fruit in tender, flaky pastry. This way, I get a forkful of juicy fruit and golden crust in every bite.

Makes one 9 x 13-inch cobbler

PIE DOUGH

3 cups all-purpose flour

½ teaspoon salt

¾ teaspoon baking powder

¾ cup vegetable shortening, chilled

About ½ cup ice water

FILLING

About 12 large ripe peaches, peeled,
    pitted, and sliced (about 10 to 12 cups)

1½ cups sugar

¼ pound (1 stick) butter,
    melted and cooled

1 tablespoon ground cinnamon

1 teaspoon freshly grated nutmeg

1 tablespoon vanilla extract

Juice of ½ lemon

ASSEMBLY

1 tablespoon ground cinnamon

Whipped cream or vanilla ice cream,
    for serving

To make the pie dough, combine the flour, salt, and baking powder in a large bowl. Using a pastry cutter or your fingertips, work the shortening into the flour until the mixture resembles coarse meal. (It's alright if some pea-size pieces of butter remain visible.) Add the ice water, a few tablespoons at a time, and mix lightly until the dough just comes together. (Add more or less water as needed.) Shape the dough into a disk, wrap in plastic wrap, and set in the refrigerator to rest and chill for about 1 hour.

Preheat the oven to 375°F. Grease a 9 x 13-inch casserole dish with vegetable shortening.

To make the filling, combine all of the ingredients in a large bowl, tossing gently.

To assemble the cobbler, divide the chilled pastry dough in half. Place one half on a lightly floured work surface and roll into a rough 12 x 16-inch rectangle. Carefully fit the dough into the prepared casserole, pressing gently into the corners and against the sides. (The dough should hang slightly over the edges of the pan.) Pour the filling into the dough-lined pan, spreading evenly. Roll the remaining half of dough into a rough 9 x 13-inch rectangle and place over the peaches. Crimp the edges of the dough to seal, cut a few vents in the top to allow steam to escape while baking, and sprinkle with cinnamon. Bake until the crust is golden brown, about 1 hour. Set on a wire rack to cool for at least 20 minutes before serving with whipped or ice cream.

Pineapple Upside-Down Cake

I have been making this cake for years, and, if I do say so myself, it is the best blend of fruit and cake I have ever tasted. I have taken the traditional recipe and tweaked it a bit.

First, most pineapple upside-down cakes are baked in a skillet or round cake pan, but I like to make mine in a rectangular baking dish. This way, I can usually include a slice or two more of pineapple, and then cut big squares of the finished cake. Next, most recipes call for canned pineapple, but, as you can guess, I encourage you to use fresh golden pineapple. It is such a treat. Finally, rather than line the baking dish with pecans and maraschino cherries, I prefer to decorate the cake with them at the end after turning it out of the pan. The cherries look fresher, and the pecans stay crunchier this way.

Makes one 9 x 13-inch cake

CAKE

4 tablespoons butter

¾ cup dark brown sugar, packed

2 tablespoons dark rum

About 8 to 10 slices ripe pineapple, about ½ inch thick

1 cup sifted all-purpose flour

1 teaspoon baking powder

⅛ teaspoon salt

3 large egg yolks

1 cup sugar

¼ cup pineapple juice

1 tablespoon dark rum

TOPPING

About ¾ cup toasted pecan halves

About ½ cup maraschino cherries

Preheat the oven to 325°F. Butter a 9 x 13-inch baking dish.

To make the cake, melt the butter in a small saucepan over low heat. Add the brown sugar and rum, stirring to combine, and pour into the bottom of the prepared baking dish. Arrange the pineapple slices on top of the butter and sugar mixture and set aside.

Stir together the flour, baking powder, and salt in a medium bowl.

Using a hand mixer, beat the egg yolks in a large bowl on medium-high speed until thickened. Gradually pour in the sugar, continuing to mix until incorporated. Reduce the mixing speed and beat in the pineapple juice and rum. (You can also do this using an electric stand mixer fitted with the whip attachment.)

Fold the flour mixture into the egg mixture and pour into the pineapple-lined pan, spreading the batter evenly. Bake until the cake is golden brown and a skewer inserted in the center comes out clean. Set on a wire rack to cool about 15 minutes.

Gently loosen the edges of the cake and turn out onto a serving platter. Arrange pecan halves around the pineapples and set cherries in the centers of the pineapples.

Serve squares of the cake warm or at room temperature.

Coconut Cake

This is, hands-down, my favorite cake. Just the sight of this tall, cloud-like cake covered with coconut makes me weak in the knees. Eating it, of course, sends me straight over the edge. Layers of coconut cake, lemon filling, and old-fashioned boiled icing all cloaked in coconut—you'll have to sit down for this one.

This cake requires several steps and takes some time to prepare. It is totally worth it, though. If you want to save time and use unsweetened shredded coconut, go ahead. I do prefer fresh coconut, though. You might be able to find pieces of fresh coconut in the supermarket ready to peel and grate. If not, whole fresh coconuts are usually available in most markets and call for only a minimal amount of elbow grease.

I find lemon filling works best in this cake. It pairs perfectly with coconut. Pineapple is delicious, too, though. If you want to try it, just substitute a cup of pineapple purée for the lemon curd.

I just know that once you try this special cake, it will become one of your favorites, too.

Makes one 9-inch cake

CAKE

3 cups sifted all-purpose flour

³⁄₄ teaspoon salt

I tablespoon baking powder

I cup vegetable shortening

2 cups sugar

I¹⁄₂ teaspoons vanilla extract

4 large eggs

I cup fresh coconut juice or canned
   coconut milk

ICING

2 cups sugar

²⁄₃ cup water

2 tablespoons light corn syrup

¹⁄₄ teaspoon cream of tartar

¹⁄₄ teaspoon salt

Preheat the oven to 350°F. Butter and flour three 9-inch cake pans.

To make the cake, stir together the flour, salt, and baking powder in a medium bowl.

Using a hand mixer, beat together the shortening and sugar in a large bowl on medium-high speed until creamy and light. Add the vanilla extract. Add the eggs, one at a time, beating well after each addition. Add the coconut juice and beat well until incorporated. (You can also do this using an electric stand mixer fitted with the paddle attachment.)

Reduce the mixing speed to medium-low and gradually add the flour mixture, stopping occasionally to scrape the sides of the bowl. Divide the batter among the prepared pans. Bake the cakes until they are golden brown and a skewer inserted in the centers comes out clean. Set on a wire rack to cool about 15 minutes. Turn the cakes out of the pans and cool completely.

To make the icing, combine the sugar, water, corn syrup, cream of tartar, and salt in a medium saucepan. Bring to a boil over medium-high heat, stirring occasionally until the sugar is

225

4 large egg whites

2 teaspoons vanilla extract

FILLING

1 cup prepared lemon curd
  (available in supermarkets)

1 cup reserved icing

ASSEMBLY

About 4 cups freshly grated coconut
  or unsweetened shredded coconut
  (see *Chef's Note*)

completely dissolved. Place a candy thermometer in the pan and continue boiling the syrup, occasionally washing down the sides with a clean pastry brush dipped in water, until it registers 240°F.

Meanwhile, begin whipping the egg whites in a large bowl. (A hand mixer is fine for this, but an electric mixer fitted with the whip attachment is better, as it allows you to keep your hands free.) Whip the whites to medium peaks on medium-high speed. (Ideally, the whites should be ready just when the sugar syrup reaches the desired temperature. If, however, you are a little early with the whites, continue beating them on the lowest speed until the sugar syrup is ready.)

Reduce the mixing speed to medium-low and immediately begin drizzling the hot sugar syrup directly down the side of the bowl into the whipped egg whites. (Pouring the sugar too quickly will cause it to splatter and harden around the bowl.) As soon as all of the syrup is incorporated, raise the mixing speed to high and continue beating the icing until it is thick, fluffy, and just lukewarm. Add the vanilla and set the icing aside momentarily, reserving 1 cup for the filling.

To make the filling, fold together the lemon curd and reserved icing in a medium bowl.

To assemble the cake, place one layer of cake on a platter or cake plate and spread with about one-half of the filling. Set another layer on top, spread with the remaining filling, and top with the third layer of cake. Coat the cake with icing and cover with grated or shredded coconut, carefully pressing it into the sides and top of the cake.

Serve slices of the cake chilled or at room temperature.

CHEF'S NOTE: Fresh coconut is so delicious that it's worth a little extra effort. Buy husked coconuts that are relatively heavy. They are moist and fresh rather than old and dry. When you shake them, you should hear the juice sloshing around. Once you get them home, drive an ice pick or screwdriver into the three holes at the top, then invert the coconut and shake out the juice. Wrap the coconut in a towel, place it on a hard surface (a concrete floor or driveway is good for this), and whack it with a hammer or mallet. Once it's in pieces, pry away the shell and remove the skin, using a paring knife or vegetable peeler. Grate the coconut in the bowl of a food processor fitted with the blade attachment or using a box grater. One medium coconut should yield about 3 cups of meat. Cover and store the coconut in the refrigerator for up to two days.

227

AH, HA!
Macaroni & Cheese

AH, HA!
MACARONI
& CHEESE

I have had some pretty amazing experiences over the years. Some have inspired me, while others have been influential, encouraging me to take a certain path or make a particular decision. There have been a few events, though, that have actually altered the course of my life. Having Oprah Winfrey announce my macaroni and cheese as the best in the country on *The Oprah Winfrey Show* was one of these truly life-changing experiences. In keeping with Oprah's often quoted "light-bulb moments," when everything suddenly becomes clear, the short time I spent in her brilliant spotlight resulted in my own "Ah, ha!" declaration and personal moment of clarity. It wasn't long before I felt the magnitude of the event. This experience catapulted me from a local to a national stage, and my life as a cook and restaurateur was forever changed.

Who would have thought that a simple casserole I had sold for years at my market stand would lead to such a whirlwind of attention and success? But then again, I have found that when life decides to take me on a really astounding journey, it doesn't usually sneak up, all quiet and polite. It downright whacks me over the head to make sure it has my attention. If that's not enough, it also sometimes throws me down a road, the likes of which I've never even seen before. I guess all of this uncertainty and craziness are what make life exciting. And there certainly was no shortage of excitement during the days surrounding my "Ah, ha! Macaroni and Cheese."

Here's how it happened: Sometime in the year 2003, without my knowing it, someone had suggested my macaroni and and cheese be considered in Oprah's search for the country's best macaroni and cheese. One Friday morning, out of the blue, I received a call from a woman saying she was a producer on *The Oprah Winfrey Show* and that I was one of five finalists in this taste test. "Five of what?" I asked. "Where did you say you are from?" I was actually getting ready to hang up on her—I didn't have a clue who she was, and, I was busy opening up my restaurant. Then it occurred to me that this might be important. Did she say *Oprah*? "Listen," I told her, "let me take your name and number and I will get right back to you." I had to pull myself together.

I collected my thoughts, sat down, and dialed the number the producer had given me. She explained that Oprah's panel of judges needed a sample of my macaroni and cheese for the tasting. "We need it by Monday morning at 10:30 a.m." Monday morning? I thought. This was some mad, crazy nonsense. "*This* Monday?" I was completely shocked. I made a couple of calls to see if this whole situation was for real. After determining that it was, I called the producer—again. She explained that I could either deliver the dish in person to Harpo Studios in Chicago where the show is taped or I could send it. "I can't FedEx macaroni and cheese!" I told her. "That's not going to work." She gave me the option of sending the ingredients and allowing their chef to put the dish together. That's *definitely* not happening, I thought. "Nobody else can make my macaroni and cheese," I blurted out. "You don't understand. This is a special dish. It is supposed to be cooked and eaten right away." I'm sure she thought I was crazy, but she was very nice, and simply said that the choice was mine and asked me to let her know what I planned to do.

As soon as I hung up with her, I was on the phone for what seemed like hours, calling friends right and left, asking their opinions on how I should get the macaroni and cheese to Oprah's Harpo Studios. "Oh, don't be playing with that," they all said. "You need to get yourself *and* the macaroni to Chicago." So that was that. I was going on a trip. I phoned my friends Brenda and Lance in Chicago to let them

know what was going down and to see if I could bake the macaroni at their place before the show on Monday. Brenda, of course, agreed right away. Lance was on board, too, but he just couldn't help giving me a hard time about it. "The only way you're gonna bake your macaroni and cheese here," he laughed, "is if you leave some at the house for us."

By Saturday, my to-do list was shrinking. After booking a Sunday flight to Chicago, I had just one more little thing to accomplish: work on my macaroni and cheese recipe. I was happy with the dish as it was; I had been making it for years, after all. But I wanted to be sure it was perfect. I called my fiancé, Tim, and our friends Frank and Jessica in a frenzy. "This is an emergency," I explained. "I need you to come over and test macaroni and cheese. I'm making it for Oprah!" What a sight we all were. The three of them were sitting at my kitchen table having a grand old time, while I was raving and swirling around them like a mad casserole scientist, draining colanders of macaroni, shredding cheese, cracking eggs, and melting butter.

I nervously set the first version in front of my jovial testers. Tim took one taste and, after about three intense seconds, declared, "This is the one! Don't mess with it any more. You got it." "Are you sure?" I asked. He couldn't possibly decide so quickly, I thought. And, anyway, I had about five more versions to go. "Here try this one, or maybe this one," I said, shoving other plates in front of him. But he was resolute, and Frank and Jessica

231

agreed with him. I had my recipe—and a kitchen filled with enough macaroni and cheese to feed a small town. While the three of them filled up on macaroni and cheese and cocktails, I committed the recipe to paper, and began preparing the ingredients for Sunday's flight to the Windy City.

Normally when I travel, I prepare for every occasion at my destination, and my neatly arranged suitcases reflect this. I carefully organize multiple outfits, matching shoes, and a variety of accessories *just in case*. That Sunday, though, Delilah The Fashionable Traveler had been snuffed out—silenced for an even greater calling than being well-dressed (if that's possible). Yes, on that day, I could hear the grand trumpets of competition rousing my sporting spirit. (Or maybe that ringing in my ears was the result of stress and anxiety.) In any case, before I knew it, I had taken on a new, albeit temporary, persona: the Get-Out-Of-My-Way-People-I'm-On-A-Macaroni-And-Cheese-Mission Woman. In place of clothes, shoes, and accessories, my Louis Vuitton suitcases were filled with plastic bags of cooked macaroni, shredded DiBruno Bros. cheese, and ice packs to keep everything cold. Even my make-up bag didn't stand a chance and was sacrificed for the extra sharp white cheddar. Of course, all of this went in the cabin with me. Please. As if I'd check the makings of my macaroni and cheese. I'm not *that* crazy.

In Chicago, Lance and Brenda picked me up at the airport along with my entourage of ingredients. They invited me out to dinner, but I decided instead to go straight to the hotel and stay in for the night. There I was, in that terrific city with lots of wonderful restaurants to explore, and I stayed in my hotel room babysitting the macaroni and cheese. Competitiveness can be a lonely business. I filled the bathtub with ice and set the bags of ingredients in it to keep them cold. Of course, I hardly slept at all that night. I woke up just about every hour checking on the bags bobbing in their extended icy bath.

The next morning, Brenda picked me up early and we went to her house to assemble and bake the macaroni and cheese. It looked gorgeous, just as I had planned. I felt relieved, but we still had to drive back into town and deliver it to the studio. Once there, I had no idea where I was going or what I was doing. I must have been a sight. Exhausted, in a fur coat and with a bandana tied around my head, I walked up to a security guard and explained, "Hi, I'm Delilah Winder. Um, I'm delivering my macaroni and cheese." I wanted to be sure and hand it in person to one of Oprah's staff. I was nervous about leaving this coddled bundle of fresh macaroni with a guard for fear that somehow, someone would mislabel it or mistake it for someone else's. After all, if babies could be switched at birth, why not macaroni and cheese? As I stood there in the middle of that busy lobby holding my box, I could just hear people thinking, 'Who's the chick in the fur with the mac and cheese?' Finally, someone from production arrived to collect my delivery. As I anxiously handed over the box, she explained that the tasters would be conducting the taste tests soon, and that someone would call me in several hours with the results.

That was that. I had delivered my lovingly prepared macaroni, and since there was nothing to do now but wait, Brenda and I went to lunch. We chose a restaurant in town, and just as we were about to order, my phone rang. It was a producer from Harpo Studios. "We're finished with the taste testing," she announced. "The judges are deciding now. Could you come and pick up your pan?" Still as hungry as we were when we sat down, Brenda and I promptly got up and returned to the studio. The security guard recognized me from before (how could he forget?), and I explained that I was picking up my pan from the taste test. He made a call and told me someone would be with me shortly.

Within a few minutes, the producer arrived with two assistants. She explained that they wanted to film me picking up the pan and receiving my thank-you gifts. Apparently, Oprah was still testing the macaroni and cheese along with some audience participants, and it would be a while before they chose the winner. "In the meantime," she said, "we'd like to introduce you to one of our other producers." I was thinking, 'Okay, I'm tired now. I haven't eaten in hours, and all this backing and forthing is getting to me. I'll just take my T-shirt and go home.'

The producer introduced herself and said, "Hello, Delilah. It's so nice to meet you. Thank you for participating in our contest. And by the way, you're our winner!" I suddenly became short of breath and then I started screaming and jumping, or maybe I jumped first and then screamed. In any case, I became a mad, crazy, basket-case and grabbed the producer. "You have *got* to be kidding me!" I yelled. "No! No! Really?" I'm sure the poor woman still has bruises from my grip.

After a few minutes, I started to calm down somewhat, but I was still shaking with excitement. Then came the biggest surprise of all. The producer explained that not only was I to be on the show the next day, but that I was also to prepare my recipe for an audience of 350 people. All of a sudden, my excited shaking stopped and I froze. "*What*?" I said in utter disbelief. "What are you talking about 350 people?" "Well," she answered, "the theme of tomorrow's show is 'Only the Best,' and Oprah is giving her top picks away to the audience. You will be there to represent the best macaroni and cheese, and Oprah is going to give everyone in the audience a taste."

Dread and fear squashed my elation with a thud. "I can't make macaroni and cheese for 350 people!" I told her. "I'm here all by myself." She explained that the show was putting me up in a suite at the Omni Hotel and that I would be able to prepare the macaroni and cheese in the hotel kitchen. "The staff are waiting for you to arrive and make the dish," she told me. "We're going to send you out shopping for ingredients. You will be able to make the macaroni just like it was today. It has to be the same, because Oprah is going to taste it, too." I thought, 'Wait a minute. I'm in a strange city, I

don't know where to shop, and I have to cook for 350 people on *The Oprah Winfrey Show*. What have I gotten myself into?'

I didn't know what I was going to do. I always buy my cheese at DiBruno Bros. in Philadelphia's Italian Market, which carries only the best and the most unique cheeses from around the world. Fortunately, Brenda and Lance are in the food business, and they helped me decide on the best place to buy ingredients in Chicago. They suggested going to a food warehouse where I could buy in bulk. "I'm not buying cheese at a warehouse!" I told them. "I'm cooking for *The Oprah Winfrey Show*!" But Brenda and Lance talked me down from the ceiling, explaining that Chicago chefs often shopped there, and that I was sure to find high-quality products that measured up to my standards. After some consideration, I changed my tune. After all, buying large quantities of cheese at a specialty shop *would* be too expensive. So we loaded up at the warehouse and supplemented some of the cheese with more expensive varieties from a local gourmet shop.

The real work began on Tuesday when I arrived at the Omni Hotel kitchen. Countless cooks helped me unload boxes of macaroni and seemingly hundreds of packages of cheese. The staff was great and assisted me at every turn. When the macaroni was cooked, the cheese shredded, the butter melted, and the eggs cracked, the cooks started assembling the big stand mixer for me. "No, no!" I yelled. "I have to mix this by hand or it won't turn out right."

I'm certain they thought I was out of my mind, but they brought out a bunch of big bowls for me instead. I was nearly up to my shoulders in creamy, cheesy macaroni for several hours before all the trays were baked and the task was finally completed.

Thank goodness someone had the good sense to send me to the spa after all that cooking. I guess the producers wanted to be sure I was free and clear of all cheese and macaroni remnants by airtime the next day, and that I at least looked presentable. I certainly was grateful for the hour or so of relaxation that included a massage, facial, and manicure. Because I never expected to win the competition, and especially because my suitcases were filled with ingredients, I hadn't packed any clothes. One of my girlfriends came to my rescue, though, and sent me an emergency FedEx package of outfits. Relaxed from the spa and with my wardrobe in tow, I arrived at Harpo Studios on Wednesday, ready to face the final phase of this journey.

I was promptly whisked away to hair and make-up, where I was primped and curled and painted. "Oprah likes her guests to look great," they told me. I guess so, but I didn't recognize myself when they finally finished with me. While I was getting ready, Art Smith, Oprah's chef, surprised me with a visit. It's rare that he meets guests, but he explained how much he enjoyed my macaroni and cheese and that he had been looking forward to meeting me. Art confirmed that Oprah raved about my macaroni and cheese—so ardently, in fact, that she actually scraped the bowl clean. She had unequivocally declared it the best in America. 'Gosh,' I thought. I even impressed myself with *that* one.

I moved from hair and make-up to the set. I was a little nervous about being on TV, but I felt ready. I was more excited than anything.

The show started, and Oprah was energetically presenting people and gifts right and left. At last, it was time for her to reveal the results of the macaroni and cheese taste test. When Oprah announced my name, the camera flashed to me, and I promptly froze. I just sat motionless. I couldn't jump or scream or laugh. I sat there dazed. I think the enormity of the previous four days crashed down on me at that very moment. Oprah responded like the pro she is, though. She walked over to me and, gently helping me up, said, "It's alright. Come on, come on over here." And then we started talking and laughing and eating. 'Ah, ha,' I said to myself. I was beginning to understand what being on Oprah's show was really all about.

The magnitude of that whirlwind weekend became clear to me almost immediately. I returned home to phone calls from national newspapers, television shows, and folks who wanted to buy my macaroni and cheese. The phone was ringing off the hook at every *Delilah's* location. My staff couldn't keep up with the calls and were getting testy. It was ridiculous. So many folks were coming to the restaurants and ordering macaroni and cheese that I couldn't make enough to satisfy them. I had to hire a cook just to make that dish, and I was spending a fortune on cheese, butter, cream, and eggs.

I also received dozens of requests to ship the macaroni and cheese frozen. I never wanted to do that, but I had little choice. These customers were relentless. I was frank and told them, "I don't know what condition the macaroni will be in when it arrives, but I'll send it." I thought maybe if I increased the price, sales would settle down. But they continued to *rise*. The insanity did start calming eventually, thank goodness. In August of 2004, though, the show replayed, and the craziness started up again. Sales still show no sign of declining.

Macaroni and cheese continues to be the biggest selling item at my restaurants. It was always popular, but winning Oprah's approval catapulted the dish and me into another realm of success. It's ironic that this simplest of comfort foods, this Southern staple that my grandmother prepared weekly in her Richmond kitchen, earned me a place in the national spotlight. I'm proud of this accomplishment, but I'm even more pleased with what it represents about my cooking in general. Choose the best ingredients, cook thoughtfully and sincerely, and even the simplest, seemingly most common dish will be worthy of a heartfelt "Ah, ha!"

237

Macaroni and Cheese

Serves 6 to 8

2 pounds elbow macaroni

12 eggs

1 cup cubed Velveeta cheese

1/2 pound (2 sticks) butter, melted

6 cups half-and-half

4 cups grated sharp yellow
cheddar cheese

2 cups grated extra sharp
white cheddar cheese

1 1/2 cups grated mozzarella cheese

1 cup grated Asiago cheese

1 cup grated Gruyère cheese

1 cup grated Monterey Jack cheese

1 cup grated Muenster cheese

1/8 teaspoon salt

1 tablespoon black pepper

Preheat the oven to 325°F.

Bring a large saucepan of salted water to a boil. Add the macaroni and cook until still slightly al dente, about 10 minutes. Drain and set aside to keep warm.

Whisk the eggs in a large bowl until frothy.

Combine the Velveeta, butter, and 2 cups of the half-and-half in a large bowl. Add the warm macaroni, tossing until the cheese has melted and the mixture is smooth. Add the remaining half-and-half, 3 cups of the sharp yellow cheddar cheese, the remaining grated cheeses, and salt and pepper, tossing until completely combined.

Pour the mixture into a 9 x 13-inch casserole or baking dish and bake for about 30 minutes. Sprinkle with the remaining 1 cup of sharp yellow cheddar cheese and bake until golden brown on top, about 30 minutes more.

Serve hot.

239

Fanciful
CELEBRATIONS

FANCIFUL
CELEBRATIONS

There is always reason to celebrate when friends and family come together to visit and enjoy a meal. I admit it doesn't take much for me to start a party. All I need is one other enthusiastic participant, and I can whip up cocktails, nibbles, and an evening of delicious food on the fly.

Large and momentous celebrations, however, call for organized menus and detailed planning. Whether I'm hosting a holiday gathering with lots of guests or a special occasion party, such as a shower or reception, I keep a few key elements in mind as I develop the menu. First, the food and drinks should reflect the character and tone of the event. Is the party formal or casual? Does the time of day call for hearty appetizers or a substantial meal? Does the party require a fanciful menu or one that is basic and comforting? The feminine breeziness of a bridal shower menu, for example, differs markedly from the soulful, often simpler dishes served at a funeral reception.

Second, the menu should harmonize with the season. Warm-weather gatherings tend to feature light, easy-to-make fare, while cooler weather parties generally call for satisfying, richer, and some-times more complex dishes. I can't imagine hosting a Fourth of July party without slices of ripe juicy tomatoes, spicy steamed crabs, and sweet-and-sour cucumber salad. And what would Thanksgiving be without hearty cornbread stuffing, silky creamed onions, and rich bourbon-nut cake?

Third, I like my menus to represent a variety of dishes. Some items will be traditional, others creative and stylish, while others I include simply because I know my guests like them. It is an absolute must, for example, that on New Year's Eve I serve such traditional fare as fried chicken, pig's feet, and black-eyed peas with rice. I can't help but prepare some of my swankier dishes as well, so I also like to include gorgeous platters of sliced roast beef tenderloin, *Bluezette* wings, and elegant chocolates. My friends, of course, have their own favorites that they request time and again. Why not serve your friends and family what they like best?

Finally, even though I admit I spend most of my time thinking about the food I will serve for a special occasion, I never forget the drinks. I like to include non-alcoholic options for people who don't drink liquor, or, of course, for children who might be attending. Specialty juices, freshly squeezed lemonade, and home-brewed iced tea, for example, are always available. For holidays such as Thanksgiving or New Year's, I like to serve a selection of wines and Champagnes. They don't have to be expensive. Just pour some of your favorites.

Cocktails, of course, either before or with the meal, are fun, too. I like to set up my bar with an assortment of liquor, slices of citrus, and an array of glasses. Sometimes my guests and I choose a signature drink for the event. Other times, it's every man for himself, and we all move about the bar, pouring, sipping, clinking glasses, and sharing each other's colorful concoctions. You will notice that my cocktail recipes make just one serving each, as is traditional. While there is nothing wrong with large bowls of spiked cider or rum punch, or blenders whizzing away with funky margaritas, for special celebrations especially, I prefer more upscale presentations. My guests and I always look forward to the creativity, fun, and imminent laughter that results from fixing our drinks one special glass at a time.

One note: Liquor is most commonly measured in ounces, as are the drinks recipes in this chapter. If you use a shot glass or jigger, which holds $1\frac{1}{2}$ ounces (3 tablespoons), you should be well on your way to making some amazing alcoholic treats!

I have always believed that holidays and special gatherings deserve thoughtfully planned menus. These events bring us together, but it is in the sharing of meals that we truly reinforce our relationships, traditions, and sense of community. The following celebrations and the menus that accompany them are colorfully varied. I hope they encourage you to experiment with your own selections of holiday or special event dishes. In the end, it hardly matters whether the food you serve is fancy or plain, innovative or traditional. Simply presenting a thoughtfully prepared meal will inspire your guests with the joy and grace of the celebration table.

243

FOURTH OF JULY

....

Steamed Blue Crabs (see page 141)

Grilled Corn on the Cob (see page 127)

Potato Salad (see page 208)

Deviled Eggs (see page 132)

Fried Green Tomatoes (see page 128)

Sliced Ripe Tomatoes

Cucumber Salad (recipe follows)

Baked Beans (recipe follows)

Spicy Shrimp (see page 53)

Roasted Pork Ribs (see page 142)

Fried Chicken (see page 175)

Cornbread (see page 130)

Rolls

Pound Cake (see page 192)

Pineapple Sherbet (see page 187)

Sliced Watermelon

Raspberry Collins

Grape Vyne Juicillini

Peach Martini

American Cooler

....

Baked Beans

Serves 10

2 (16-ounce) bags dried navy
    or Great Northern beans

1 cup light brown sugar, packed

1/2 cup blackstrap molasses

2 tablespoons yellow mustard

2 tablespoons Dijon
    or whole-grain mustard

2 tablespoons tomato paste

2 tablespoons Worcestershire sauce

1 piece salt pork or fatback
    (about 2 inches square), cubed

6 strips bacon

1 onion, peeled and chopped

At least 8 hours before cooking and baking the beans, pour them into a large bowl, add water to cover by about 1/2 inch, and set aside to soak for at least 8 hours or overnight.

The next day or when you are ready to proceed with the dish, drain the beans and set aside momentarily.

Stir together the brown sugar, molasses, mustards, tomato paste, and Worcestershire sauce in a small bowl.

Heat a large heavy-bottomed saucepan or Dutch oven over medium-high heat. Place the cubes of salt pork or fatback in the pan and sauté until browned and crisp. Remove and reserve the browned bits. Add the bacon to the pan and cook until golden brown and crisp. Remove the bacon to paper towels and drain all but about 3 tablespoons of the rendered fat from the pan, reserving the remaining fat.

Return the pan to medium-high heat, add the onion, and sauté until softened and golden brown. Stir in the reserved drained beans and brown sugar mixture and pour in water to just barely cover the beans. Reduce the heat to low, cover, and simmer for 1 hour, stirring occasionally.

Meanwhile, preheat the oven to 250°F.

Pour the simmered beans into a large casserole dish, stir in the browned salt pork or fatback pieces, the remaining rendered fat (about 1/4 cup), and crumble the browned bacon overtop. Bake for about 40 minutes.

Just before serving the beans, remove any large pieces of salt pork or fatback.

Cucumber Salad

Serves 10

10 cucumbers, peeled and sliced into
   $\frac{1}{2}$-inch-thick slices

1 cup apple cider vinegar

$\frac{1}{2}$ cup sugar

1 Vidalia onion, peeled and thinly sliced
  (optional)

Salt & freshly ground black pepper

Toss together the cucumbers, vinegar, sugar, and onion in a large bowl. Season with salt and pepper, cover, and set aside for at least 1 hour or overnight.

To serve, strain the cucumbers, reserving the liquid. Place the cucumbers in a serving bowl and drizzle with the reserved liquid.

247

Raspberry Collins

Serves 1

1 ½ ounces gin*
½ ounce DeKuyper Raspberry Pucker
Juice of ½ lemon
Club soda, as needed
Fresh raspberries, for garnish

Combine the gin, Raspberry Pucker, and lemon juice in a shaker and shake vigorously. Pour into a tall glass over ice, top with club soda, and garnish with raspberries.

   *Note: I prefer Plymouth gin in this recipe. Liquor is most commonly measured in ounces. The easiest way to do this is to use a shot glass or jigger, which holds 1 ½ ounces (3 tablespoons).

Grape Vyne Juicillini

Serves 1

1 ½ ounces vodka*
½ ounce Triple Sec
2 ounces Juici Grape Vyne Sparkling Beverage

Combine all of the ingredients in a shaker and shake vigorously. Pour into a sugar-rimmed martini glass.

   *Note: I prefer VOX vodka in this recipe.

248

Peach Martini

Serves 1

1½ ounces peach vodka*
¾ ounce DeKuyper Amaretto
Juice of ½ lemon
¾ ounce half-and-half
Sliced almonds, for garnish

Combine all of the ingredients in a shaker and shake vigorously. Strain into a chilled martini glass and garnish with almonds.

*Note: I prefer Absolut vodka in this recipe.

American Cooler

Serves 1

1½ ounces bourbon*
2 ounces orange juice
1 tablespoon lime juice
1 teaspoon confectioners' sugar
Orange slice, for garnish

Combine all of the ingredients in a shaker filled with cracked ice and shake vigorously. Strain into a tumbler or an old-fashioned glass filled with crushed ice and garnish with an orange slice.

*Note: I prefer Knob Creek bourbon in this recipe.

249

JESSICA'S
BRIDAL SHOWER

....

Smoked Fish Platter:
Salmon, White Fish, Trout

Hard Cheeses with
Fresh Grapes and Crackers

Soft Cheeses with Candied Pecans,
Fresh Figs, and Crackers

Deviled Eggs Garnished with Caviar (see page 132)

Olives, Pickles, and Onions
Marinated in Balsamic Vinaigrette

A selection of Pastries such as Key Lime Tarts,
Sweet Potato Cheesecake Tarts, Fresh Berry Tarts,
Flourless Chocolate Tarts with Pecans

Mini Crab Cakes (recipe follows)

Shrimp Cocktail

Passiontini

Ruby Pomegranate Martini

Mimosa Italia

....

Mini Crab Cakes

Serves 8 to 10

SAUCE

½ cup prepared tartar sauce

2 teaspoons ketchup

½ teaspoon lemon juice

About ⅛ teaspoon ancho chili powder

CRAB CAKES

1 tablespoon butter

½ red or yellow bell pepper, cored,
    seeded, and finely chopped

2 pounds lump crabmeat

1 tablespoon chopped fresh flat-leaf parsley

1 tablespoon chopped fresh dill

1 tablespoon chopped scallion

2 eggs, lightly beaten

1 tablespoon Old Bay seasoning

½ teaspoon cayenne pepper

2 tablespoons dry breadcrumbs

1 cup vegetable oil, for frying

To make the sauce, stir together all of the ingredients in a small bowl and set aside while preparing the crab cakes.

To make the crab cakes, melt the butter in a small sauté pan over medium-high heat. Add the pepper and sauté until softened, about 2 to 3 minutes. Remove from the heat and set aside to cool.

Combine the cooled pepper with the crabmeat, herbs, scallion, eggs, spices, and breadcrumbs in a large bowl, tossing gently to prevent breaking the pieces of crabmeat. Shape the mixture into about 16 small balls, about the size of golf balls, and press gently into small patties.

Heat the oil in a large sauté pan over medium-high heat. Place as many crab cakes in the pan as you can without crowding the pan (there should be about 1 inch between each cake), and sauté on each side for about 2 minutes until golden brown. Remove the crab cakes to a paper-towel-lined baking sheet to drain and keep warm while frying the remaining cakes.

Arrange the crab cakes on a large platter and serve with sauce.

Passiontini

Serves 1

1½ ounces raspberry vodka*
½ ounce DeKuyper Island Blue Pucker
½ ounce Triple Sec
1½ ounces white cranberry juice, or to taste

Combine all of the ingredients in a shaker and
shake vigorously to combine. Strain into a chilled
martini glass.

   *Note: I prefer VOX vodka in this recipe.

Ruby Pomegranate Martini

Serves 1

1½ ounces Ruby Red Vodka*
1½ ounces pomegranate juice
Simple Syrup (see page 194), to taste
Lime wedge, for garnish

Combine all of the ingredients in a shaker filled
with ice and shake vigorously. Strain into a chilled
martini glass and garnish with a lime wedge.

   *Note: I prefer Absolut vodka in this recipe.

Mimosa Italia

Serves 6

4 ounces DeKuyper Amaretto
3 cups orange juice
1 (750-ml) bottle sparkling wine*

Stir the amaretto and orange juice together in a
pitcher. Pour into six champagne flutes (filling
each about halfway) and top with sparkling wine.
   *Note: I prefer Asti sparkling wine in this recipe.

253

CHRISTENING

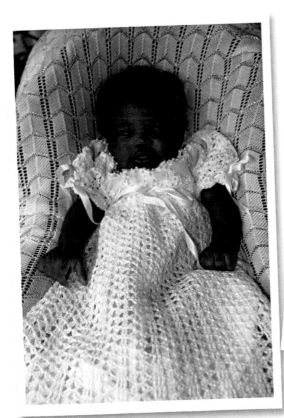

···

Tea Sandwiches: Tuna,
Cream Cheese with Olives, Ham,
Smoked Salmon with Boursin,
Egg Salad, Chicken Salad

Fresh Fruit Kebabs

A selection of Pastries such as Key Lime Tarts,
Sweet Potato Cheesecake Tarts, Fresh Berry Tarts,
Flourless Chocolate Tarts with Pecans

Coffee, Tea, Fresh Lemonade

···

FUNERAL

....

Mustard Catfish
with Rémoulade (see page 55)

String Beans with Braised
Smoked Turkey (recipe follows)

Mashed Sweet Potatoes (see page 162)

Bibb Salad with Buttermilk Dressing
(see page 58)

....

String Beans with Braised Smoked Turkey

Serves 8

2 smoked turkey wings

¼ teaspoon dried red pepper flakes, or to taste

1 tablespoon black pepper

Salt

2 pounds string beans, trimmed

4 tablespoons butter

Place the turkey wings in a large saucepan or Dutch oven, sprinkle with red pepper flakes and black pepper, and season with salt. Pour water overtop just to cover the wings and bring to a boil over high heat. Reduce the heat to low and simmer until the meat falls off the bones, about 1 to 2 hours. Remove the wings, reserving the cooking liquid in the pan. Pull the turkey from the bones and return the turkey to the pan, discarding the bones.

Bring the cooking liquid and turkey to a simmer over low heat, toss in the beans, and cover, simmering until the beans are tender, about 20 to 25 minutes. Stir the butter into the beans, simmer for another 5 minutes, and season with additional salt and pepper as needed.

To serve, pour the beans, turkey, and cooking juices onto a large serving platter.

259

NEW YEAR'S EVE

....

Fried Chicken (see page 175)

Herb-Roasted Lamb Chops (see page 73)

Roasted Beef Tenderloin (recipe follows)

Bluezette Wings (recipe follows)

Spicy Shrimp (see page 53)

Hot Crab Dip (recipe follows)

Pig's Feet (recipe follows)

Collard Greens (see page 208)

Black-eyed Peas with Brown and White Rice

Potato Salad (see page 208)

Macaroni and Cheese (see page 235)

Mashed Sweet Potatoes (see page 162)

Rolls

Assorted Chocolates

Fresh Strawberries

Champagne, Wine, Cocktails

Coffee

....

Roasted Beef Tenderloin

Serves 6

1 cup olive oil

4 sprigs rosemary, 2 stemmed and
chopped and 2 left whole

2 tablespoons chopped fresh thyme

4 cloves garlic, peeled and chopped

1 onion, peeled and quartered

1 teaspoon freshly ground black pepper

1 (5½-pound) whole beef tenderloin,
trimmed and tied (ask the butcher to
do this for you)

At least 8 hours before roasting the tenderloin, combine all of the ingredients in a large zip-top bag, coating the tenderloin completely with the marinade. Set in the refrigerator to marinate for at least 8 hours or overnight.

The next day or when you are ready to proceed with the dish, remove the tenderloin from the refrigerator and set aside to warm to room temperature in the bag. Preheat the oven to 450°F.

Put the tenderloin in a medium roasting pan, pour the marinade overtop, and roast for about 1 hour for medium-rare, or longer to desired doneness. Remove from the oven, loosely cover with aluminum foil, and set aside to rest for about 5 to 10 minutes.

To serve, slice the tenderloin into 1/2-inch-thick slices and arrange on a platter along with the rosemary sprigs and quartered onion.

Bluezette's Buffalo Wings

Serves 4 to 6

SAUCE

2 pounds (8 sticks) unsalted butter

6 cups Red Hot sauce or Goya hot sauce

¼ cup Tabasco sauce

2 cups mild ancho chili powder

1 teaspoon cayenne pepper

1 teaspoon Worcestershire sauce

1 pineapple, peeled, cored, and roughly chopped

2¼ cups pineapple juice

2 cups honey

WINGS

Vegetable oil, for frying

24 chicken wings

To make the sauce, melt the butter in a large saucepan over medium heat. Stir in the hot sauce, Tabasco sauce, chili powder, cayenne pepper, and Worcestershire sauce, mixing until smooth.

Place the chopped pineapple in a blender and puree until smooth. Add the juice and honey and continue to blend until incorporated. Pour the pineapple mixture into the hot sauce mixture and simmer, stirring frequently, until thickened to the consistency of thick barbecue sauce, about 45 minutes.

Meanwhile, fill a large saucepan about two-thirds full with vegetable oil and heat over medium-high heat. (The oil will appear to shimmer on the surface when it is ready.) Carefully drop about 6 or 8 wings at a time into the oil and fry until just barely golden, about 15 minutes. (The wings will not be fully cooked at this point.) Remove the wings to a paper-towel-lined baking sheet to drain while frying the remaining wings.

Preheat the oven to 350°F.

Toss together the thickened sauce and fried wings in a large bowl and arrange in a single layer on a large baking sheet. Bake until lightly browned and caramelized, about 40 minutes. Serve hot on a large platter.

CHEF'S NOTE: I recognize that just looking at the amount of butter in this sauce might give you heart palpitations, but don't worry so much. First, they are Buffalo wings, after all. This is fun food and not meant to be incorporated into a weekly diet regimen. Second, this recipe makes a lot of sauce. Even after it cooks down, you're probably looking at a good 10 to 12 cups or so. Use what you need for the number of wings I suggest here, and then just store the rest in the refrigerator.

Hot Crab Dip

Serves 6 to 10

DIP

6 pounds crabmeat (a mixture of lump
  and flaked, if desired)

2 tablespoons chopped fresh dill

2 tablespoons chopped fresh flat-leaf parsley

2 tablespoons chopped scallion

1 yellow bell pepper, cored, seeded, and
  chopped (optional)

1 teaspoon salt

1 teaspoon cayenne pepper

Juice of 1 lemon

1 cup shredded mozzarella cheese

1 cup shredded spicy cheese (such as
  Pepper Jack or cheddar with hot peppers)

1 cup Boursin (triple-cream cheese
  with herbs)

TOASTS

1 large baguette, sliced into
  ¼-inch-thick slices

About ½ cup olive oil

About 2 tablespoons granulated garlic

Preheat the oven to 350°F.

To make the dip, toss all of the ingredients together in a large bowl, transfer to a large casserole dish, and bake until bubbly and golden brown, about 20 to 30 minutes.

Meanwhile, to make the toasts, arrange the baguette slices on a large baking sheet. Brush with olive oil, sprinkle with granulated garlic, and toast in the oven just until golden, about 5 minutes. Turn the toasts, brush again with olive oil, and sprinkle with granulated garlic. Return to the oven for about 2 to 5 minutes more, just until the second sides are golden.

Serve the dip hot in the casserole dish surrounded by toasts.

264

Pig's Feet

Serves 4 to 6

6 pig's feet, split lengthwise

¼ cup kosher salt, plus more as needed

About 1½ gallons cold water

1 cup apple cider vinegar

2 onions, 1 halved and skin on,
   1 peeled and quartered

4 ribs celery, halved, divided

1 head garlic, halved widthwise and skin on

2 cups pickling spices

1 tablespoon dried red pepper flakes

6 cloves garlic, peeled

Hot sauce, for serving

Yellow mustard, for serving

To clean the pig's feet, scrub them with kosher salt under cold running water to remove any impurities. In a large container, combine the water, ¼ cup of salt, and ½ cup of vinegar, then add the cleaned feet, and set aside for at least 1 hour. Drain the pig's feet, scrub again with additional kosher salt, and rinse.

Place the soaked and rinsed feet in a large saucepan or Dutch oven, cover with cold water, and toss in the halved onion, ½ of the celery, and the head of garlic. Bring to a boil over medium-high heat. Reduce the heat to medium-low, cover, and simmer for 45 minutes. Drain the pig's feet, discarding the liquid and aromatics, and rinse again.

Layer the pig's feet in the large saucepan or Dutch oven, and sprinkle them with pickling spices and red pepper flakes. Toss in the remaining celery and onion, and the garlic cloves, pour in the remaining vinegar, and add cold water just to cover. Bring the liquid to a boil over medium-high heat. Reduce the heat to medium-low, cover, and simmer until the pig's feet are very tender, about 2 to 3 hours.

To serve, arrange the pig's feet, celery, onion, and garlic on a large platter and serve with hot sauce and mustard.

265

MARIE'S
THANKSGIVING
DINNER

....

Broiled Grapefruit (recipe follows)

Roast Turkey with Gravy

Glazed Ham or Prime Rib

Cornbread Stuffing (recipe follows)

Macaroni and Cheese (see page 235)

Collard Greens with Cornmeal Dumplings (recipe follows)

Candied Yams with Marshmallows

Mashed Potatoes (see page 121)

Creamed Onions (recipe follows)

Molded Orange Jell-O Salad

Cranberry Sauce

Relish Tray of Pickles, Stuffed Olives, and Celery

Hot Rolls (recipe follows)

Bourbon-Nut Cake (recipe follows)

Sweet Potato Pie

Coconut Cake (see page 225)

....

Broiled Grapefruit

Serves 8

4 grapefruits, halved

½ cup light brown sugar, packed

8 maraschino cherries

Preheat the broiler.

Section the grapefruit flesh using a small serrated or grapefruit knife. Arrange the halves, cut sides up, on a baking sheet. Divide the brown sugar among them, spreading it evenly over the exposed sections. Set under the broiler, watching carefully until the sugar is bubbly and caramelized.

To serve, arrange the grapefruits on a serving platter and set a maraschino cherry in the center of each one.

268

Cornbread Stuffing

*Makes about 8 cups, or enough to fill
a 12- to 15-pound turkey*

4 tablespoons butter

2 medium onions, peeled and finely
chopped

4 ribs celery, finely chopped

2 loaves white bread, torn roughly into
1-inch pieces

1 (9-inch-square) Cornbread (see page
130), broken roughly into ½-inch pieces

About 1 cup chicken broth, or as needed

Salt & black pepper

1 teaspoon dried thyme

1 teaspoon dried marjoram

½ teaspoon dried rubbed sage

½ teaspoon granulated garlic

½ teaspoon onion powder

Preheat the oven to 325°F. Butter two large casserole dishes.

Melt the butter in a medium-sized roasting pan over medium heat. Add the onions and celery, sautéing until softened and translucent. Add the white bread and cornbread pieces and pour in the chicken broth to moisten, adding more as needed. Stir to incorporate with the vegetables. Season with salt and pepper, stir in the herbs and spices, and continue to cook, stirring occasionally, until the bread pieces are lightly browned, about 5 minutes.

Pour the stuffing into the prepared casserole dish and bake until lightly browned, about 45 minutes. (If you're using this stuffing to stuff your turkey, pack the warm stuffing loosely in the cavity of the bird and roast immediately. DO NOT let the turkey sit for any amount of time once it is filled with warm stuffing. Bake any extra stuffing separately in a casserole dish.)

Serve hot.

269

Collard Greens with Cornbread Dumplings

Serves 6

COLLARD GREENS

2 smoked turkey wings, cracked at the
joints and skins split to expose the meat

2 leeks, trimmed and roughly chopped

1½ teaspoons dried red pepper flakes

1 tablespoon granulated garlic

1 tablespoon Lawry's Seasoned Salt

1½ teaspoons black pepper

4 cups water

6 bunches fresh collard greens, stemmed
and roughly chopped

DUMPLINGS

1½ cups white or yellow cornmeal

¼ cup all-purpose flour

1 tablespoon salt

1 teaspoon sugar

1 cup boiling water

To make the collard greens, combine the turkey wings, leeks, red pepper flakes, garlic, seasoned salt, pepper, and water in a large stockpot and bring to a boil over high heat. Reduce the heat to medium-low and simmer until the turkey meat is tender and begins to fall off the bones, about 45 minutes.

Add the collard greens, stirring frequently at first to incorporate into the liquid. Reduce the heat to low, cover the pot, and simmer until the greens are very tender and most of the liquid has evaporated, about 3 hours.

When the greens are just about done, begin making the dumplings. Stir together the cornmeal, flour, salt, and sugar in a medium bowl. Slowly pour in the boiling water, stirring constantly to form a stiff dough.

To finish the dish, drop teaspoons of the dough into the simmering collard greens, cover the pan, and simmer until the dumplings are puffed and fully cooked, about 30 minutes.

Serve the greens, residual cooking liquid, turkey (bones and all, if desired), and dumplings and collard greens on a large platter.

Creamed Onions

Serves 5 to 6

12 to 15 pearl onions

4 tablespoons butter

3 tablespoons all-purpose flour

1 teaspoon salt

⅛ teaspoon black pepper

1 cup light cream

1 cup milk

Chopped fresh flat-leaf parsley, for garnish
  (optional)

Bring a medium saucepan of lightly salted water to a boil. Drop in the pearl onions and boil for about 1 minute. Lift the onions out of the water using a slotted spoon and set immediately in a bowl of ice water to stop the cooking. Drain the cooled onions, slip off and discard their skins, and set aside momentarily.

Melt the butter in a medium sauté pan over medium-high heat. Stir in the flour, salt, and pepper to form a paste (roux) and cook for about 1 minute. Whisk in the cream and milk, reduce the heat to low, and stir constantly with a wooden spoon until thickened to a medium gravy consistency, about 3 to 5 minutes. Toss in the onions and simmer until heated, about 2 minutes.

To serve, pour the onions and sauce into a serving dish and garnish with parsley.

271

Hot Rolls

Makes 36

6 cups all-purpose flour

1 teaspoon salt

2 teaspoons baking powder

2½ cups hot water

½ cup sugar

¼ pound (1 stick) butter, at room
   temperature

1 (¼-ounce) package active dry yeast

Stir together the flour, salt, and baking powder in a large bowl.

Pour ½ cup of the hot water into a smaller bowl and set aside to cool until just warm to the touch. Pour the remaining two cups of hot water in a large bowl. Add the sugar and butter, stirring until the butter is just about melted. Sprinkle the yeast over the smaller bowl of warm water, stirring to dissolve, and set aside to proof for about 3 minutes.

Stir the proofed yeast into the sugar and butter mixture. Add the flour mixture, mixing to make a soft and slightly sticky dough, incorporating more flour if the dough appears too wet. Cover the bowl with a clean dishtowel and set aside in a warm place to rise until doubled in size, about 1 hour.

Grease three 9-inch square pans.

Turn the risen dough out onto a lightly floured work surface and divide into 36 pieces. Roll each piece into a ball and arrange 12 dough balls in each pan. Cover the pans with clean dishtowels and set aside again in a warm place until the rolls double in size, about 45 minutes.

Meanwhile, preheat the oven to 350°F.

Bake the rolls until puffed and golden, about 20 minutes. Set on wire racks to cool the rolls in the pan for about 5 minutes before turning them out of the pan.

Serve the rolls warm or at room temperature.

Bourbon-Nut Cake

Makes one 9- or 10-inch cake

CAKE

4 cups all-purpose flour, divided

1 tablespoon plus 1 teaspoon
  baking powder

½ teaspoon salt

½ pound (2 sticks) butter

2 cups sugar

6 eggs

1 cup bourbon

4 cups chopped pecans or walnuts

GLAZE

½ cup confectioners' sugar, sifted

1 tablespoon bourbon

Juice of ½ lemon

Preheat the oven to 350°F. Butter and flour a 9- or 10-inch tube pan.

Sift 3½ cups of the flour along with the baking powder and salt into a medium bowl.

Using a hand mixer, beat together the butter and sugar in a large bowl on medium-high speed until creamy and light. Add the eggs, one at a time, beating well after each addition. (You can also do this using an electric stand mixer fitted with the paddle attachment.)

Reduce the mixing speed to medium-low and alternately add the flour mixture and bourbon, beginning and ending with the flour and stopping occasionally to scrape the sides of the bowl.

Toss the nuts with the remaining ½ cup flour in a medium bowl and incorporate into the batter. Pour the batter evenly into the prepared pan. Bake until the cake is golden brown and a skewer inserted near the center comes out clean, about 1 hour and 15 minutes.

Meanwhile, to make the glaze, stir together the sugar, bourbon, and lemon juice in a small bowl until smooth.

Set the cake on a wire rack to cool in the pan for about 15 minutes. Turn the cake out of the pan and drizzle with the glaze while still warm.

Serve the cake warm or at room temperature.

273

INDEX

274

276

Ackee and Salt Cod, 48
Banana Pancakes, 45
Barbecue Pulled Pork Sandwich with
        Cole Slaw, 56–57
Bibb Salad with Buttermilk Dressing, 58
Blueberry Buckwheat Pancakes, 46
Callaloo, 49
Fried Oyster and Caesar Salad, 59–60
Fritters, 49
Late Night Burger, 54
Mustard Catfish with Rémoulade, 55
Poached Eggs with Spinach and
        Crabmeat, 51–52
Spicy Shrimp, 53
Stuffed Bluefish, 61
Sweet Potato Cheesecake, 63

J
Jam, grape, 190
Jerk Chicken, 116–117
Jerk Shrimp with Grits, 71–72
Johnny Cakes, 206

K
Knives, essential, 32
Kosher salt, 25

L
LaBelle, Patti, 116
Lamb
        Herb-Roasted Lamb Chops, 73
        Roasted Leg of Lamb with Peaches and
                Mint, 158
Lard, 24
Late Night Burger, 54
Lemonade, strawberry, 147
Lemon Chess Pie, 221
Lemon curd, in Coconut Cake, 225–227
Lemon pepper, 25
Limeade, 193–194
Lobster
        Fried Lobster Tail with Corn, Okra, and
                Tomatoes, 155–156
        Grilled Shellfish with Vegetables,
                113–115
        Lobster Stuffed with Crab and Bay
                Scallops, 138–139

M
Macaroni and cheese
        Oprah Winfrey Show and, 230–237
        recipe, 239
Marmalade, cherry, 75
Martinis. See Beverages, alcoholic
Mashed potatoes. See Potatoes; Yams
Mayonnaise, 28
Meal. See Flour and meal
Mimosa Italia, 253
Mini Crab Cakes, 252
Mint, Roasted Leg of Lamb with Peaches
        and, 158
Mousse, Crème Brûlée with Bananas and
        Chocolate, 77–79
Mushrooms
        Late Night Burger, 54
        Turkey Loaf with Mushrooms and
                Caramelized Onions, 120
Mussels, in Grilled Shellfish with Vegetables,
        113–115
Mustard
        about, 28
        Mustard Catfish with Rémoulade, 55
Mustard greens, in Collard Greens, 208
My Mother's Cold Plate Dinner, 204

N
Navy beans, stewed, 99
New Year's Eve menu, 261
Nutmeg, 27
Nuts. See Pecans; Walnuts

O
Ochs, Harry, 73
Oils and fats, 24
Okra
        Fried Lobster Tail with Corn, Okra, and
                Tomatoes, 155–156
        Fried Okra, 129
        Grilled Shellfish with Vegetables,
                113–115
Old Bay Seasoning, 25
Onions
        Creamed Onions, 271
        Late Night Burger, 54
        Onion Gravy, 177
        Turkey Loaf with Mushrooms and
                Caramelized Onions, 120
The Oprah Winfrey Show, 230–237
Oxtails, braised, 100
Oysters, fried, 59–60

P
Palm oil, 24
Pancakes
        Banana Pancakes, 45
        Blueberry Buckwheat Pancakes, 46
Panko breadcrumbs, for Skewered Coconut
        Shrimp, 69
Paprika, 26
Parties. See Entertaining
Passiontini, 253
Pastrami, in Cold Plate Dinner, 204
Pastry dough, for Cherry Turnovers, 84–85
Peaches
        Peach Cobbler, 222
        Peach Preserves, 189
        Peach Wine, 195–197
        Pineapple, Ginger, and Peach Smoothie,
                146
        Roasted Leg of Lamb with Peaches and
                Mint, 158
Peach Martini, 249
Peanut oil, 24
Pears
        Poached Pear Salad, 205
        Salad with Cider Vinaigrette and
                Poached Pears, 126
Peas. See Black-eyed peas
Pecans
        Bourbon-Nut Cake, 273
        Veal Chop with Bourbon Applesauce
                and Pecan Wild Rice, 122–124
Pepper, types of, 25
Peppers (bell), in Grilled Shellfish with
        Vegetables, 113–115
Pies. See Desserts
Pig's Feet, 265
Pimento wood, 116
Pineapple
        Bluezette's Buffalo Wings, 263
        Pineapple, Ginger, and Peach Smoothie,
                146
        Pineapple Sherbet, 187
        Pineapple Upside-Down Cake, 223

277

278

279

Photography Credits

© John Romeo: Front and back covers, inside back cover, and pp. 3, 20-21, 26, 29 (right), 32 (right), 42, 47, 50, 62, 70, 72, 74, 76, 80, 89, 98, 101, 102, 110, 112, 114, 119, 121, 123, 131, 133, 135, 139, 140, 154, 164-165, 170, 173, 174, 176, 178, 181, 182, 184, 185, 186, 191, 196, 204, 206, 215, 217, 219, 224, 228-229, 247, and 266.

© Christopher McGlinn: pp 29 (left), 30, 32 (left), 34, 37, 60, 106, 127, 143, 147 (right), 149 (top right, middle left, bottom right), 194, 212, 232, 235, and 238.

© Raymond Holman, Jr: pp 38-39, 65, 66 (top and bottom right), 79, 145, 166, 169, 254, 256, and 259.

© Brand X Pictures: pp 124, 137, 147 (left), 149 (top left & middle right), 156 (left), 198-199, 203,

Peter Haigh © Digital Vision: pp 95, 105 (left), 149 (bottom left), 156 (right)

© Digital Stock pp: 105 (right), 117 (right),

© PhotoDisc: pp 90-91

© Patrick Paul: pp 53

© Frank Reynolds: pp 66 (bottom left)

© Carley Mento: pp 250

© Jim Holmes: pp 260 NY eve

The following photos are used courtesy of the author:
pp 83, 85, 117 (left), 153, 244

Notes

Notes

Notes

Notes